A REVOLUTIONARY PILGRIMAGE

Carpenters' Hall, Philadelphia

A Revolutionary Pilgrimage

Being an Account of a Series of Visits to Battlegrounds and
Other Places Made Memorable by the War of the Revolution

Written and Illustrated by Ernest Peixotto

HERITAGE BOOKS
2008

HERITAGE BOOKS
AN IMPRINT OF HERITAGE BOOKS, INC.

Books, CDs, and more—Worldwide

For our listing of thousands of titles see our website at
www.HeritageBooks.com

Published 2008 by
HERITAGE BOOKS, INC.
Publishing Division
100 Railroad Ave. #104
Westminster, Maryland 21157

Copyright © 1917 Ernest Peixotto

All rights reserved. No part of this book may be reproduced or transmitted in any form or by any means, electronic or mechanical, including photocopying, recording or by any information storage and retrieval system without written permission from the author, except for the inclusion of brief quotations in a review.

International Standard Book Numbers
Paperbound: 978-0-7884-1402-2
Clothbound: 978-0-7884-7059-2

TO
WILLIAM BUNKER
OF THE STURDY STOCK
THAT DEFENDED ITS LIBERTIES IN THE
WAR OF THE REVOLUTION
THIS BOOK
IS AFFECTIONATELY INSCRIBED

PREFACE

SOME years ago I systematically visited the scenes and battle-fields connected with the Revolution, undertaking a sort of pilgrimage—a series of journeys that covered a period of almost fourteen months, my motive being to furnish illustrations for Henry Cabot Lodge's "Story of the Revolution."

The only book I could procure to guide me was Lossing's classic "Field-Book of the Revolution," an admirable work, indeed, but so bulky, so unwieldy, and so verbose that it makes rather complicated reading. Besides, in many particulars it is now quite out of date. Many of the scenes have radically changed since 1850; many of the landmarks he describes have disappeared; while, on the other hand, much has been done by patriotic people to mark and make interesting the Revolutionary battle-grounds since his day.

While engaged upon this pilgrimage I met many people—local authorities, men of importance, who had made special researches into the history of their own particular region and were kind enough to give me pamphlets and articles that they had written or data that they had collected—material that seemed to me most interesting. So, as there appeared to be no recent book devoted to

PREFACE

the topographical history of the Revolution, I made up my mind to write one, but one busy period after another has hitherto prevented the accomplishment of that purpose. During this past year, however, I have again gone over the ground, and to my illustrations that originally appeared in "The Story of the Revolution" I have added a number of others and particularly a number of maps which I hope may be of real assistance to the reader in following the narrative.

Now that a new wave of patriotism has swept over the land and created a revival of the "American spirit," as it is called, the moment seems peculiarly propitious to awake anew the story of the deeds of our ancestors—the men who risked their lives and staked their all to found our nation and make its ideals possible.

I wish to thank all those who helped me on my wanderings—and they are many—the kind friends and the chance acquaintances who made these journeys interesting and pleasurable and aided so much in giving me an opportunity to see things and to unearth documents that I should otherwise have surely overlooked.

E. P.

NEW YORK, 1917

CONTENTS

	PAGE
INTRODUCTORY	1
AROUND BOSTON	7
I. THE BEGINNING	9
II. LEXINGTON AND CONCORD	17
III. BUNKER HILL	39
TICONDEROGA AND LAKE CHAMPLAIN	49
TO THE PLAINS OF SARATOGA	67
I. TICONDEROGA TO FORT EDWARD	69
II. THE GREEN MOUNTAINS	76
III. THE MOHAWK VALLEY	87
IV. SARATOGA	101
DOWN THE HUDSON	115
ABOUT NEW YORK	145
IN THE JERSEYS	173
I. TRENTON	175
II. PRINCETON	191
III. MORRISTOWN	204

CONTENTS

	PAGE
ROUND ABOUT PHILADELPHIA	213
I. Chadd's Ford and the Brandywine	215
II. Germantown	228
III. Valley Forge	236
PHILADELPHIA	247
CAMPAIGNS IN THE CAROLINAS	271
I. Charleston	273
II. Through South Carolina	289
III. Guilford Court House	307
THROUGH VIRGINIA	315
I. Williamsburg	317
II. Yorktown	329
III. Hampton Roads	341
MOUNT VERNON	345
WASHINGTON	361

LIST OF ILLUSTRATIONS

Carpenters' Hall, Philadelphia	*Frontispiece*
	PAGE
The Old North	11
Lexington Green at the Present Time	19
Buckman Tavern	20
The Boulder and Harrington House	21
Major Pitcairn's Pistols	23
The Wright Tavern, Concord	25
Barrett House, near Concord	27
Concord Bridge	29
Daniel French's Statue of the "Minuteman"	32
Flag Carried by the Bedford Militia at Concord	34
Grave of British Soldiers near the Bridge at Concord	35
Vicinity of the Washington Elm, Cambridge	47
The Ruins of Fort Ticonderoga	55
Ruins of the Officers' Quarters at Ticonderoga	56
Ruins of Old Fort Frederick, Crown Point	60
Map Illustrating Burgoyne's Campaign	63
Map of Ticonderoga	65
Battle Monument, Bennington	80
The Catamount Tavern, now completely destroyed	81
The Ravine near Oriskany	91
Old Stone Church at German Flats	95

LIST OF ILLUSTRATIONS

	PAGE
General Herkimer's House and Grave	98
Castle Church, near Danube	99
The Home of General Philip Schuyler at Old Saratoga	103
Cellar in the Marshall House, Schuylerville, which was Used as a Hospital by the British	108
Old Battle Well, Freeman's Farms	113
The Hudson River at West Point	124
Parts of the Great Chain which was Stretched across the Hudson	125
Old Fort Putnam, Showing the Magazines	131
Stony Point and the Medal Awarded to Anthony Wayne	135
Headquarters at Tappan from which the Order for André's Execution was Issued	138
'76 Stone House in which André was Imprisoned	140
Stone Marking the Place of André's Execution	142
Old Houses on State Street, New York City	148
Tomb of Alexander Hamilton, Trinity Churchyard	149
The Monument to Montgomery, St. Paul's Church	151
Washington's Pew, St. Paul's Church	152
Map of Operations near New York City	153
View from Old Fort Putnam (now Fort Greene), Brooklyn	156
Battle Pass, Prospect Park, Brooklyn	159
The Jumel Mansion	165
Site of Fort Washington, Looking toward Fort Lee	171
The Point at Which Washington Crossed the Delaware River	179
Map of Operations around Trenton and Princeton	184
Old King Street (now Warren Street), Trenton	188

LIST OF ILLUSTRATIONS

	PAGE
The Old Quaker Meeting House, near Princeton	192
Stony Brook Bridge, near Princeton	193
House and Room in Which General Mercer Died	197
Nassau Hall, Princeton	199
Washington's Headquarters, Morristown	207
Map of Vicinity of Philadelphia	217
Washington's Headquarters, near Chadd's Ford	219
Lafayette's Headquarters, near Chadd's Ford	221
Birmingham Meeting House, near Chadd's Ford	225
The Chew House, Germantown	231
The Old Potts House at Valley Forge	239
View from Fort Huntington, Looking toward Fort Washington	242
Bell Used in Camp at Valley Forge	243
The Assembly Room, Carpenter's Hall	251
Independence Hall, Chestnut Street Front	255
Room in Which the Declaration of Independence was Signed	257
View of Independence Hall from the Park Side	258
Stairway in Independence Hall	259
The Betsy Ross House	261
The Pringle House, Charleston	275
St. Michael's Church	276
Statue of William Pitt, Charleston	277
Charleston Harbor	280
Fort Moultrie	282
Map of Campaigns in the Carolinas, Showing Cornwallis's March from Charleston to Virginia	291

LIST OF ILLUSTRATIONS

	PAGE
Cornwallis's Headquarters at Camden, S. C.	295
Monument to Daniel Morgan, Spartanburg	305
The Battle-field at Guilford Court House	311
The Home of the President of William and Mary College, Williamsburg	319
Bruton Church and the George Wythe House	321
Hall in Carter's Grove	323
British Intrenchment at Yorktown, and Map Showing the Position of the French and American Troops	330
York River, Seen from the Inner British Works and Looking toward Gloucester Point	333
The Moore House	335
Principal Street in Yorktown, Showing Monument Commemorating the Surrender	336
Governor Nelson's Home	337
Washington's Home at Mount Vernon	349
Room in Which Washington Died	357
Tomb of Major L'Enfant at Arlington	367

INTRODUCTORY

INTRODUCTORY

I PROPOSE, on this Revolutionary Pilgrimage, to take the reader, step by step, to all the important localities connected with our War of the Revolution. We shall start at Lexington and Concord, and finish at Yorktown. En route, we shall visit battle-fields and historic sites, and see them as they appear to us to-day. We shall also note what has been done to commemorate the events that took place upon them and perpetuate their memories. We shall see traces of old redoubts; the ruined walls of Ticonderoga; the streets of Trenton; the spot where Washington crossed the Delaware; the buildings and churches wherein historic events were enacted—the places associated with Washington, Stark, Greene, Marion, Lafayette, and the other heroes of the Revolution.

I propose also to take with us, as guides, eye-witnesses of the events they describe—those who have left us the best records of what they themselves saw—authors long since silent, contemporaries, sometimes illiterate, of the events they write about, and, in some instances, the chief actors in them; so that we shall read upon the spot, for example, Paul Revere's own account of his "Midnight Ride," Ethan Allen's own narrative of the taking of

INTRODUCTORY

Ticonderoga; a Princeton student's account of the events that took place about his college; a Quaker's graphic recital of what he saw of the battle of the Brandywine; Major André's own description of the "Mischianza," and Cornwallis's personal despatches of the siege of Yorktown.

Thus I hope to make my story vivid and living. For the clarity of my text, I shall omit some of the less important campaigns and treat the main episodes as nearly in chronological order as my journey will permit. For, primarily, I shall tell my story by geographical sections, starting in New England and ending in the South.

Professor Albert Bushnell Hart wrote, in the "American Historical Review," more than a decade ago, that "too little attention has been paid to the geographical and topographical side of American history, and a prime duty of Americans is the preservation and marking of our historical sites."

I heartily agree with this point of view. My chief hope in writing this book is that, by stimulating interest in Revolutionary landmarks, it may indirectly contribute to their worthy and lasting preservation.

Through the admirable work of local chapters of the Sons and Daughters of the Revolution and of the Order of the Cincinnati, as well as of such active associations as the Society for the Preservation of Virginia Antiquities, many historic houses have been rescued from oblivion or destruction, appropriately "restored," and marked with tablets, the best form of inscription for identifica-

INTRODUCTORY

tion. These patriotic societies have also placed upon many of the battle-fields of the Revolution unobtrusive "markers," showing positions of troops and sites of interest. But much more can be done.

Many of us know the historic spots round about our own particular locality. The New Englander, for instance, knows Bennington and Lexington; the New Yorker, Oriskany and Fort Edward, but could many of them tell me, I wonder, in what State the battles of the Cowpens and King's Mountain were fought—both turning-points in the Revolution? And do most of us realize that Valley Forge and the field of Guilford Court House are to-day public parks, set out with memorial arches and monuments?

The custom of visiting battle-fields is very prevalent in Europe. Monuments and historic tablets are national methods of education, aiding to visualize the events they commemorate and serving to impress them upon the public mind. From them and their stories, people inspire themselves with patriotism and inculcate it in their children. In America such is far less the case. The Civil War veterans make pilgrimages to the scenes of their struggles, it is true, but otherwise few of us look backward. Our eyes are riveted upon the future, forgetting that we may learn many important lessons from the teachings of the past.

Let us, then, in these momentous days, read again the story of our nation's birth; of the sacrifices and abnegation of our forefathers before our country became so

INTRODUCTORY

rich. Let us read again the story of our Revolution, and inspire ourselves anew with the fine old ideals of the "Spirit of '76."

There is much of interest to be seen on our Revolutionary Pilgrimage—surprisingly much, as I think I shall be able to prove, and in these days of automobiles it is an easy matter to visit these historic spots. When I first went over the ground, some years ago, it was quite a different matter, for many of the places were remote from railways, and it took hours of driving to reach them. Because of motors also, the hotels have been much improved since then, many of the old roadhouses having been resurrected and converted into prosperous hostelries, well equipped for comfort and good cheer.

I have personally visited all the localities described in this book—first, some years ago, as I state in my preface, and again, recently, to refresh my memory and ascertain what further has been done to mark the Revolutionary sites. Both tours were singularly interesting, and I wish my reader the same pleasure that I had, if he should elect to undertake a similar journey.

AROUND BOSTON

AROUND BOSTON

I

THE BEGINNING

OUR pilgrimage will naturally begin in Boston, for in Boston and its vicinity the first organized resistance to British oppression was made; while the old city still conserves more mementoes of the days that preceded the actual outbreak of hostilities than any other in our country.

The lion and the unicorn on the old State House gable had looked down upon the Boston massacre, when, on a clear March night in 1770, the new-fallen snow was tinged with the blood of unarmed citizens; near the corner of Washington and Essex Streets once stood the Liberty Tree, in whose shade the "Sons of Liberty" used to meet and discuss their grievances. From the door of the Old South Meeting House—still one of the city's venerated landmarks—a crowd of men, disguised as savages, set out for Griffin's wharf, where they boarded the *Dartsmouth*, the *Eleanor*, and *Beaver* and dumped their cargoes of tea into the harbor.

Through a window above the pulpit of this same meeting-house, Doctor Warren was introduced on the fifth anniversary of the Boston massacre, that is, on the 5th of March, 1775, and its walls echoed the ringing

REVOLUTIONARY PILGRIMAGE

sentences, bold and prophetic, of his oration to the townspeople:

"Our streets are again filled with armed men; our harbor is crowded with ships of war, but these cannot intimidate us; our liberty must be preserved, it is dearer than life. . . . Our country is in danger; our enemies are numerous and powerful, but we have many friends and, determining to be free, heaven and earth will aid the resolution. You are to decide the important question, on which rests the happiness and liberty of millions yet unborn. Act worthy of yourselves."

Thus events were shaping to a crisis, and the town was a centre of patriotic ferment. John Hancock and Samuel Adams were busy. Paul Revere and his friends were holding their meetings at the Green Dragon Tavern, and carefully watching the movements of the British troops.

Near where this tavern once stood, in the North End, —once Boston's "Little Britain," now its "Little Italy," —fronting the small triangular North Square, still stands a humble dwelling. When Paul Revere bought it, in 1770, it was nearly a hundred years old, and it still looks almost as it did when first built. A patriotic group, the Paul Revere Memorial Association, has cleared away excrescences, replaced the old diamond-shaped, leaded windowpanes, and the square, fat chimney, and closed the shops that once disfigured its front, so that now the house has again assumed the appearance it had when Paul Revere occupied it in 1775. His own flintlock hangs above the

AROUND BOSTON

living-room mantel; his toddy-warmer is on the kitchen shelf; and prints from his copper-plates and his advertisements in the "broadsides"—the single-sheet newspapers of the day—are displayed in the rooms up-stairs. From this very house, as we see it to-day, he set forth on his famous "midnight ride."

But a few minutes' walk away, over in Salem Street, Christ Church, now known as the Old North, rears its shapely spire. So conspicuously did this once tower above the houses on Copp's Hill that by it mariners used to shape their course up the bay.

If you are agile enough you still may climb this steeple. A flight of wooden stairs leads first to the bell-ringer's chamber, then on to the bell-loft itself, where hang eight bells, whose inscriptions, cast in the bronze, tell their remarkable history. On number one you read: "This peal of bells is the gift of generous persons to Christ Church, Boston, New England, Anno 1744"; on number three: "We are the first ring of bells cast for the British Empire in

THE OLD NORTH
The Signal Lanterns of PAUL REVERE displayed in the steeple of this church April 18 1775 warned the country of the march of the British troops to LEXINGTON and CONCORD.

REVOLUTIONARY PILGRIMAGE

North America"; and on number eight: "Abel Rudhall of Gloucester cast us all. Anno 1744." Their joyful voices sounded the repeal of the Stamp Act and proclaimed Cornwallis's surrender and, in between, many another event of those stirring Revolutionary days.

From the loft in which they hang I mounted again, by a succession of hazardous ladders, to a gallery above them, and thence to the lantern that forms the crowning feature of the steeple, turning a round-headed window to each point of the compass. The sun poured merrily into the eastern window, through which I could see far down the bay, with its shipping and necks of land. From the south window I could discern the sky-scrapers and big office-buildings of the modern city, and the gilded dome of the State House shining conspicuously on the top of Beacon Hill. The west window revealed, above the tree-tops of Copp's Hill burying-ground, the Charles River, with its terminals and dockyards, and Cambridge spreading out beyond; while, to the north, the Bunker Hill monument pointed like a giant finger upward above the red houses of Charlestown.

From my conspicuous point of vantage I realized so well how far the beacons, placed within this lantern, could cast their fitful beams—how plainly they could be seen from all the countryside. And this was Paul Revere's thought when he agreed with Colonel Conant, in Cambridge, to place his signal lanterns in the Old North steeple.

I shall now let Paul Revere himself tell the story of

AROUND BOSTON

these lanterns, and of his famous ride on the night of the 18th of April, 1775.*

"In the fall of 1774 and winter of 1775, I was one of upwards thirty, chiefly mechanics, who formed ourselves into a committee for the purpose of watching the movements of the British soldiers and gaining every intelligence of the movements of the tories. We held our meetings at the Green Dragon Tavern. We were so careful that our meetings should be kept secret, that every time we met, every person swore upon the bible that they would not discover any of our transactions but to Messrs. HANCOCK, ADAMS, Doctors WARREN, CHURCH, and one or two more. . . .

"The Saturday night preceding the 19th of April about 12 o'clock at night, the boats belonging to the transports were all launched, and carried under the sterns of the men-of-war. . . . On Tuesday evening, the 18th, it was observed that a number of soldiers were marching towards the bottom of the Common. About 10 o'clock, Dr. Warren sent in great haste for me and begged that I would immediately set off for Lexington, where Messrs. Hancock and Adams were, and acquaint them with the movement and that it was thought they were the objects. . . .

"The Sunday before, by desire of Dr. Warren, I had been to Lexington to Messrs. Hancock and Adams who were at the Rev. Mr. Clark's. I returned at night through Charlestown; there I agreed with a Colonel Conant, and some other gentlemen, that, if the British went out by water, we would shew two lanthorns in the north church steeple; and if by land, one, as a signal;

* A letter from Colonel Paul Revere to the corresponding secretary, in the "Collections of the Massachusetts Historical Society," for the year 1798.

REVOLUTIONARY PILGRIMAGE

for we were apprehensive it would be difficult to cross the Charles River, or get over Boston Neck. I left Dr. Warren, called upon a friend,* and desired him to make the signals. I then went home, took my boots and surtout, went to the north part of the town where I had kept a boat; two friends rowed me across Charles River, a little to the eastward where the Somerset man of war lay. It was then young flood, the ship was winding, and the moon was rising. They landed me on the Charlestown side. When I got into town, I met Colonel Conant and several others; they said they had seen our signals. I told them what was acting and went to get me a horse; I got a horse of Deacon Larkin. . . .

"I set off upon a very good horse; it was then about eleven o'clock, and very pleasant. After I had passed Charlestown Neck, and got nearly opposite where Mark was hung in chains, I saw two men on horseback, under a tree. When I got near them, I discovered they were British officers. One tried to get ahead of me, and the other to take me. I turned my horse quick and galloped toward Charlestown Neck, and then pushed for Medford road. . . . The one who chased me, endeavoring to cut me off, got into a clay pond, near where the new tavern is now built. I got clear of him, and went through Medford, over the bridge, and up to Menotomy. In Medford, I awaked the Captain of the minute men; and after that I alarmed almost every house till I got to Lexington. I found Messrs. Hancock and Adams at the rev. Mr. Clark's. . . ."

Now, before he proceeds, let us follow him thus far upon his road. According to his narrative, he crossed

---

* His old friend, Captain John Pulling, a merchant of Boston and a vestryman of Christ Church.

AROUND BOSTON

the Charles somewhere in the vicinity of present-day Charlestown Bridge, passed via the Neck into Cambridge, and started out to Lexington by the main road, now called Massachusetts Avenue. But, meeting the officers, he turned back, took the Medford Road through Somerville, and across the Mystic lowlands.

This route to-day forms part of the city's suburbs, and is built up until you attain the Mystic River, where first you reach open country. Following it recently, I found the Mystic lowlands newly parked and set out with lawns and avenues of trees. Soon we came into the twisting streets of old Medford, with its comfortable houses shaded by towering elms—one of those pleasant towns that impart such charm to the environs of Boston, its newer homes interspersed with just enough old dwellings to give variety and create the special atmosphere that characterizes the older settlements of Massachusetts.

At Medford Common we turned sharp to the left and made for West Medford, where a sign-board, nailed to a tree, told us we were really upon the right trail and following "Paul Revere's Ride." We crossed the Mystic "over the bridge," as he says, with the Mystic Lakes lying off to the right, and then came "up to Menotomy," now Arlington, its old name, however, perpetuated upon the sign of one of the local banks.

Here at Arlington we met the main road from Boston, to which I have alluded—Massachusetts Avenue—the road that Paul Revere started to take when he fell in with the officers, and the one that the British troops did

REVOLUTIONARY PILGRIMAGE

take later in the night, when they set out for Lexington in the darkness, marching in secrecy and silence, to arrest "Messrs. Hancock and Adams and then, at Concord, to seize the military stores known to be collected there."

II

LEXINGTON AND CONCORD

MASSACHUSETTS AVENUE leads directly through Arlington and East Lexington to Lexington Green. As you turn its last elbow and pass the historic Munroe Tavern* you perceive straight before you, Henry Kitson's bronze statue of the Minuteman, gun in hand, peering down the road from the top of a great boulder, watching expectantly for the British Regulars.

And thus did the minutemen, warned by Paul Revere and by William Dawes, another messenger who arrived a little later, stand in the gray dawn of the 19th of April, expectant, calm, and firm, grimly awaiting the arrival of the redcoats.

Revere, after warning the people of Lexington, had endeavored to reach Concord and spread the alarm there, but half-way he was intercepted by a British patrol and taken back to Lexington where the officers relieved him of his horse and left him.

He thus resumes his narrative in a sworn statement that I have before me in a facsimile of his original handwriting:

"I then went to the house where I left Messrs. Adams and Hancock, and told them what had happened; their

*See page 37.

REVOLUTIONARY PILGRIMAGE

friends advised them to go out of the way; I went with them about two miles a cross road; after resting myself, I sett off with another man to go to the Tavern to enquire the News; when we got there, we were told the troops were within two miles. We went into the Tavern to git the Trunk of papers belonging to Col. Hancock; before we left the house, I saw the Ministerial Troops from the Chamber window. We made haste and had to pass thro' our Militia, who were on a green behind the meeting house, to the number as I supposed of about 50 or 60. I went thro' them; as I passed, I heard the commanding officer speake to his men to this purpose, 'Lett the troops pass by, and don't molest them, without they begin first.'

"I had to go a cross road, but had not got half gun shot off, when the Ministerial troops appeared on right behind the Meeting House; they made a short halt, when one gun was fired; I heard the report, turned my head, and saw the smoake in front of the Troops, they immediately gave a great shout, ran a few paces, and then the whole fired."

This, his account, agrees perfectly with recorded history. The tavern to which he alludes, still fronts upon the Green, and is known as the Buckman Tavern. In it the militia assembled that morning, and from it marched forth to take their place upon the Common. Their line is marked by a rough boulder that bears upon its face Captain Parker's words, substantially as Revere records them: "Stand your ground; don't fire until fired upon, but if they mean to have a war let it begin here."

If you place yourself beside this boulder, it will take

AROUND BOSTON

but little imagination to reconstruct the scene. The big, barn-like meeting-house stood near the statue of the Minuteman, where a tablet marks its site. The old wooden belfry, so clearly shown in Doolittle's primitive engraving of the scene, stood near it. "The Ministerial

Lexington Green at the Present Time

troops appeared on right behind the Meeting House" and formed their line with Major Pitcairn at their head. The first shot was fired from his pistol. Jonathan Harrington, one of the patriots who fell at the first volley, dragged himself to his house, that still stands behind you, and died at his wife's feet.

Beyond, a little way up the Woburn Road, stands the home of the Reverend Jonas Clark, in which Hancock and Adams were sleeping when awakened by Paul Revere. This Clark house is the most interesting of all

REVOLUTIONARY PILGRIMAGE

Buckman Tavern

the present-day structures of Lexington, and we gratefully owe its preservation from destruction to the efforts of the Lexington Historical Society. Its oldest portion, the one-story ell, was built in 1698 by the Reverend John Hancock, who reared his five children in it. His second son, grown a wealthy Boston merchant, built on the main portion of the house for his father, who died in it

AROUND BOSTON

in 1752. Three years later the Reverend Jonas Clark, who had married one of Hancock's granddaughters, moved in to become the village pastor.

Edward Everett, who knew Clark, recalls his sympathetic voice, "to which all listened with reverence and delight," and describes him as a clergyman who "enlightened and animated the popular mind," a learned theologian, a correct and careful writer. As we have just seen, he was related by marriage to the John Hancock of the Revolutionary period, who had spent many of his boyhood days in this old home of his grandfather.

On the 18th of April, 1775, there was another guest in the house besides the two distinguished patriots who occupied the large room on the ground floor. This was Dorothy Quincy, John Hancock's betrothed, whom he

The Boulder and Harrington House

REVOLUTIONARY PILGRIMAGE

married in the following August—the one romantic note in all this grim Lexington tragedy.

Paul Revere tells us that Hancock and Adams left Mr. Clark's house after his second warning. But the pastor remained, and he has written for posterity a clear account of what he himself saw from his own house, for at that time there was nothing but open country between the parsonage and the village green. I quote the following extracts from his little-known narrative:

"At half an hour after four (in the morning) alarm guns were fired and the drums beat to arms; the militia were collecting together. About 50 or 60, or possibly more, were on the parade, others coming toward it. In the mean time the troops, having stolen a march upon us, and, to prevent any intelligence of their approach, having seized and held prisoners several persons whom they met unarmed, seemed to come determined for murder and bloodshed; and that whether provoked to it or not! When within half a quarter of a mile of the meeting house, they halted and the command was given to prime and load; which being done, they marched on till they came up to the east end of said meeting house, in sight of our militia, (collecting as aforesaid) who were about 12 or 13 rods distant. . . . Immediately upon their appearing so suddenly and so nigh Captain Parker, who commanded the militia, ordered the men to disperse and take care of themselves; and not to fire.—Upon this our men dispersed;—but many of them not so speedily as they might have done.

"About the same time, three officers . . . advanced to the front of the body and . . . one of them cried

AROUND BOSTON

out 'Ye villains, ye rebels, disperse. Damn you disperse' or words to that effect. . . . The second of these officers, about this time, fired a pistol toward the militia as they were dispersing . . . which was immediately followed by a discharge of arms from said troops, succeeded by a very heavy and close fire upon our party, dispersing, so long as any of them were within reach. Eight were left dead upon the ground! Ten were wounded. The rest of the company, through divine goodness, were (to a miracle) preserved in this murderous action! . . . One circumstance more; before the brigade quitted Lexington, to give a further specimen of the spirit and character of the officers and men of this body of troops. After the militia company were dispersed and the firing ceased, the troops drew up and formed in a body on the common, fired a volley and gave three huzzas by way of triumph, and as expression of the joy of victory and glory of conquest! Of this transaction I was a witness, having at that time a fair view of their motions, and being at a distance of not more than 70 or 80 rods from them."

Major Pitcairn's Pistols

Treasured in the Clark house, from which the patriot-minister watched this scene, I found the bell-clapper that sounded the alarm from the wooden belfry, and the very drum that William Diamond beat to assemble the militia that April morning. There, too, is the identical brace of pistols that belonged to Major Pitcairn, and from which he fired the first shot of the war—weapons that

REVOLUTIONARY PILGRIMAGE

he lost later in the day, together with his horse and accoutrements, when he was wounded in a skirmish at Fisk's Hill. The pistols were sold to Nathan Barrett, of Concord, who in turn presented them to General Israel Putnam, and he carried them throughout the war.

Half an hour after giving their "three huzzas," the British troops took up their march again and proceeded to Concord, six miles away, with the purpose of seizing the military stores collected there in the Barrett house.

Thither we shall now follow them by the same road that they took—a highway that winds up and down through a rough and broken country, interspersed with little groves of pines and cedars. Stone walls and apple-orchards border the road, and over them at times, on the hill-crests, you see out to far distances and obtain views of rolling fields dotted here and there with farmhouses.

About midway to Concord we noticed a tablet recording the fact that here "ended the midnight ride of Paul Revere," for it was at this spot that he was stopped by the British patrol. Longfellow, in the celebrated poem that has made of Revere's name a household word, takes him farther than he went:

"It was two by the village clock,
When he came to the bridge in Concord town,"

which lines are not borne out by fact, as Paul Revere never reached old Concord.

AROUND BOSTON

We did, however, and as the hilly road from Lexington finally led us into the town memories other than those connected with the Revolution for a moment crowded my brain. There, to the right, rose the gables of "The Wayside" that was Hawthorne's home; then we passed

The Wright Tavern, Concord

Orchard House and the School of Philosophy, so intimately connected with the Alcotts, and opposite the calm white house set in pine-trees where Ralph Waldo Emerson wrote his "Essays."

But as soon as we reached Concord Green the Revolutionary atmosphere returned, for the great white meeting-house, now somewhat modernized, the old burying-

REVOLUTIONARY PILGRIMAGE

ground with its slate headstones, and, most of all, the Wright Tavern, all vividly recall the events that preceded the Concord fight. At the tavern that still turns its shingle to the road and retains much of its old-time appearance, Major Pitcairn, the sinister hero of the day, stopped for his glass of toddy and gave vent to his idle boasts.

When making the accompanying drawings I spent a fortnight in this ancient hostelry, seduced by the charm of a neat room "up-chamber," with its view, through chintz curtains and small window-panes, of the great white meeting-house opposite, where the First Provincial Congress met. Indeed, so charming a place is Concord that I recall that sojourn with the greatest pleasure.

To reach the battle-ground, you follow Monument Street until you pass, upon your right, an old house with a bullet still embedded in its wall. Then you turn toward the river, beside the Old Manse, hallowed by so many memories, "worthy to have been one of the time-honored parsonages of England, in which, through many generations, a succession of holy occupants pass from youth to age and bequeath each an inheritance of sanctity to pervade the house and hover over it as with an atmosphere," to quote Hawthorne's own description of it. Its back windows overlook the Old North Bridge and the battle-field. From one of them—a window in the study upon the second floor, in which her grandson, Ralph Waldo Emerson, later wrote his "Na-

AROUND BOSTON

ture," and in which Hawthorne prepared for the press his "Mosses from an Old Manse"—Phœbe Bliss Emerson, wife of the parish minister and grandmother of Ralph Waldo, watched the battle that memorable April morning.

Her direct descendants still occupy the Manse, and have preserved its rare and subtle atmosphere intact, for the portraits that hang in the hall, the antique furniture, the panelling and the hand-printed wall-papers of the old rooms still compose a perfect picture of the life of long ago.

Recently, when we were visiting some friends who live just out of Concord, these people were among the guests at dinner. Later in the evening, I read to them the following account of the Concord fight, a document that I unearthed, reproduced in facsimile, and of which they had never heard, nor had any of the other Concord people that I met. It was written by an Amos Barrett, but what relation, if any, he was to Colonel

Barrett House, near Concord

REVOLUTIONARY PILGRIMAGE

James Barrett, who commanded the Concord minutemen, I have not been able to ascertain.

His is the most graphic eye-witness's account of the battle that I have been able to find. He prefaces his story by telling of the march of the British troops through Cambridge and Lexington toward Concord, and then continues:

"We at Concord heard that they were coming. The bell rung at three o'clock for alarm. As I was a minute man, I was soon in town and found my captain and the rest of my company at the post. It wasn't long before there was another minute company. (One company, I believe, of minute men was raised in almost every town, to stand at a minute's warning.) Before sunrise there were I believe 150 of us and more of all that was there. We thought we would go and meet the British. We marched down towards Lexington about a mile or mile and a half and we see them a-coming. We halted and staid till they got within about 100 rods, then ordered to the about face and marched before them with our drums and fifes going and also the British. We had grand music. We marched into town and over the north bridge a little more than half a mile and then on a hill not far from the bridge, where we could see and hear what was a-going on. . . .

"While we were on the hill by the bridge, there were 80 or 90 British came to the bridge and there made a halt. After a while they began to tear the planks from the bridge. Major Buttrick said if we were all his mind, he would drive them away from the bridge—they should not tear that up. We all said we would go. We, then, were not loaded. We were all ordered to load, and had

Concord Bridge

AROUND BOSTON

strict orders not to fire till they fired first, then to fire as fast as we could. We then marched on. Capt. Davis' company marched first, then Capt. Allen's minute company, the one I was in, next. We marched 2 deep. It was a long corsay (causeway) being round by the river.

"Capt. Davis had got I believe within 15 rods of the British when they fired 3 guns, one after another. I see the ball strike in the river on the right of me. As soon as they fired them, they fired on us. The balls whistled well. We then were all ordered to fire that could fire and not kill our own men. It is strange there were no more killed but they fired too high. Capt. Davis was killed and Mr. Osmore (Hosmer) and a number wounded. We soon drove them from the bridge, when I got over, there were 2 lay dead and another almost dead. We did not follow them. There were 8 or 10 that were wounded and a-running and hobbling about, looking back to see if we were after them.

"We then saw the whole body coming out of town. We were then ordered to lay behind a wall that run over a hill and when they got near enough Maj. Buttrick said he would give the word fire. But they did not come so near as he expected before they halted. The commanding officer ordered the whole battalion to halt and officers to the front march. The officers then marched to the front. There we lay behind the wall, about 200 of us, with our guns cocked, expecting every minute to have the word, fire. Our orders were if we fired, to fire 2 or 3 times and then retreat. If we had fired, I believe we would have killed almost every officer there was in the front; but we had no orders to fire and they wan't again fired (on). they staid about 10 minutes and then marched back and we after them. After a while we found them marching back toward Boston. We were soon after them.

REVOLUTIONARY PILGRIMAGE

"When they got about a mile and a half to a road that comes from Bedford and Bildrica (Billerica) they were waylaid and a great many killed. When I got there, a great many lay dead and the road was bloody." *

This account, I think, gives a clear idea of the successive phases of the fight; the assembling of the various companies on Concord Green; their march to meet the British; their retirement to the hill beyond the North Bridge; their assault upon the troops who attempted to destroy it; the arrival of reinforcements for the British, and the beginning of their retreat.

The battle-ground is still a secluded spot, propitious for meditation. The placid river, well named Concord, flows silently by, threading its way through the meadows.

Daniel French's Statue of the "Minuteman"

* Captain Amos Barrett was afterward at Bunker Hill and at Burgoyne's surrender. He himself says: "I was in the whole of it from Concord to Bunker Hill." I have corrected some of his errors of orthography, but left enough to give color to the picturesque narrative.

AROUND BOSTON

As I sat sketching, I could perceive no sound above its murmur, but the rustling of the leaves, the chirping of birds, or the squeak of a squirrel cracking nuts in the trees above my head. An old-fashioned monument, by the bridge-head, marks the position of the British troops and is thus inscribed:

> Here
> On the 19th of April, 1775
> was made the first forcible resistance to
> BRITISH AGGRESSION
> On the opposite bank stood the American
> Militia, and on this spot the first of the enemy fell
> in the WAR OF THE REVOLUTION
> which gave Independence to these United States.
> In gratitude to God, and in the name of freedom
> This Monument is erected
> A.D. 1836.

But a few steps from it lie the three British soldiers who fell in the fight, buried within an enclosure marked off by stone posts, connected by a chain. Since I made my drawing their graves have been designated with a tablet. The bridge has been rebuilt recently, but upon the same old lines. Beyond it stands Daniel French's fine bronze statue of the "Minuteman" alive, alert, with one hand upon his plough, the other firmly grasping his flint-lock as he hurries off to assembly. Behind him rises the gentle slope of Battle Lawn, as it is called, "the hill not far from the bridge," to which Amos Barrett refers, and on which he took up his position with the minutemen.

There was, as far as is known, but one flag that waved

REVOLUTIONARY PILGRIMAGE

over the "embattled farmers" that April morning. I knew of its existence and had seen it before and made a drawing of it. But I wished to refresh my memory. So one morning we motored over to Bedford, only a few miles from Concord, and drew up before an old house railed off from the road by prim white palings. There I found the gentleman who had been so kind to me upon my former visit. He took us over to the town hall, and led us down into the basement. Hanging his hat upon an electric bulb, so that he would "not forget to put out the electric lights again," he took us to a great safe built in the wall. This he opened and disclosed an inner safe. It, in turn, contained a smaller compartment, especially made to receive the flag, which is placed between two plates of glass so that both sides can be seen. It is a piece of handsome crimson damask, upon which has been painted a mailed arm and hand grasping a dagger, surrounded by a ribbon on which is the singularly appropriate device: *Vince aut morire*.

Flag Carried by the Bedford Militia at Concord

While we were looking at it he told us its story. It was made in England, and sent out to the militia of Middlesex County about 1670. It became one of their accepted standards, and as such was used by the Bedford company. It belonged by inheritance to the Page family, and Nathaniel Page was cornet and color-bearer at the

AROUND BOSTON

time of the Concord fight. When aroused by the early morning summons of the 19th of April, he seized it and hurried off to join his company—the Bedford Company—which was assembling at the Fitch Tavern.

Our kind host, Mr. Jenks (whose mother was a Fitch), then led us back to his own home again—once the Fitch Tavern, the house behind the white palings, to which I have alluded—and we entered the very room in which the minutemen assembled that April morning. In its corner still stands the cupboard from which drinks were served, and here Jonathan Wilson, the company's captain, who was killed later in the day, uttered his well-known words: "It's a cold breakfast, boys, but we'll give the British a hot dinner; we'll have every dog of them before night."

Grave of British Soldiers near the Bridge at Concord

REVOLUTIONARY PILGRIMAGE

The house is filled with souvenirs, and we went about with our friend and his sister and saw their family treasures: portraits and furniture, books and mementos; the frocks and slippers that once set off the charms of their great-grandmother; the fans and hair combs that are now carefully laid away in cabinets.

You will remember that Captain Amos Barrett concludes his narrative with these two sentences: "When they [the British] got about a mile and a half to the road that comes from Bedford and Bildrica [Billerica] they were waylaid and a great many killed. When I got there a great many lay dead and the road was bloody." These words refer to the fight at the crossroads that are now known as Merriam's Corner.

After the fight at the North Bridge the British commander, Colonel Smith, seeing the militia gathering from every side, and apprehending very serious trouble, had already despatched a messenger for reinforcements, when at about noon he decided to start back by the way he had come, and reach Boston while yet he could. Here, at Merriam's Corner, he was first set upon by the militia companies. Carved upon a stone, at the crossroads we read:

> The British troops
> retreating from the
> Old North Bridge
> were here attacked in flank
> by the men of Concord
> and neighboring towns
> and driven under a hot fire
> to Charlestown.

AROUND BOSTON

These words sound the key-note of the disastrous retreat. The minutemen, in deadly earnest, enraged at the death of their comrades, hiding behind fences and barns, utilizing every point of vantage, picked off the British soldiers, who, worn by their long night march and by the various events of the day, dusty and bedraggled, harassed incessantly by the fire of their hidden enemies, plodded doggedly on, finally making their way back to Lexington, but leaving many of their number lying upon the road.

In Lexington, fortunately for them, they were met by the reinforcements sent out by General Gage from Boston, with Lord Percy in command. He had taken up his position at the Munroe Tavern, already mentioned, and had planted two field-pieces on the high ground near it. He had formed his nine hundred men into a hollow square, and into this living fortress the jaded regulars retreated, so exhausted that many fell upon the ground, with their "tongues hanging out," to take a moment's respite.

But not for long. To reach the protection of Boston before night was imperative. So, tired and hungry, they resumed their march again, fighting intermittent skirmishes all the way, until, toward nightfall, they reached Cambridge with their enemies still hanging close upon their heels. Here they found the bridge across the Charles torn up, so, retreating over the Neck, they finally attained Charlestown, where they encamped for the night on Bunker Hill, with two hundred and seventy-three of their number missing.

REVOLUTIONARY PILGRIMAGE

Thus closed that memorable day—the day that stirred men to decisive action, and from which may be dated "the liberty of the American world."

I feel that I cannot better terminate this chapter devoted to its stirring events than by quoting the sentence with which Richard Henry Dana concluded his oration, delivered at Lexington on the 19th of April, 1875, before the President of the United States and a distinguished company, met to celebrate the hundredth anniversary of the fight:

"God grant, that, if the day of peril shall come, the people of this republic, so favored, so numerous, so prosperous, so rich, so educated, so triumphant, may meet it—and we can ask no more—with as much intelligence, self-control, self-devotion, and fortitude as did the men of this place, in their fewness, simplicity, and poverty, one hundred years ago!"

III

BUNKER HILL

THE 19th of April, 1775, was followed by a month or two of feverish activity in and around Boston, and, indeed, throughout all the American colonies. Tidings of the fights at Lexington and Concord spread like wild-fire through the land. East and west, north and south, as the message flew from the Green Mountain intervales to the cypress swamps of the Carolinas, patriots sprang to arms.

The Rhode Island Assembly voted an "army of observation," and appointed Nathaniel Greene, an ironmaster, who was destined to become second only to Washington himself in the high command, as its brigadier. Twelve hundred men from the New Hampshire Grants, with gallant John Stark at their head, marched into the camp at Cambridge; while Israel Putnam led the men of Connecticut as they came to join their comrades near Boston. So that soon the American lines extended from Prospect Hill, to the north of Cambridge, all the way to Roxbury, both wings being protected by intrenchments.

Meanwhile, the British garrison in Boston had also been reinforced by the arrival of fresh regiments from England, with three distinguished generals—Howe, Clin-

REVOLUTIONARY PILGRIMAGE

ton, and Burgoyne—names we shall often meet hereafter. But this proud army and the governor himself found themselves besieged within their own city, quite surrounded by land if not by sea. It was a serious situation, and the British generals decided to combat it by fortifying Dorchester Heights on the one hand, and Bunker Hill on the other, thus threatening both American flanks.

This intention became known to the patriots, so, to forestall the scheme, a little army was paraded in the camp at Cambridge on the evening of the 16th of June —a clear, warm night—and furnished with picks and shovels. President Langdon of Harvard offered up a prayer, and the citizen-soldiers set out for Charlestown. There they halted on Bunker Hill, but the engineers decided that Breed's Hill, just beyond, was better suited to their purpose. In grim silence, Colonel Gridley traced the lines for the intrenchments, and the men fell to work with their picks and shovels in the darkness.

Not a word was spoken, for there, directly below them in the river, lay the three British frigates—the *Somerset*, *Lively*, and *Falcon*—and the "all's well" of the ships' sentries came clearly to the workers' ears, from time to time, to tell them that as yet they were undiscovered. So they toiled on vigorously through the night, and by dawn had thrown up a long intrenchment with a redoubt on the very spot where the mighty Bunker Hill Monument now raises its granite shaft.

Their activities were not discovered until daylight re-

AROUND BOSTON

vealed their breastworks to the watch on the *Lively*, who instantly gave the alarm. Soon the booming of this ship's guns was waking the people of Boston, who crowded the streets and flocked to points of vantage in the North End, where, torn by conflicting emotions—Whigs praying for the "rebels," Tories for the "regulars"—they prepared to watch the impending battle from housetops and steeples.

Meanwhile General Gage had called a council at his headquarters, a house that stood until quite recently in Hull Street, nearly opposite Copp's Hill burying-ground and within a stone's throw of the Old North Church. With his officers he then crossed over to the old graveyard to watch events and direct them.

So, to Copp's Hill burying-ground let us follow him. This ancient cemetery, occupying the highest hill in North Boston, has retained its old-time character intact. A great proportion of the graves that we see in it to-day were there at the time of the Revolution. There lie the Hutchinsons, father and grandfather of the last royal governor; there are interred

The REVEREND DOCTORS
INCREASE, COTTON
& SAMUEL MATHER

as the inscription upon their simple tombstone records; there, "buried in a stone grave 10 feet deep," lies that stanch old patriot, Captain Daniel Malcolm, "one of the foremost in opposing the Revenue Acts in America."

REVOLUTIONARY PILGRIMAGE

"You may bang the dirt and welcome, they're as safe
 as Dan'l Malcolm
Ten foot beneath the gravestone that you've splintered
 with your balls!"*

And, indeed, his and many another tombstone in the old graveyard still bear traces of the bullets that flew that afternoon.

At the time of the battle there was a battery of six guns in Copp's Hill burying-ground, placed near the Mather tomb. General Gage took up his position beside this battery and, through his glasses, could plainly see the Americans and Prescott walking upon the parapet talking to and encouraging his men.

To-day, of course, the view across the Charles has changed radically since the time of the Revolution. Breed's Hill, then an open pasture, is now part of a crowded city. Factories, terminals, docks, and houses have obliterated all the ancient landmarks. Yet, from this point of vantage, I think, can still be obtained the best idea of the battle of Bunker Hill.†

The north slope of Copp's Hill pitches steeply down to the river. Directly below, at the ferry where Paul Revere had crossed and where Charlestown Bridge now spans the river, lay the *Somerset* man-of-war, the largest of the British ships. Old Charlestown stood by the waterside just beyond, under the shadow of Breed's Hill, upon which the monument now stands so conspicuously.

* "Grandmother's Story of Bunker Hill," by Oliver Wendell Holmes.
† See decorative cover lining.

AROUND BOSTON

Near the present navy-yard the *Lively* and *Falcon* lay at anchor. To the foot of the eminence farther off to the right, then called Morton's Hill, the British troops were ferried over, landed, and formed for the attack.

By this time it was three in the afternoon. The day was warm, the sky cloudless. Deliberately, the grenadiers and light infantry deployed their lines, and then, three deep, in the blistering sunshine, began the toilsome ascent of Breed's Hill. Silently the patriots waited behind their breastworks, watching them coming. And the word went round: "Wait till you see the whites of their eyes." "Aim at the handsome coats; pick off the commanders!"

We all know the rest of the story: how the regulars mounted in grim, serried ranks; how the provincials waited until they were within fifty yards, then poured down upon them one deadly volley after another; how the gallant redcoat ranks faltered, staggered, and broke; how they were rallied by their officers for a second attack and, with General Howe leading, mounted once more over the bodies of their fallen comrades, and how again, before the deadly aim of the patriot-soldiers, their lines broke and they fell back to the shore.

Meanwhile, hot shot, flung into Charlestown, had set it on fire. General Clinton, who, with General Burgoyne, had been watching the battle from Copp's Hill, now rushed down to the waterside and, with reinforcements, crossed over to aid his comrades. Slowly and painfully the British troops reformed their ranks and bravely faced their redoubtable enemy a third time.

REVOLUTIONARY PILGRIMAGE

The American ammunition was now almost exhausted; their muskets were unprovided with bayonets. This time the British were able to push home their attack and, at the point of the bayonet, carry the intrenchments by storm.

Burgoyne remained on Copp's Hill until the end of the battle and, in a letter to Lord Stanley, thus describes what he saw:

"And now ensued one of the greatest scenes of war that can be conceived. . . . Howe's corps, ascending the hill in the face of intrenchments, and in a very disadvantageous ground, was much engaged; and to the left, the enemy pouring in fresh troops by thousands over the land; and in the arm of the sea, our ships and floating batteries cannonading them; straight before us a large and noble town in one blaze: the church steeples, being made of timber, were great pyramids of fire above the rest; behind us, the church steeples and heights of our camp covered with spectators. The enemy all anxious suspense; the roar of cannon, mortars, musketry; the crash of churches, ships upon the stocks, and whole streets falling together in ruin to fill the ear; the storm of the redoubts, with the objects above described, to fill the eye; and the reflection, that, perhaps a defeat was a final loss to the British Empire in America, to fill the mind,— made the whole a picture and complication of horror and importance, beyond anything that came to my lot to be a witness to. I much lament my nephew's absence; it was a sight for a young soldier that the longest service may not furnish again."

Among some letters by British officers collected by Samuel Adams Drake, I found this one written by

AROUND BOSTON

Adjutant Waller to his brother in England. It shifts us to a nearer point of view, and gives a picture of the storming of the redoubt, his battalion, the Royal Marines, according to Colonel Carrington's plan of the battle, having occupied the extreme left of the British line.

"CAMP OF CHARLESTOWN HEIGHTS
"22d. June, 1775.

"MY DEAR BROTHER,—Amidst the hurry and confusion of a camp hastily pitched in a field of battle, I am sat down to tell you I have escaped unhurt, where many, so many, have fallen. The public papers will inform you of the situation of the ground and the redoubt that we attacked on the heights of Charlestown. I can only say that it was a most daring attempt, and that it was performed with as much gallantry and spirit as was ever shown by any troops in any age.

"Two companies of the first battalion of marines and part of the 47th regiment, were the first that mounted the breastwork; and you will not be displeased when I tell you that I was with those two companies who drove their bayonets into all that opposed them. Nothing could be more shocking than the carnage that followed the storming of this work. We tumbled over the dead to get at the living. . . . The rebels had 5000 to 7000 men, covered by a redoubt, breastworks, walls, hedges, trees, and the like; and the number of the corps under General Howe (who performed this gallant business) did not amount to fifteen hundred. We gained a complete victory, and intrenched ourselves that night, where we lay under arms, in the front of the field of battle. . . . I suppose, upon the whole, we lost, killed and wounded, from eight hundred to one thousand men.

REVOLUTIONARY PILGRIMAGE

"We killed a number of the rebels, but the cover they fought under made their loss less considerable than it would otherwise have been. The army is in great spirits, and full of rage and ferocity at the rebellious rascals who both poisoned and chewed the musket-balls, in order to make them the more fatal."

But the "rebellious rascals" did not disperse, nor was the "victory" so "complete" as Adjutant Waller thought. Instead, the patriots, encouraged by the battle, tightened their lines about Boston, and the city was more closely besieged than ever.

On the 2d of July, by decision of Congress, General George Washington arrived at Cambridge to assume command of the American army. The simple ceremony attending his investment as commander-in-chief took place next day under the historic elm, now blasted and torn by lightning, that still stands at the north end of Cambridge Common. Washington made his headquarters at Craigie House, which had been prepared for his reception, and which remains one of the landmarks of the college town, though now better known as the Longfellow House. It is still occupied by the poet's eldest daughter, whose presence lends distinction to the old demesne. I shall not soon forget my visits to it, nor my pleasure and interest in seeing, with her and members of her family, the treasures of that mansion-house, so rarely marked by memories.

Washington at once proceeded to strengthen his position. He fortified the heights about Cambridge—Pros-

AROUND BOSTON

pect, Cobble, and Ploughed Hills—and extended his redoubts as far as Winter Hill on the left to the heights of Roxbury on the right. Then, one night in March, 1776, "with an expedition equal to that of the Genii belonging

Vicinity of the Washington Elm, Cambridge

to Aladdin's lamp," to quote the words of a British officer, the Americans threw up two redoubts on Dorchester Heights, a position of such importance that from it and from their battery on Nook's Hill over Boston Neck, they commanded both the city and the bay.

REVOLUTIONARY PILGRIMAGE

The British admiral admitted that he could no longer "keep a ship in the harbor," and Howe's position in Boston became untenable. So, on the 17th of March, he embarked his army on a fleet of transports, and set sail for Halifax. Three days later Washington entered the streets of Boston at the head of his army, and was rapturously greeted by the patriotic citizens.

TICONDEROGA AND LAKE CHAMPLAIN

TICONDEROGA AND LAKE CHAMPLAIN

WHILE these events were taking place in and around Boston, the other colonies were also active. Only three weeks after the skirmishes at Lexington and Concord, Ethan Allen took Ticonderoga.

Our next pilgrimage, then, will be to the scene of this exploit—one of the most daring and spectacular in the early annals of the Revolution. Though born in Connecticut, Ethan Allen migrated to the New Hampshire Grants at a very early age, and settled in Bennington. There, in pre-Revolutionary days, he used to frequent the Green Mountain Tavern (to which I shall have occasion to refer later) and in its tap-room he and Seth Warner cemented their friendship during the controversies over the New York border.

At the outbreak of the Revolution they both longed to express their patriotism in some great deed of heroism, and the story of their hopes and of what they did is best told, I think, in Ethan Allen's own language—his "Narrative," * a document that gives us a fine glimpse of this

* "Ethan Allen's Narrative of the Capture of Ticonderoga and of his Captivity and Treatment by the British." Written by himself (Bennington, 1849). In the preface to the fifth edition I find this statement by the senior publisher, Chauncy Goodrich: "It is given in the plain language of its self-educated author without any alteration. The senior publisher has been intimately acquainted with his widow, who died about ten years since, and has been assured by her that this narrative is printed as he wrote it without alteration; and that it shows more of his true character than all else ever written of him."

REVOLUTIONARY PILGRIMAGE

blunt, honest patriot—not the illiterate, coarse fellow he is sometimes depicted, but a frank, red-blooded frontiersman. His narrative is dated Bennington, March 25th, 1779, so was written just after he returned from his captivity:

"Ever since I arrived at the state of manhood, and acquainted myself with the general history of mankind, I have felt a sincere passion for liberty. The history of nations, doomed to perpetual slavery, in consequence of yielding up to tyrants their natural-born liberties, I read with a sort of philosophical horror; so that the first systematical and bloody attempt at Lexington, to enslave America, thoroughly electrified my mind, and fully determined me to take part with my country. And, while I was wishing for an opportunity to signalize myself in its behalf, directions were privately sent to me from the then colony (now state) of Connecticut, to raise the Green Mountain Boys, and, if possible, to surprise and take the fortress of Ticonderoga.

"This enterprise I cheerfully undertook, and after first guarding all the several passes that led thither, to cut off all intelligence between the garrison and the country, made a forced march from Bennington, and arrived at the lake opposite Ticonderoga, on the evening of the ninth day of May, 1775 with two hundred and thirty valiant Green Mountain Boys, and it was with the utmost difficulty that I procured boats to cross the lake. However, I landed eighty-three men near the garrison, and sent the boats back for the rear guard, commanded by Col. Seth Warner, but the day began to dawn, and I found myself under a necessity to attack the fort, before the rear could cross the lake."

TICONDEROGA

He then harangued his men, explaining the danger of the enterprise, and, like Pizarro, asked all who dared to follow him to "poise their firelocks."

"The men being, at this time, drawn up in three ranks, each poised his firelock. I ordered them to face to the right, and at the head of the center file, marched them immediately to the wicket-gate where I found a sentry posted, who instantly snapped his fusee at me; I ran immediately toward him and he retreated through the covered way into the parade within the garrison, gave a halloo, and ran under a bomb-proof. My party, who followed me into the fort, I formed on the parade in such a manner as to face the two barracks which faced each other.

"The garrison being asleep, except the sentries, we gave three huzzas which greatly surprised them. One of the sentries made a pass at one of my officers with a charged bayonet, and slightly wounded him. My first thought was to kill him with my sword; but, in an instant, I altered the design and fury of the blow to a slight cut on the side of the head; upon which he dropped his gun, and asked quarter, which I readily granted him, and demanded of him the place where the commanding officer kept; he shewed me a pair of stairs in the front of a barrack, on the west side of the garrison, which led up a second story in said barrack, to which I immediately repaired, and ordered the commander, Capt. De La Place, to come forth immediately, or I would sacrifice the whole garrison; at which the Capt. came instantly to the door with his breeches in his hand; when I ordered him to deliver me the fort; he asked me by what authority I demanded it; I answered him '*In the name of the great Jehovah and the Continental Congress.*'

REVOLUTIONARY PILGRIMAGE

"The authority of the Congress being very little known at that time, he began to speak again; but I interrupted him, and with my drawn sword over his head, again demanded an immediate surrender of the garrison; which he then complied, and ordered his men to be forthwith paraded without arms, as he had given up the garrison. In the mean time some of my officers had given orders and in consequence thereof, sundry of the barrack doors were beat down and about a third of the garrison imprisoned, which consisted of the said commander, a Lieut. Feltham, a conductor of artillery, a gunner, two sergeants, and forty four rank and file; about one hundred pieces of cannon, one thirteen inch mortar and a number of swivels.

"This surprise was carried into execution in the grey of the morning of the tenth of May, 1775. The sun seemed to rise that morning with a superior lustre; and Ticonderoga and its dependencies smiled on its conquerors, who tossed about the flowing bowl, and wished success to Congress, and the liberty and freedom of America. Happy it was for me, at that time, that the then future pages of the book of fate, which afterward unfolded a miserable scene of two years and eight months imprisonment, were hid from my view."

Now that we have his story, let us visit the place. The ruins of old Fort Ticonderoga, the key to all the waterways at the south end of Lake Champlain, are still among the most impressive in our country.

I have not visited them in some years—in fact, not since the time when I made the drawings that accompany this chapter. I have never wanted to go again, for the memory of that visit has been tinged with a flavor of

TICONDEROGA

adventure and romance that, I feared, might be dispelled if I visited the locality again under changed conditions. At that time I had noticed the advertisement of a summer hotel near the old fort—an account that read most attractively—as these advertisements always do.

The Ruins of Fort Ticonderoga

So, to stay at this hotel, we left the train at the station of Fort Ti, expecting to take the steamer across the lake. But, upon inquiry, the captain said: "That pier's rotten; I wouldn't risk my boat there for anything. And, besides, there's a sea running." "But how are we going to get across?" I asked. "Oh, I guess you can get the station agent to row you over; he's got a boat."

And with that he rang his engine-bell, and the steamer

REVOLUTIONARY PILGRIMAGE

floated slowly north, settling down close upon the water, like a big white duck. The train we had just left was flying toward the tail of the lake, leaving a billowy cloud of smoke behind it. The little station was deserted. Presently the agent appeared with our luggage. Yes, he'd take us "over the lake in about two hours." He'd his "dinner to eat and his job to finish."

The two long hours slipped by in the shadow of Mount Defiance. Then he beckoned to us, and we descended to a little cove where a boat lay between the rocks. Our trunk, bags, and sketching outfit were loaded in the bow and we in the stern, and we pushed off. He rowed a strong stroke, and, despite a head wind and the white-

Ruins of the Officers' Quarters at Ticonderoga

TICONDEROGA

caps, we soon could discern the ruins of the old fort and its bastions firmly planted on the rocks, with the walls of its barracks silhouetted against the sky.

Our boatman had been most incommunicative. Finally he headed for the shore and, with a vigorous stroke or two, drove the nose of the boat on a pebbly beach and dumped out our luggage. In a moment, still quite silent, he was off again, gliding over the lake, leaving us stranded like two pilgrims on a desert shore. Not a house nor habitation was in sight.

We took our smaller belongings and walked up a path some three hundred yards or more, when, set in a fine grove of locust-trees, we made out a large white house— a great colonial mansion with tall columns to its central portico, and long wings at each side leading to end-pavilions. This was the summer hotel of which I had read. On entering, however, we found only a shiftless fellow in his shirt-sleeves in the vast corridor. "Yes, this is the hotel; do you want a room?" And he led us off to one of the end-pavilions and assigned us a large chamber. When we went in to dinner we found ourselves the only guests! The shiftless one was the proprietor, and his wife the cook.

Well, we stuck it out eight days. We had adventures, too. One night a party of drunken yachtsmen landed and fired pistols right and left to give vent to their enthusiasm. There was not a lock or key to any of our doors, which gave directly on verandas, and we did not know at what moment these roisterers might make irrup-

REVOLUTIONARY PILGRIMAGE

tion into our room. So I made barricades of bureaus and tables as the unsteady steps echoed up and down the empty corridors, at times approaching, then disappearing in dim distances, as with pistol-shots and loud huzzas they "tossed about the flowing bowl."

The climax to our visit was reached upon the eighth day, when our proprietor announced, with some perturbation, that there would be no dinner as his wife had run away! So he drove us to the train, and we proceeded to Port Henry and Crown Point. I have never heard what became of the hotel.

Luckily, however, my drawings were completed. Luckily, also, we had lingered long enough, undisturbed, among the ruins to absorb their every detail. We had traced the underground passage (as you still may do) through which Ethan Allen led his men from the sallyport. We had found its orifice upon the parade-ground between the barracks. We had explored these "two barracks which faced each other," as Allen describes, and beyond had visited the old French lines of Fort Carillon.

From the bastions, high above the river, we had enjoyed wide prospects. To the north stretched Lake Champlain, so narrow that we saw both banks, so long that it reached the far horizon. From the west the waterway came in from Lake George; toward the south and east, Mount Defiance and Mount Independence reared their wooded slopes, with the village of Ticonderoga lying at their feet, while, beyond, the hills of Vermont, dotted

TICONDEROGA

with farms, stretched off to the line of the distant Green Mountains.

As the sun dropped and the shadows lengthened, how the past came back—especially in the moonlight, when a spirit of romance, born of the quiet of the night, hovered over the place, and the ghosts of its dead heroes seemed to walk again among the trees as the wind softly stirred their rustling leaves—the men of the French and Indian Wars—brave Montcalm, its commandant, who died so gloriously before Quebec; General Abercrombie and his gallant young lieutenant, the Viscount Howe; Rogers and Stark of the Rangers; and Lord Jeffrey Amhurst, who took the proud fortress from the French—then the men of '75: Ethan Allen, Seth Warner, Benedict Arnold, St. Clair, and Burgoyne! So its ruined ramparts seemed to speak of gallant deeds. . . .

After Ethan Allen had seized the fortress, he sent Seth Warner to the north to capture Crown Point. This was done without trouble or bloodshed. Benedict Arnold, who had accompanied the enterprise, hot-headed and ambitious, now wished to make the conquest of Lake Champlain complete. So, with fifty men, he seized a schooner, mounted some guns upon it, and captured St. John's at the head of the lake, thus driving the last British soldier from its shores.

Lake Champlain now remained undisputably in American hands for nearly two years. A new star fort was built on the summit of Mount Independence, opposite Ticonderoga, and both places were well garrisoned.

REVOLUTIONARY PILGRIMAGE

In March, 1777, Sir Guy Carleton, the military governor of Canada, received a message from London requesting him to detach all the troops that he could spare, put them in charge of Lieutenant-General John Bur-

Ruins of Old Fort Frederick, Crown Point

goyne, and send them south "with all expedition" to Albany to join Sir William Howe's forces, and "aid him in putting down the rebellion."

Thus Burgoyne's campaign was launched—a campaign we shall now follow to its final issue on the plains of Saratoga.

It was to proceed in two divisions. A smaller one, under Lieutenant-Colonel St. Leger was to go by way of

TICONDEROGA

the Mohawk Valley (and we shall follow its movements later). The main column, with General Burgoyne himself in command, was to move south by way of Lake Champlain. On the 12th of June Sir Guy Carleton reviewed this proud army of invasion before he sent it forth upon its career. The picture that it made as it sailed down the placid waters of Lake Champlain is thus vividly described* by Thomas Anburey, a British officer who accompanied the expedition:

"I cannot forbear picturing to your imagination one of the most pleasing spectacles I ever beheld. When we were in the widest part of the lake, whose beauty and extent I have already described, it was remarkably fine and clear—not a breeze was stirring—when the whole army appeared at one view in such perfect regularity as to form the most complete and splendid regatta you can possibly conceive. . . .

"In the front the Indians went with their birch canoes, containing twenty or thirty in each; then the advanced corps in regular line with the gun-boats; then followed the *Royal George* and *Inflexible*, towing large booms which are to be thrown across two points of land, with the other brigs and sloops following; after them the first brigade in a regular line, then the Generals Burgoyne, Phillips and Riedesel in their pinnaces; next to them were the second brigade, followed by the German brigades; and the rear was brought up with the sutlers and followers of the army. Upon the appearance of so formidable a fleet you may imagine they were not a

---

* "Travels through the Interior Parts of America in a series of Letters." By an Officer.

REVOLUTIONARY PILGRIMAGE

little dismayed at Ticonderoga, for they were apprised of our advance, as we every day could see their watch-boats."

This splendid army consisted of more than seven thousand troops, commanded by efficient officers and provided with exceptional artillery. About half of its soldiers were German mercenaries. Its weak point, as we shall see, lay in its lack of pioneers, horses, and provisions for its transport.

A preliminary camp was established on the Boquet River above Crown Point, and here in answer to a proclamation about four hundred Indians joined the expedition. Thence an advance was made on Crown Point, which surrendered without opposition. The army then divided into two columns. One, the British troops under Brigadier-General Fraser, marched down the west shore of the lake; the other, the German troops under General Riedesel, followed the east shore; while Burgoyne himself sailed with the fleet.

The British column arrived before Ticonderoga on the 1st of July, and on the following day the Americans abandoned the old French works, burned their defenses, and retired into the main fortress. Its garrison, as well as that upon the star fort on Mount Independence opposite, was commanded by General Arthur St. Clair, who had under his orders a total of about twenty-five hundred continentals, and nine hundred poorly equipped militia. He decided that he could hold the fort, but only for a short time, as supplies, clothing, and military stores were all deficient.

TICONDEROGA

General Schuyler, who commanded the Northern Department, and had just inspected the defenses at Ticonderoga, also foresaw its probable downfall, for he wrote: "The insufficiency of the garrison at Ticonderoga, the improper state of the fortifications, and the want of discipline in the troops, give me great cause to apprehend that we shall lose that fortress."

His fears proved only too well-founded. Baron Riedesel's troops drew close about the foot of Mount Independence from the north and east, while the British, crossing to Sugar Loaf Hill, which had always been deemed inaccessible for artillery, in the dead of night, succeeded in placing a battery upon its summit. This new position they called Fort Defiance, and from it they could command both Ticonderoga and Mount Independence from an elevation several hundred feet higher than either.

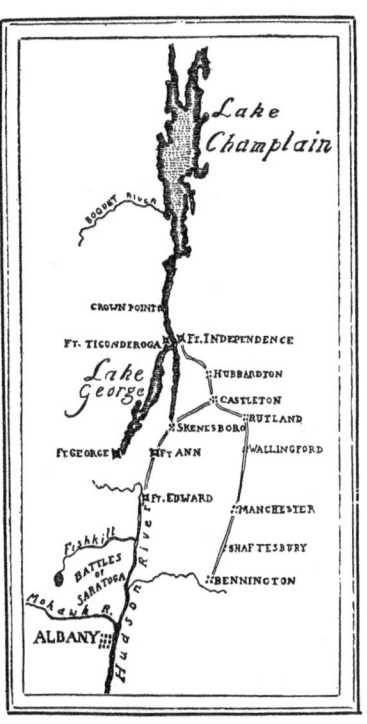

Map Illustrating Burgoyne's Campaign

REVOLUTIONARY PILGRIMAGE

With their glasses, they could plainly watch the movements of every soldier in both forts.

Under so startling a menace, a council of American officers decided it was best to evacuate while yet the south slope of Mount Independence was open for retreat.

Lake Champlain, roughly speaking, is shaped like a thin fish swimming north, with two long ends to its tail. Lake George* is one of these ends; the other is a narrow waterway, South River, that extends down as far as Whitehall or Skenesborough, as it then was called. A temporary bridge of floats, protected by a boom of heavy timbers, clinched with bolts, had been built by the Americans to impede navigation into this south arm of the lake and to connect Fort Ticonderoga with Mount Independence.

When the evacuation was decided upon, it was arranged that the Ticonderoga garrison would cross this bridge, and joining that of Fort Independence march by land to Skenesborough via Castleton. The baggage, ammunition, and stores, with the invalids, under the escort of a battalion of troops under Colonel Long, was to go in batteaux to the same destination by the narrow south end of the lake. The retreat was to be effected during the night of the 5th of July.

And now we have our second picture of Ticonderoga. The guns of the fort, to quiet suspicions, were keeping up a desultory fire upon the battery on Mount Defiance.

* The old Indian name for Lake George was "Horican," or "Tail of the Lake."

TICONDEROGA

Meanwhile, though a young moon was shining, the American garrison, at three in the morning, in stealthy silence, crossed the bridge unseen, and arrived at the foot of Mount Independence. The troops from the fort above came down to join them, but just at this critical moment some one, contrary to orders, set fire to the house of General de Fermoy, commander of Fort Independence, and the flames, leaping aloft, revealed the American columns to the British sentries.

The boats got off and the garrison marched away, but all knew that their movements had been discovered. The British drums beat to arms. Quick orders rang in the night. When day broke all was astir, and a pursuit rapidly organized. General Fraser, with an advance corps of light infantry, started after the fleeing garrison, General Riedesel following with his Germans.

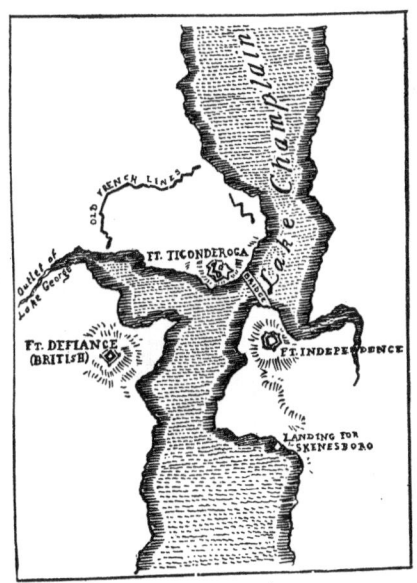

Map of Ticonderoga

Meanwhile a passage had been cut through the boom

REVOLUTIONARY PILGRIMAGE

and bridge, and the British frigates moved with all speed down the South River, in pursuit of the American shipping. It was a critical moment, and every one knew it.

TO THE PLAINS OF SARATOGA

TO THE PLAINS OF SARATOGA

I

TICONDEROGA TO FORT EDWARD

FIRST we shall follow Burgoyne and his floating column to Skenesborough. So swiftly did he move, and so hotly did he pursue Colonel Long and the American flotilla, that he reached the south end of the lake only two hours behind the Americans. These had had no time to organize, and, besides, what could they do against such a formidable enemy? So, abandoning all hope of resistance, they set fire to the mills, shipping, dwellings, and to the stores that they had saved at such pains, and all went up together in one vast brasier, whose flames, mounting aloft, licked up the mountain-side, devouring trees, shrubs, and houses, in one great conflagration. The little American column, meanwhile, hopelessly outnumbered, hastened onward to Fort Ann, eleven miles to the south.

Burgoyne remained at Skenesborough for some time, waiting for General Fraser and organizing his advance. He stayed with Major Skene, a noted loyalist, from whom the town took its name, and who was able to give him much information about the country and the people, some of it, as events proved, of value, some of it not.

Skenesborough is now called Whitehall. It is situated

REVOLUTIONARY PILGRIMAGE

at the point where the south end of Lake Champlain is tapped by the Champlain Canal, that connects it with the Hudson River, thus affording an unbroken waterway from New York to Canada. The situation of the town is highly picturesque. A hill with a rounded top but very steep sides, well-wooded, rises abruptly above it, holding upon its declivities some of the buildings. A big, black cannon planted among them on a ledge, points its nose up the lake to remind you of the one-time importance of this strategic point.

The main portion of the town clusters about the base of this hill, its shapely church spires telling handsomely against the green slopes behind them. The principal street, parked in places, borders the canal, whose locks are alive with tugs and barges. Beyond, long lines of freight-cars fill the railway yards and emphasize the consequence of this long waterway—the whole aspect of the place being strongly reminiscent of some busy canal town in Flanders: Dinan or Namur, for example.

Burgoyne's route to the Hudson is almost identical with that now followed by the Champlain Canal. Thus far all had gone well with him, and his success had equalled his most sanguine hopes. The first act of his drama— "the first period of this campaign," as he himself calls it—had ended brilliantly here at Skenesborough. In the second act his troubles were to begin—troubles that commenced as soon as he left Major Skene's house.

A fine state highway takes one to-day along the Champlain Canal, landing you finally, twenty-five miles away,

TO THE PLAINS OF SARATOGA

at Fort Edward. From it you obtain an excellent idea of the topography of the region through which Burgoyne now began this advance. At first the valley is quite narrow, hemmed in by a succession of wooded hills; then it widens enough to reveal the lofty hills that surround Lake George upon the one hand, and the distant Green Mountains on the other.

A mile or two north of Fort Ann, the canal, railroad, and highway together penetrate a narrow defile, rocky and clothed only with stunted cedars. Here Colonel Long with his detachment, reinforced by troops sent forward by General Schuyler, made his first stand against the pursuing British. The Americans were almost successful in their defense, for at first they flanked their enemy, got in his rear, and "made a very vigorous attack, and they certainly would have forced us," states Major Forbes of of the Ninth, "had it not been for some Indians that arrived and gave the Indian whoop." This turned the tide, the Americans gave way, fell back to and burned Fort Ann, that was untenable before so strong an adversary, and retreated to Fort Edward, where they joined forces with General Schuyler's command.

Fort Ann of to-day is a pleasant village, set on a hillock with nothing in particular, except its name, to distinguish it from other villages in its vicinity. Beyond it, the valley widens out even more, until it becomes quite level, and rapidly takes on the characteristics of the broad Hudson valley, peaceful, pastoral, rather uncultivated, with distant mountains lying along far horizons.

REVOLUTIONARY PILGRIMAGE

In the days of the Revolution it was wooded, and Schuyler had used every artifice to impede his enemy's advance. Thomas Anburey writes:

"The country between our late encampment at Skenesborough and this place, was a continuation of woods and creeks, interspersed with deep morasses; and to add to these impediments, the enemy had very industriously augmented them, by felling immense trees, and various other modes, so that it was with the utmost pains and fatigue that we could work our way through them. Exclusive of these, the watery grounds and marshes were so numerous, that we were under the necessity of constructing no less than forty bridges to pass them, and over one morass there was a bridge of near two miles in length."

The Americans had also rounded up all the live stock of the region so that Burgoyne's foraging parties brought him no supplies. This was striking the British army in its weakest spot, for, as I have said, it was deficient in stores, and the farther it went from its bases, the more acute this problem became.

The road from Fort Ann to Fort Edward takes us through the large modern town of Hudson Falls, above which is Glenn's Falls, where the Hudson, though now harnessed by machinery and almost screened by a new viaduct, tumbles in a series of broad cascades a distance of sixty feet. Beside these rushing waters, "in one place white as snow, in another green as grass," as Hawk-eye himself describes them, dwelt Uncas, last of the Mohicans,

TO THE PLAINS OF SARATOGA

for it was here, by the portages between the Hudson and the lakes, that Fenimore Cooper lays his famous story.

Having forced its way from the west through a series of rocky defiles, and having here made its impetuous descent, the Hudson turns abruptly to the south, and spreads out serene and placid as it takes its lazy way to the sea.

Just below this sharp bend lay Fort Edward, that played so prominent a part in the annals of the French and Indian Wars. Now a modern town of some consequence covers its site. The star-shaped fort used to stand upon the east bank of the Hudson, high above the river, its ramparts protected by it as well as by Fort Edward Creek, which here flows in.

After his long struggle across the intervening country, Burgoyne came down to Fort Edward by way of Sandy Hill, at which place occurred the unfortunate murder of Jane M'Crea, that did so much to alienate loyalists and patriots alike from the British cause—an event that fits well into the setting of this country so linked with Indian myths and murders. The exact facts connected with Jane M'Crea's death have always been more or less shrouded in mystery, so that, around her tragic story, many fictions have been woven and many a harrowing tale been told.

Anburey, in a letter, dated "Camp at Fort Edward," and written a few days after the tragedy, thus recounts the facts as he heard them:

REVOLUTIONARY PILGRIMAGE

"To those who have been averse to our employing Indians, a melancholy instance was lately afforded that will sharpen their arguments against the maxim, and, as the matter will be greatly exaggerated, when the accounts of it arrive in England, I shall relate to you the circumstance, as it really happened. . . .

"A young lady, upon the approach of our army, was determined to leave her father's house and join it, as a young man, to whom she was on the point of being married, was an officer in the provincial troops. Some Indians, who were out upon a scout, by chance met her in the woods; they at first treated her with every mark of civility they are capable of and were conducting her into camp, when, within a mile of it, a dispute arose between the two Indians, whose prisoner she was, and words growing very high, one of them, who was fearful of losing the reward for bringing her safe into camp, most inhumanly struck his tomahawk into her skull, and she instantly expired.

"The situation of the General whose humanity was much shocked at such an instance of barbarity, was very distressing and critical; for however inclined he might be to punish the offender, still it was hazarding the revenge of the Indians, whose friendship he had to court rather than seek their enmity. . . . The General shewed great resentment to the Indians upon this occasion and laid restraints upon their dispositions to commit other enormities."

Indeed, this incident pained Burgoyne exceedingly, and occasioned him no end of trouble. When reproached with it by General Gates, he sent this fine reply: "I could not be conscious of the foul deeds you impute to me for

TO THE PLAINS OF SARATOGA

the whole continent of America; though the wealth of worlds were in its bowels and a paradise upon its surface."

In the latter part of July, he moved down from Sandy Hill to Fort Edward, where his soldiers, for the first time, beheld the Hudson, so long the goal of their desires. They were greatly heartened by this sight for their troubles now seemed nearing their end.

Meanwhile General Schuyler, unable to face Burgoyne with his scant army, had retired down the river and taken up his position near Stillwater, above the mouth of the Mohawk River, and not far from busy, present-day Mechanicsville. Both generals now busied themselves with preparations for the conflict which seemed inevitable. And while they remain thus in close proximity, let us return to see what became of the garrison of Ticonderoga that started south through the mountains of Vermont.

II

THE GREEN MOUNTAINS

THIS quest will take us through the Green Mountain region—as delightful a motor trip as one could desire—the stretch from Rutland to Bennington, in particular, being a long succession of beautiful landscapes, framed with mountains whose contours reminded us, as our French chauffeur expressed it, of his own "native Pyrenees." Like the verdant Pyrenean slopes, they are wooded to their summits—whence their name. At their feet, knolls and hillocks are clothed with stately oaks, elms, and maples, to which now and then groves and clumps of hemlocks add a sombre note. But in the valleys the fields are lush and green, and aglow, especially in June, with the brightest wild flowers.

It was to these mountains of Vermont, as I have stated, that the Ticonderoga garrison escaped on its road to Castleton. But they were hotly pursued by Fraser's corps, while Riedesel, with his Hessians, followed close behind. The American main column, under St. Clair, pushed on rapidly—threading the narrow "intervales" of the Green Mountains, whose mazes they knew so well, and attained Castleton in safety.

TO THE PLAINS OF SARATOGA

The rear-guard, however, under gallant Seth Warner, remained behind at Hubbardton. Here, early on a hot, summer morning, they were overtaken by Fraser's troops and a fierce battle ensued. The Americans were so favorably posted, and poured such a well-directed fire into the British ranks that they would have carried the day had not Riedesel arrived at the opportune moment and, with flags flying and fifes playing, thrown his fresh troops into the conflict. The tide quickly turned, and the American defeat was complete. Their broken regiments fled in every direction—some over the mountains to Rutland; others to join their comrades at Castleton. When these latter reached St. Clair and told of their disaster, he collected every fugitive he could find and hastened forward to General Schuyler on the Hudson, joining him about five days later.

Castleton to-day has an air of real distinction. It is set in a valley hemmed in by mountains of picturesque and fantastic contour. Many of its houses are very old. Porticos with tall, white columns alternate with simple clapboarded fronts to form an interesting main street that is shaded by noble elms. Just as you leave it to proceed to Rutland, a tablet marks the site of Fort Warren, the scene of a conflict.

Through a gateway formed by Mount Handy on the north and Mount Herrick on the south we now entered the valley of the Otter and Rutland lay before us, its tall church spires rising finely above the general mass of its buildings. We crossed a long bridge that spans

REVOLUTIONARY PILGRIMAGE

the river and important railway yards, descended its main street—a busy thoroughfare—and drew up before the hotel.

Rutland was always a favorite recruiting place for the Green Mountain Boys, as well as their haven of refuge after their forays. This fact is commemorated by a bronze statue by Porter that has recently been erected by the Daughters of the Revolution, up under the lofty trees that shade a handsome avenue in the residential district of the city. A powerful, manly fellow, clad in shirt and homespuns, stands upon a great pile of boulders that strongly suggests a mountain-top. His head is turned, and the action brings into play the big muscles of the neck and chest; his attitude is alert and vigilant; his pose striking and instinct with life; and it is indeed good to see, in so remote a locality, such a real contribution to the art that commemorates the Revolution. The simple inscription, too, is perfect: "To the Green Mountain Boys."

From Rutland southward the road follows the Otter River, threading a beautiful valley, hemmed in between the Taconic Ridge on the one side and the main range of the Green Mountains on the other. The day we motored down it was showery, and gray clouds hung thick at times about the mountains, hiding one peak and revealing another; screening one range entirely and crawling over another in long, white filaments, that hung like ghosts among the trees, and by their air of mystery enhanced the sense of height.

TO THE PLAINS OF SARATOGA

At Wallingford I noted a granite boulder by the church engraved with these words: "In memory of the Revolutionary soldiers who went from Wallingford." Beyond we passed the Nichols Farm that dates from 1778. Now and then we came upon important marble quarries, and frequently saw the sign "Maple and nut candy," that hinted at another industry of the countryside.

Then we entered the main street of Manchester-in-the-Mountains, that alluring resort situated at the foot of Mount Equinox. Sidewalks of marble border the broad avenue, and towering elms of great age shade it. The white colonnades of the Equinox House—reminiscent of Jefferson's dream at the University of Virginia—invited us to linger, as well as the mid-Victorian atmosphere of its spacious rooms, with their brocaded hangings and old-fashioned rosewood furniture. "Here in summer," in naïve fashion says good Colonel Jack Graham, who wrote of Vermont in 1797, "the kind breezes, which whisper among the trees, and press between the mountains, refresh the weary traveller and render this place, if I may venture to use such an expression, the habitation of the Zephyrs."

But despite these allurements, so real and so substantial, we remained firm to our purpose and pushed on to Bennington, our objective for the night.

We soon reached Shaftesbury, beyond which we climbed quite a steep grade. Then from a summit we beheld, for the first time, the valley of Bennington lying spread beneath us—a rarely beautiful landscape, built upon a

REVOLUTIONARY PILGRIMAGE

great scale and worthy the brush of Inness or of Constable. Lofty, purplish mountains, wreathed in clouds, enclosed a broad stretch of country whose undulations were clothed with stately trees. In the centre, the focal point of the picture, placed high upon an eminence, the tall shaft of the Bennington Monument shot upward, rising handsomely against the vast blue dome of Mount Anthony.

We passed by an outlying village or two, and then, at the very door of the city, as it were, were treated to a novel sight—a deer (it was nearing sunset) leaping the fences, one after another, and even the railway tracks, as he made for the depths of the woods beyond. Then we obtained a near view of the monument, and of Mount Anthony, finely silhouetted against the western sky, where the clouds were now breaking, and shafts of light shot forth, giving promise for the morrow.

We drew up before the homelike Walloomsac Inn, on the hill, not far from the monument, and a few minutes later were dining in a charming home near by and talking of Bennington, its history and its attractions.

The town certainly possesses

Battle Monument, Bennington

TO THE PLAINS OF SARATOGA

that evanescent something that we call "atmosphere." Its modern section, to be sure, at the foot of the hill, with the shops and newer dwellings, is not particularly attractive; but the old quarter, up above, is still to a remarkable degree redolent of other days. Most of its houses are a century old, and many are, architecturally, of great interest, with their pilastered corners, delicate dentillated cornices, fanlights, and well-spaced window openings.

The Catamount Tavern, now completely destroyed

Directly opposite the inn stands a handsome church, and up the shaded avenue the soaring monument appears. There is scarcely a house on Monument Avenue that has not weathered its hundredth winter. Half-way up it a bronze catamount marks the site of the Green Mountain Tavern, to which I have alluded in a preceding chapter as the place in which Ethan Allen and Seth Warner planned their attack upon Ticonderoga. Crouched upon its sign-board, a stuffed catamount used to snarl toward New York State, with which the New Hampshire Grants were then in controversy concerning

REVOLUTIONARY PILGRIMAGE

the boundary. From this sign the place became known as the Catamount Tavern. To it, after his thrilling adventures and his visit to Washington at Valley Forge, Ethan Allen returned, arriving, as he further recounts in his "Narrative," upon

"the evening of the last day of May to their [the Green Mountain Boys'] surprise, for I was thought to be dead, and now my joy and theirs was complete. Three cannon were fired that evening and next morning, Colonel Herrick gave orders, and fourteen more were discharged, welcoming me to Bennington, my usual place of abode; thirteen for the United States and one for young Vermont.

"After this ceremony was ended, we moved the flowing bowl, and rural felicity, sweetened with friendship, glowed in each countenance, and with loyal healths to the rising States of America, concluded that evening and with the same loyal spirit, I now conclude my narrative."

His friend, Seth Warner (done in granite, I am sorry to say), stands upon a pedestal at the head of the avenue, directly in front of the gigantic monument that commemorates the Battle of Bennington, a mighty shaft, not, strictly speaking, a work of art, but certainly most impressive, dominating an extended landscape of great beauty.

Upon the ground where it stands there was a storehouse in the days of the Revolution. When Burgoyne reached Fort Edward his need of supplies and horses became very acute. On August 6, he records: "At ten o'clock this morning, not quite enough provisions for the consumption of two days." Major Skene, who ac-

TO THE PLAINS OF SARATOGA

companied him, knew of this storehouse at Bennington, and that in it were collected great quantities of military supplies. He also persuaded Burgoyne that there were many Tories in the district who were only too anxious to join the British forces if he would but send an expedition in their direction.

This Burgoyne now resolved to do. He selected Colonel Baume to carry out his purpose, and sent him with about five hundred men, mostly Hessians, to collect horses to mount the dragoons and to seize the stores at Bennington.

Meanwhile the Green Mountain Boys had been gathering to watch his movements, and when this expedition started out they hastily organized. John Stark, who held no regular commission in the American army at that time, was persuaded to lead them, and he sent word to Seth Warner, at Manchester, asking him to co-operate as speedily as possible. The improvised army quickly collected at Bennington and marched forthwith to meet Baume's column.

The Hessians had advanced to within a few miles of Bennington, but when they heard that important forces were coming out to meet them they intrenched themselves upon a steep hill situated in a bend of the Walloomsac River. Riedesel's dragoons and the Rangers were posted upon the top of this hill, while Baume's other troops took up positions down by a ford, with the Canadians and Tories thrown out across the stream as outposts on the Bennington Road.

REVOLUTIONARY PILGRIMAGE

Stark led his men to a spot a little farther up the river, where a stone now marks his camp—a stone graven with his well-known words: "There are the red-coats; and they are ours, or this night Molly Stark sleeps a widow." From this place of encampment, on the morning of the 16th of August, he led forth his men. He sent Colonel Hubbard and Colonel Stickney against the troops stationed at the ford; Colonel Herrick marched his regiment around to the back of the hill; Colonel Nichols was stationed to the east, while Stark reserved for himself the main assault up the steep declivity. All the attacks were delivered with precision and exceeding vigor. The British outposts were forced in and driven up the hill until the various American regiments, uniting from all sides at once, stormed the breastworks on the top with conspicuous gallantry. Though Baume's picked troops were stationed here, they were soon overcome and Baume himself mortally wounded.

Stark, in his report to the Council of New Hampshire, thus sums up the further progress of the battle:

"Our people behaved with the greatest spirit and bravery imaginable. Had they been Alexanders or Charleses of Sweden they could not have behaved better.

"The action lasted two hours; at the expiration of which time we forced their breastworks at the muzzle of their guns; took two pieces of brass cannon, with a number of prisoners; but before I could get them into proper form again, I received intelligence that there was a large reenforcement within two miles of us, on the march, which occasioned us to renew our attack; but, luckily

TO THE PLAINS OF SARATOGA

for us, Colonel Warner's regiment came up, which put a stop to their career. We soon rallied, and in a few minutes, the action became very warm and desperate, which lasted until night. We used their cannon against them, which proved of great service to us.

"At sunset, we obliged them to retreat a second time; we pursued them till dark, when I was obliged to halt for fear of killing our men."

Congress, having passed over Stark before, now commissioned him a full brigadier-general, and the State of Massachusetts voted him "a complete suit of clothes becoming his rank, together with a piece of linen."

The day after our arrival in Bennington we set out to visit the battle-ground which lies about six miles to the west of the city, near the town of North Hoosick. Before reaching it we came upon a sign that indicates the site of the house to which Colonel Baume was taken and in which he died. From a point just above this, where a power-house stands by a railway embankment, you gain, I think, the best idea of the battle-field as a whole.

Directly in front of you rises the steep hill upon which the dragoons and Rangers were posted with the Walloomsac skirting its base. From the other side of the embankment you can see a great maple-tree that stands by the ford which the Canadians defended, and from the top of the hill you look down on the positions taken by the American militia: Herrick to the north, Nichols to the east, Stickney and Hubbard to the south.

REVOLUTIONARY PILGRIMAGE

Somewhere I found this poetic version of the view from this hilltop, penned by a romantic Hessian, who escaped capture by fleeing to the forest he describes:

"The fields looked green and refreshed (after a night of rain) the river was swollen and tumultuous and the branches were all loaded with dew-drops which glittered in the sun's rays, like so many diamonds. Nor would it be easy to imagine any scene more rife with peaceful or even pastoral beauty. Looking down from this summit of the rising ground, I beheld immediately beneath me a wide sweep of stately forest, interrupted at remote intervals by green meadows or yellow cornfields, whilst here and there, a cottage, a shed, or some primitive edifice reared its modest head, as if for the purpose of reminding the spectator, that man had begun his inroads upon nature, without as yet taking away from her simplicity and grandeur."

Except that the "green meadows and yellow cornfields" are now more extensive and the forests of smaller size than formerly, his description of this view quite fits it to-day, and well conveys the charm of this Walloomsac Valley. The battle-field, I hear, has recently been acquired by the State, and a monument is to be erected upon the historic hill where Stark's New Englanders made the first successful attack of the war upon an intrenched enemy.

His victory, so complete and so substantial, was most heartening to the patriots and greatly strengthened their cause; while to Burgoyne it was a bitter blow, frustrating all his hopes of replenishing his supplies.

III

THE MOHAWK VALLEY

ON almost the same day that saw this British expedition defeated at Bennington St. Leger's column reached the end of its career up in the Mohawk Valley. In my chapter on Ticonderoga I alluded to this expedition, explaining that it was to invade New York State from the west, descending by way of the Mohawk to join Burgoyne at Albany.

It had successfully ascended the St. Lawrence River to Lake Ontario, crossed that lake, moved up the Oswego and Oneida Rivers to Oneida Lake, and from Sylvan Beach had made its way up Fish Creek, so that at the beginning of August it was but a short portage from the Mohawk.

On the Mohawk River, where the city of Rome now stands, was the principal American outpost in the Mohawk Valley, Fort Stanwix. This fort had just been strengthened and renamed, in honor of the general of the Northern Department, Fort Schuyler. It was commanded by Colonel Peter Gansevoort, who, with reinforcements that had just reached him, had a garrison of about a thousand men.

REVOLUTIONARY PILGRIMAGE

It is indeed difficult for the traveller who journeys nowadays down the Mohawk Valley in a Pullman car to picture it as it was in the days of the Revolution. Its broad fields and well-tilled acres, its peaceful villages and thriving towns in no way even remotely suggest the pathless forests that then clothed the banks of the river, affording safe hiding-places for the cruel savages that infested them—the red men that played so conspicuous a part in the Revolutionary history of this wild district. In these forests the ferocious tribesmen depicted by Fenimore Cooper had free rein for the practice of their barbarous warfare, and they and the Tories of the region, particularly numerous and particularly bitter, vied with each other in deeds of cruelty.

St. Leger was taking advantage of these circumstances and was using the Indians and Tories in great numbers, allowing the former the practice of their savage customs, the unrestrained use of the scalping-knife and tomahawk.

When he finally left his boats at Fish Creek and started through the forest to invest Fort Schuyler, he organized his column in masterly fashion. A diagram of his plan of march was afterward found among the papers in his writing-desk, and shows his troops thus ingeniously disposed: first came five files of Indians, walking singly, spaced well apart and flanking the British flag. These were led by Joseph Brant, a full-blooded Mohawk, whose Indian name, Thayendanega, signified strength; a savage fighter, noted for his many cruelties, but so shrewd, withal, and of such conspicuous ability that he held a

TO THE PLAINS OF SARATOGA

colonel's commission from the British king. More than four hundred paces behind these Indians came the advanced guard, and a hundred paces behind these the two main columns of regulars, also in single file, with files of Indians flanking them to the right and left, as well as covering their rear. By this clever disposition, protected on all sides by a curtain of redskins, St. Leger was able to march through the pathless forest without fear of ambuscade or surprise of any kind.

He arrived before Fort Schuyler on the 3d of August, with his strange array of British regulars, Hessian chasseurs, Canadians, Royal Green Tories, and warriors from all the tribes of the Six Nations. He instantly summoned the garrison to surrender under dire threats of reprisal. Gansevoort indignantly refused, and sat tight behind his breastworks. So St. Leger drew in his lines and laid siege to the fortress, the Indians keeping up a hideous howling throughout the night to intimidate the garrison.

Meanwhile General Nicholas Herkimer, who lived farther down the valley in an old brick house still standing, had called up the militia of Tryon County to organize and hasten to the relief of Fort Schuyler. They eagerly responded, collecting at Fort Dayton, in the German Flats, where the thriving town of Herkimer now stands.

Herkimer sent a messenger to Gansevoort apprising him of his movements, and requesting the commander of the fort to co-operate by making a sortie upon his approach. He then advanced beyond Utica and there

REVOLUTIONARY PILGRIMAGE

awaited the three signal-guns that were to tell him that his messenger had arrived in safety at the fort. This messenger, however, was delayed for a whole day or more, and some of Herkimer's younger officers, impetuous and impatient, wanted to move on. The old man tried to restrain them, but under their repeated taunts—they called him a coward and a Tory—he finally gave in and, against his own good judgment, ordered an advance.

St. Leger, informed of Herkimer's approach, sent forth a strong column, composed largely of Tory troops and Indians, under Brant, to waylay him en route and entrap him in an ambush. For this purpose Brant selected a ravine near Oriskany, about eight miles east of Fort Schuyler. He disposed his troops and his Indians in a wide circle, completely hidden by the dense woods, leaving only the road from Utica open.

Into this sort of funnel the unsuspecting Americans marched on a dark, sultry morning, crossing the marshy bottom of the ravine by means of a narrow causeway of earth and logs, where the road in the foreground of my picture now traverses the hollow. When the marching column was well within the trap, Brant gave the signal, the circle tightened and closed in, and from every side, with war-whoop, spear, and tomahawk, the Indians sprang forth, while the British troops poured in a hot fire from the cover of the woods.

At first the Americans were dismayed by this sudden onslaught, but under brave, cool Herkimer's leadership they quickly rallied and desperately defended themselves.

TO THE PLAINS OF SARATOGA

Their general was soon severely wounded but, propped against a tree, continued to give his clear, calm orders. The Americans now formed into circles so as to face their encircling foes, and were fighting with the greatest obstinacy and bravery, when the clouds that had been gathering heavily all morning suddenly, with a terrific peal of thunder, broke into a torrent of rain. The firing ceased as both sides sought shelter for a while and prepared for a second trial of strength.

Johnson's Greens, a Tory regiment recruited in the district, now came up to reinforce the British. The sight of these men, many of whom were their neighbors

The Ravine near Oriskany

and erstwhile friends, infuriated the Americans to such a degree that, as soon as the rain had ceased, they leaped upon their enemies in a fierce hand-to-hand encounter, fighting venomously with bayonets and knives. The struggle now became imbued with all the bitterness of civil warfare and was one of the fiercest and, in proportion to the numbers engaged, the bloodiest of the war.

But now the Indians, seeing many of their number lying prone upon the ground, while the patriots still held firm, began to give way and, yelling, fled to the woods. The Tories and Canadians soon followed their example and retreated in confusion, with the Americans in hot pursuit. But the patriots were too weakened in numbers to push on, or to continue their march to the fort, so they, too, fell back toward Fort Dayton, carrying their wounded with them. Among these was gallant Herkimer, who died a few days later in his own house.

During this battle the garrison of Fort Schuyler had made its sortie, as prearranged; and, though it succeeded in capturing much plunder, including six British flags, it failed, of course, to unite with the relief column. St. Leger now again demanded a surrender. Gansevoort's answer was a flat refusal, so St. Leger began to push forward his parallels.

Gansevoort then sent messengers to General Schuyler, asking for aid, and these, after many hardships, succeeded in reaching the commander at Stillwater, where we left him encamped. He quickly assumed the responsibility

TO THE PLAINS OF SARATOGA

of sending a relief force, even at the risk of weakening his own scant army, and Arnold volunteered to command it.

Rumors of its advance and of its strength, these latter exaggerated, now reached St. Leger. The Indians, too, heard these reports and wanted to retreat, so they

"artfully caused messengers to come in one after another, with accounts of the near approach of the rebels; one and the last affirmed that they were within two miles of Captain Lernoult's post." When their stories were not entirely credited "they grew furious and abandoned; seized upon the officers' liquor and cloaths in spite of the efforts of their servants and became more formidable than the enemy we had to expect." *

Finally they fled in all directions, and the British commander, believing Arnold's force near, suddenly in the dead of night lifted the siege and, abandoning his artillery and baggage, retreated precipitately to Oswego.

Thus the Mohawk Valley expedition met its fate on almost the same day that witnessed the British defeat at Bennington, and as the British Annual Register rightly observes:

"The Americans represented this affair and the affair at Bennington as great and glorious victories. Nothing could excel their exultation and confidence. Gansevoort and Willet, with General Stark and Colonel Warner, who had commanded at Bennington, were ranked among those who were considered as the saviours of their country."

* Report of Lieutenant-Colonel Barry St. Leger, dated Oswego, August 27, 1777.

REVOLUTIONARY PILGRIMAGE

At Oriskany there is little but the lay of the land to remind one of the savage struggle that took place in the depths of the forest. A monument commemorates the battle, but the field whereon it took place has lost its forests, and is now rolling country dotted only here and there with trees. No vestige remains of Fort Schuyler in the busy present-day city of Rome, and no trace of Fort Dayton is to be found at Herkimer.

But the flavor of these Revolutionary conflicts lingers in the valley for him who will seek it out. This is especially true farther down near the thriving town of Herkimer, which, as I have said, stands upon the site of old Fort Dayton, where Herkimer organized his expedition for the relief of Fort Schuyler.

His father, John Jost Herkimer, who had come to the Mohawk Valley from the Lower Palatinate on the Rhine, was one of the oldest residents of the German Flats, as this district is called, and had built himself a stone house, since destroyed, which was included in the stockaded area of Fort Herkimer, that stood in a fine position on the south side of the river, about a mile and a half east of Fort Dayton. Also within these stockades stood the old Stone Church that I have drawn—a stout edifice, almost a fortress in itself, originally but one story high, the masonry about the windows plainly showing the addition to its walls. It was built by the Lutheran settlers of the region, and its services were always conducted in German.

In these surroundings the Revolutionary patriot grew

Old Stone Church at German Flats

It was built in 1767 and formed part of the stockade defense of Fort Herkimer, and was often used as a place of refuge from the raids of Tories and Indians

TO THE PLAINS OF SARATOGA

up and remained until his father gave him "five hundred acres whereon he built a fine residence on the south bank of the river below the Little Falls."

Below the town of Herkimer the valley narrows and exchanges its pastoral aspect for that of a rugged gorge, in which the city of Little Falls stands beside the cascades of the river. From this place I found it was but a short drive to Danube, where this Herkimer house still stands, close by the south bank of the river—a big, sturdy edifice built of brick and still retaining much of its old-time character. It was from this homestead that the brave old general started out for Oriskany, and to it that he was afterward carried, wounded, to die, some say through the carelessness of an unskilled doctor, who might have saved him from the hemorrhage that killed him.

He lies on a hillock just behind the house in a little family burying-ground. His grave is the one marked with a flag in my drawing, and to the right of it appears the base of the monument erected to his memory.

A mile or two below the Herkimer house lies Castle Church, one of those houses of worship due to the generosity of Sir William Johnson. In this mission church Brant, the Mohawk leader, who lived near by, received his first lessons from Kirkland and other missionaries, and here he was employed as an interpreter to give instruction to his tribesmen. But at the beginning of the Revolution he espoused the British cause; all his teachings were forgotten and his innate savagery burst

REVOLUTIONARY PILGRIMAGE

forth again as he led his fierce warriors upon their bloody forays against the Whig settlers of the region.

Farther down the valley, but still upon the river, lies Fonda, which is the most convenient point upon the railroad from which to visit Johnson Hall.

General Herkimer's House and Grave

This great baronial manor was, up to the time of the Revolution, the most important house in the Province of New York outside of New York City. It was built by Sir William Johnson in 1760, and in it the baronet lived like a feudal lord with his "wives and concubines, sons and daughters of different colors." One of these wives was Mary Brant, sister of the Mohawk chieftain.

Sir William was handsome and dignified, and his haughty manners and fine speeches so won the Indians

TO THE PLAINS OF SARATOGA

to him that he possessed a remarkable ascendancy over them, to which is largely due their loyalty to the British cause during the Revolution. He died in 1774, very suddenly, in his sixtieth year, and his funeral was the

Castle Church, near Danube

most elaborate that the colonists of the region had ever witnessed, nearly two thousand mourners, including all the colonial dignitaries and Indian sachems, accompanying the funeral procession.

He was succeeded in his lands and titles by his son, Sir John, a man of much smaller calibre, who fled to Canada at the outbreak of the Revolution, and whose lands were then sequestrated. To this is to be ascribed his implaca-

REVOLUTIONARY PILGRIMAGE

ble hatred of the patriots, as well as that of his friend Brant, whose enmity toward the Whig settlers of the valley was unrelenting.

Johnson Hall has retained much of its original aspect. The manor-house has been somewhat disfigured by the addition of bay windows, porches, and a "cupola," but its simple, original lines are still plainly visible. It is flanked by stone blockhouses of very solid structure, pierced, just under the roofs, by loopholes for muskets. When Sir William occupied it, the residence and these blockhouses were surrounded by a twelve-foot breastwork, thus constituting a veritable fortress.

After its sequestration Johnson Hall was owned for many years by successive members of the Wells family, and was still inhabited, when I was last there, by a member of that family. On the stair rail in the hall are regular marks, cut with a hatchet, which are said to have been made by Brant as a signal to the Indians neither to pillage nor burn the house of his friend.

In Johnstown, the nearest township to the hall, still stand the court-house and the old stone jail, that up to the time of the Revolution were the only places for the administration of justice west of Albany.

IV

SARATOGA

WE left Burgoyne stationed upon the Hudson at Fort Edward. By the defeat of his Bennington expedition, and the dispersal of St. Leger's troops in the Mohawk Valley, the second act of his drama—begun so auspiciously on Lake Champlain—was now ending with heavily clouded skies.

Unfortunate commander! One cannot but pity him —this high-strung soldier-poet who, through no fault of his own, saw with each advance his line of communication grow thinner and weaker; who listened in vain for an encouraging word of the advance of General Howe from the south—the man he had been despatched to join; who felt the toils tightening about him; who saw his own army dwindle with each reverse, while his enemy's grew stronger daily.

For, inspirited by their victories at Oriskany and Bennington, the militia was flocking into Schuyler's camp at Stillwater, while several regiments of Continentals, despatched from the Highlands, also joined him. All seemed to augur the success of his deep-laid plans. At this crucial moment, when these plans seemed upon the very point of fruition, General Schuyler—able and ardent patriot, the only one of his generals for whom Washington signed himself "your affectionate friend"—suddenly found himself, through Congressional intrigue and cabal, superseded as commander of the Northern Department by Horatio Gates, the schemer and ambitious politician.

Without a word of protest, like the gentleman he was, he handed over his command to his successor, to whom Congress now allowed all that it had refused to him. Morgan's famous riflemen were sent to Stillwater, where the Americans had laid out their camp, and intrenched it under Kosciusko's direction.

By the beginning of September the main armies were about to confront each other, for Burgoyne had advanced down the Husdon as far as Batten Kill and was preparing to cross the river. Thomas Anburey, the British officer whom I have before quoted, writes:

"The bridge of boats was soon constructed and thirty days provisions brought up for the whole army. On the 13th instant, we passed Hudson's River, and encamped on the plains of Saratoga, at which place there is a handsome and commodious dwelling-house, with out-houses, an exceeding fine saw and grist-mill, and, at a small distance, a very neat church, with several houses round it, all of which are the property of General Schuyler."

This collection of houses, then called Saratoga, now forms part of Schuylerville, a town upon the Hudson about eleven miles from Saratoga Springs, with which it is connected by a fine State road. The "handsome and commodious dwelling-house" was burned during the

TO THE PLAINS OF SARATOGA

battle that ensued, but it was quickly replaced by another that still stands almost hidden by the trees, just over the bridge that spans the Fishkill near Victory Mills, where the stream tumbles, in a series of cascades, into the great, calm Hudson.

The Home of General Philip Schuyler at Old Saratoga

This Schuyler House, though still occupied, has the air of a haunted manse. We had been informed, before visiting it, that no one was at home. Yet on peering through one of the windows, I was startled to perceive, hobbling about on two canes, across the kitchen floor, an elderly woman, bent and feeble, but with eyes so bright and piercing, and a chin so long and sharp, as to recall some aged witch of old—a figure singularly befitting this house so fraught with memories.

REVOLUTIONARY PILGRIMAGE

The British encamped around this spot, near the Fishkill, on the 14th of September, 1777, and only a few miles of woodland now separated the two hostile armies.

I present the following quaint extracts from the "Journal" of Elijah Fisher, a native of Norton, Massachusetts, and later a member of Washington's life-guard, first, because it is a good summary of the events of the month that followed, and, second, because it is such a curious example of the orthography of an American soldier of the period:

"*Sept.* 19*th*. The Enemy made an attact on the Left wing of our army and the Engagement was begun at half past two in the afternoon by Col. Morgan's Riflemen and Lite Infintry— . . .

"*Oct.* 7*th*. We had the secent Engagement begun at one in the afternoon and the Enemy got wosted and our army Drove them and took Gen. Bergoine's adecamp and the General's Doctor and five hundred tents and five hundred Prisoners officers and solgers and Drove the others. . . .

"*The* 8*th*. The next Day Gen. Gates gave the Enemy three Days to git off with themselves. . . .

"*The* 17*th*. Gen Burgoin and his howl army surrendered themselves Prisoners of Ware and Come to Captelate with our army and Gen. Gates."

Such is an abstract of the Battles of Saratoga. Now let us look at them in more detail, and visit the fields whereon they took place.

"On the nineteenth [of September]" says Anburey, "the army marched to meet the enemy in three divisions;

TO THE PLAINS OF SARATOGA

the German line flanked the artillery and baggage pursuing the course of the [Hudson] river through the meadows; the British line marched parallel to it at some distance through the woods forming the center division, whilst the advanced corps, with the grenadiers and light infantry of the Germans made a large circuit through the woods and composed the right hand division.

"The signal guns for all the columns to advance were fired between one and two o'clock." . . .

Here we have the advance to the first battle of Saratoga—Riedesel's left wing by the river, the main British column in the centre, Fraser's advanced corps on the right.

The Americans first came in contact with Fraser's corps, and by three o'clock the main action was centring round Freeman's Farm, a house advantageously placed upon a hillock. About it the battle ebbed and flowed, eddying back and forth between two ravines that lead down toward the river. The Americans "behaved with great obstinacy and courage," says the Earl Balcarras, their enemy, and they held their own for some time, until, at the critical moment, General Riedesel was able to bring his troops up from the river into the main action, and with the cannon of Captain Pausch (whose Journal, by the way, gives us an excellent description of the battle) did much to decide the final issue of this first conflict, the results of which Anburey thus sums up:

"Just as the evening closed in, the enemy gave way on all sides and left us masters of the field, but darkness prevented a pursuit. . . .

REVOLUTIONARY PILGRIMAGE

"Notwithstanding the glory of the day remains on our side, I am fearful the real advantages resulting from this hard fought battle will rest with the Americans, our army being so much weakened by this engagement as not to be of sufficient strength to venture forth and improve the victory."

Such indeed proved the case. For a fortnight or more, the two armies lay watching each other, like two giants preparing for a death-grapple, yet awaiting a propitious first hold. Then the British could afford to delay no longer. To remain in camp was to starve. So, at all costs, Burgoyne determined to try to force his way through Gates's army and reach Albany.

On the 7th of October he moved forward again, and a second desperate battle ensued over practically the same terrain as the first engagement. The Americans attacked the entire British line as soon as the action began. Under the impact of their furious onslaughts even the British grenadiers wavered. Gallant Fraser tried, for a long time, to steady his men, but, despite his efforts, before the repeated attacks of Morgan's riflemen —those stanch backwoodsmen—the British lines began to break.

At this juncture Arnold, who had had a quarrel with Gates and resigned his commission dashed, like one intoxicated, with impetuous fury to the head of his former troops and, cheered to the echo, led them like a whirlwind upon the broken lines of the British left. Fraser, trying to withstand the shock, was mortally wounded.

TO THE PLAINS OF SARATOGA

Arnold, too, pushing into the very heart of Breyman's redoubt, was severely wounded just as the battle finished in complete victory for the patriots.

Thomas Anburey was on camp duty that day, so saw nothing of the battle itself, but he thus graphically describes the beginning of the end, as his comrades began to return:

"Nor can you conceive the sorrow visible on every face as General Fraser was brought in wounded, your old friends, Campbell and Johnston, of our regiment, on each side of his horse, supporting him. . . .

"Early in the morning General Fraser breathed his last and at his particular request, was buried without any parade, in the great redoubt, by the soldiers of his own corps. About sunset the corpse was carried up the hill, the procession was in view of both armies."

The great redoubt here mentioned was on one of three mound-like hills, that we shall soon visit, down by the Hudson. The night of the second battle found the defeated British forces compactly collected around these hills near Wilbur's Basin, broken, crippled, and laden with wounded. The following evening, abandoning almost everything, Burgoyne retreated in a heavy rain up the river bank and back to his old camp at Saratoga. But even there he was not safe, for, like a wild animal tracked to its lair, he was soon surrounded by vastly superior forces.

At the north end of his camp stood a house that had always belonged to the Marshall family. It still stands

REVOLUTIONARY PILGRIMAGE

at the extreme north end of Schuylerville, quite in the open country, shaded by great pine-trees, and overlooking the placid Hudson. Its exterior has been modernized, so I have chosen to make a sketch of the cellar—the very

Cellar in the Marshall House, Schuylerville, which was Used as a Hospital by the British

one described by Madame Riedesel, the devoted wife who followed her husband, the German general, through this entire campaign and whose letters give so vivid an account of her Saratoga experiences. The rafters she describes, pierced by cannon-balls, can still be seen, and from the porch you may look across the river and see,

TO THE PLAINS OF SARATOGA

as she did, the hills where the American soldiers stationed themselves to fire upon the house:

I quote from her "Letters":

"About two o'clock in the afternoon the firing of cannon was again heard, and all was alarm and confusion. My husband sent me a message telling me to betake myself forthwith into a house which was not far from me. I seated myself in the calash with my children, and had scarcely driven up to the house, when I saw on the opposite side of the Hudson River, five or six men with guns, which were aimed at us. Almost involuntarily I threw the children on the bottom of the calash and myself over them. At the same instant the churls fired, and shattered the arm of a poor English soldier behind us, who was already wounded, and was on the point of retreating into the house. Immediately after our arrival, a frightful cannonade was begun, principally directed against the house in which we had sought shelter, probably because the enemy believed, from seeing so many people flocking around it, that all the generals made it their headquarters. Alas! it harbored none but wounded soldiers, or women!

"We were finally obliged to take refuge in a cellar in which I laid myself down in a corner not far from the door. My children laid down on the earth with their heads upon my lap, and in this manner we passed the entire night. A horrible stench, the cries of the children, and yet more than all this, my own anguish prevented me from closing my eyes.

"On the following morning the cannonade began again, but from a different side. I advised all to go out of the cellar a little while, during which time I would have it

REVOLUTIONARY PILGRIMAGE

cleaned, as otherwise we should all be sick. . . . After they had all gone out and left me alone, I for the first time surveyed our place of refuge. It consisted of three beautiful cellars, splendidly arched. . . . I had just given the cellars a good sweeping and had fumigated them by sprinkling vinegar on burning coals and each one (the wounded) had found his place prepared for him—when a fresh and terrible cannonade threw us all once more into alarm. . . . Eleven cannon balls went through the house, and we could plainly hear them rolling over our heads. One poor soldier, whose leg they were about to amputate, having been laid upon a table for this purpose, had the other leg taken off by another cannon ball, in the very middle of the operation. . . . I was more dead than alive, though not so much on account of my own danger, as for that which enveloped my husband, who, however, frequently sent to see how I was getting along, and to tell me he was still safe. . . . In this horrible situation we remained six days. Finally, they spoke of capitulating, as by temporizing for so long a time, our retreat had been cut off. . . .

"On the 17th of October the capitulation was consummated. The generals waited upon the American general-in-chief, Gates, and the troops laid down their arms, and surrendered themselves prisoners of war. . . .

"At last my husband sent to me a groom with a message that I should come to him with our children. I, therefore, again seated myself in my dear calash; and in the passage through the American camp, I observed, with great satisfaction, that no one cast at us scornful glances. On the contrary, they all greeted me, even showing compassion on their countenances at seeing a mother with her little children in such a situation. . . .

"When I approached the tents, a noble looking man

TO THE PLAINS OF SARATOGA

came toward me, took the children out of the wagon, embraced and kissed them, and then, with tears in his eyes, helped me also to alight. 'You tremble,' said he to me, 'fear nothing.' 'No,' replied I, 'for you are so kind, and have been so kind to my children, that it has inspired me with courage.' He then led me to the tent of General Gates, with whom I found Generals Burgoyne and Phillips, who were on an extremely friendly footing with him. Burgoyne said to me, 'You may now dismiss all your apprehensions, for your sufferings are at an end.' . . . All the generals remained to dinner with General Gates. The man who had addressed me so kindly, came up and said to me, 'It may be embarrassing to you to dine with all these gentlemen; come now with your children into my tent, where I will give you, it is true, a frugal meal, but one that will be accompanied by the best of wishes.' 'You are certainly,' answered I, 'a husband and a father, since you show me such kindness.' I then learned that he was the American General Schuyler."

Schuylerville, named for this gallant gentleman, or Saratoga, as it used to be called, is a pretty town ranged for the most part along one broad thoroughfare running parallel to the river. Though haunted with memories of the Indian Wars, one event stands pre-eminent in its history: it was the scene of Burgoyne's surrender.

This important ceremony, by which the Americans took possession of nearly six thousand prisoners, with their arms and accoutrements, besides thirty-five pieces of the best artillery then known, took place down near the old Schuyler House, to which I have already alluded. The troops laid down their arms in the low-lying field

REVOLUTIONARY PILGRIMAGE

just north of the Fishkill, and Burgoyne delivered his sword to Gates to the south of that stream, where the commanding general's marquee stood upon a height.

A great obelisk, visible far and near, commemorates this event—a monument due to the incessant labor of a group of patriotic citizens of the locality, and by its size and costly appearance giving evidence of their zeal.

To visit the scene of the battles we took the new State road that leads southward to Mechanicsville. As soon as we had passed Quaker Springs we were on historic ground, for here we began to follow the route of Fraser's column to their position in the first battle. From here down to the river, that can be seen off to the east, extended the lines of Burgoyne's army.

The woods that then clothed the rolling hills have largely disappeared, for now trees only follow the hedgerows. The battle-ground to-day has a serene, pastoral aspect, its hillocks dotted, here and there, with scattered farms set in well-tilled fields. To the east, across the Hudson, rises Willard's Mountain, whence the Americans observed the British movements.

We soon reached Freeman's Farm, now Brightman's, around which both battles raged. Its site is marked by a tablet, and a small monument to the north indicates the position of Breyman's Hill, the Hessian redoubt, where Colonel Breyman was killed and Arnold wounded in his last spectacular assault.

Farther down the road to the south you come upon a stone erected to Daniel Morgan's memory by his great-

TO THE PLAINS OF SARATOGA

granddaughter, and thus inscribed: "Here Morgan, reluctant to destroy so noble a foe, was forced by pathetic necessity to defeat and slay the gentle and gallant Fraser." Now a broad panorama unfolds itself southward, and the hills called Bemis's Heights become plainly visible—the hills upon which the Americans lay intrenched before the battle. As we approached the great ravine across which both conflicts eddied, we found a stone that marked the position of Fort Neilson, a fortified log barn that formed the apex or north salient of the American camp. Just beyond it another stone, near a farmhouse, indicates the position of Gates's headquarters.

We then descended rapidly toward the river and came to the site of the old Bemis House that gave its name to these historic heights. It stood near the present-day Bemis's Heights Tavern, just below which lies the village of Stillwater.

We had now reached the southern extremity of the battle-field. To complete the circuit you should here turn north along the river and ascend to Wilbur's Basin, where

Old Battle Well, Freeman's Farms

REVOLUTIONARY PILGRIMAGE

stand the three hills by the river, on one of which was the Great Redoubt where General Fraser was buried. John Taylor's house, to which he was carried and in which he died, used to stand near by. Around these three hills, under the guns of the Great Redoubt, the defeated British army huddled after the second battle, and from this point started on their retreat back to the place of their first encampment, struggling along up the river in a driving rain by way of Do-ve-gat, or Coeville, to the heights just north of Saratoga, where they finally surrendered.

So ended Burgoyne's campaign, begun so splendidly and attended with such brilliant hopes. The third act of his drama was finished in disaster and defeat, and the remnants of his proud army marched off to Cambridge as prisoners of war.

No American, I think, can visit these plains of Saratoga without a certain thrill of patriotic pleasure—pride in the courage of his ancestors, who here made their first great capture of the war; humbling an army of veterans; lifting the gloom from Howe's capture of Philadelphia; and flashing the news of their triumph across the sea, by swift sailing ship from Boston, throwing "Turgot and all Paris into transports of joy," and thus influencing the French King himself to espouse the American cause. The surrender at Saratoga was one of the most decisive events of the war.

DOWN THE HUDSON

DOWN THE HUDSON

AFTER the surrender of Burgoyne the chief actors in the Saratoga drama set out for Albany. As there was some difficulty in procuring suitable quarters for the captured commander and his military family in the small city of that day, General Schuyler generously offered his own house for their use, and his invitation was accepted. "He wrote his wife to prepare everything for giving him (Burgoyne) the best reception and his intentions were perfectly fulfilled." *

Of the arrival of the party and of their stay in Albany Madame Riedesel has this to say:

"The day after this, we arrived in Albany, where we had so often longed to be. But we came not as victors! We were, nevertheless, received in the most friendly manner by the good General Schuyler, and by his wife and daughters, who showed us the most marked courtesy, as, also, General Burgoyne, although he had—without any necessity, it is said—caused their magnificently built houses† to be burned. . . . Even General Burgoyne was deeply moved at their magnanimity and said to General Schuyler 'It is to me, who have done you so much injury, that you show so much kindness!' 'That is the fate of war,' replied the brave man, 'let us say no more

* Marquis de Chastellux, "Travels in North America."
† At Schuylerville or Saratoga.

about it.' We remained three days with them, and they acted as if they were very reluctant to let us go."

The old Schuyler mansion, in which they all stayed, still stands toward the south end of Albany, on a hill not very far from the river. Until quite recently it has been used as an orphan asylum, but the State has now bought it, and is restoring it to its original appearance. It is an ample residence, built of buff bricks with white woodwork, and is finely set in a large square of land, shaded by aged chestnut-trees.

An octagonal entry that juts from the façade serves as a sort of vestibule from which you enter at once a great square hall, with a drawing-room at one side and the dining-room at the other. Both rooms, with their handsome fireplaces, recalled to my mind the account given by de Chastellux of the visit he paid to the house toward the close of the Revolution:

"A handsome house half way up the bank, opposite the ferry, seems to attract attention and to invite strangers to stop at General Schuyler's who is the proprietor as well as architect. I had recommendations to him from all quarters, but particularly from General Washington and Mrs. Carter. I had besides given the rendezvous to Colonel Hamilton who had just married another of his daughters, and was preceded by the Vicomte de Noailles and the Comte de Damas who I knew were arrived the night before."

Making his way, cold and hungry, across the Hudson through the floating ice, he was wishing he might be

DOWN THE HUDSON

asked to share the proverbial hospitality of General Schuyler, when

"the first person we saw on shore was the Chevalier de Mauduit who was waiting with the general's sledge, into which we quickly stepped and were conveyed in an instant into a handsome saloon, near a good fire, with Mr. Schuyler, his wife and daughters. Whilst we were warming ourselves, dinner was served, to which every one did honor, as well as to the Madeira which was excellent and made us completely forget the rigor of the season and the fatigue of the journey.

"General Schuyler's family was composed of Mrs. Hamilton, his second daughter, who has a mild agreeable countenance; of Miss Peggy Schuyler, whose features are animated and striking; of another charming girl, only eight years old, and of three boys, the eldest of whom is fifteen and are the handsomest children that you could wish to see."

As may easily be imagined the old Schuyler House is filled with memories. Lafayette, Steuben, Rochambeau, and other distinguished foreigners, as well as most of the celebrated Americans of that day, were, at one time or another, the general's honored guests. In it Alexander Hamilton was married to Miss Elizabeth Schuyler, and, as de Chastellux tells us, was living there at the time of his visit. The large chambers above and the comfortable rooms below have all been occupied by persons of distinction. In one of the latter Burgoyne was lodged.

"His bed was prepared in a large room; but, as he had a numerous suite, or family, several mattresses were

REVOLUTIONARY PILGRIMAGE

spread on the floor for some of his officers to sleep near him. Mr. Schuyler's second son, a little spoilt child of about seven years old, very forward and arch, as all American children are, but very amiable, was running all the morning about the house. Opening the door of the saloon, he burst out a laughing on seeing all the English collected, and shutting it after him, cried '*Ye are all my prisoners:*' this stroke of nature was cruel and rendered them more melancholy than the preceding evening." *

In the broad light of day, in its present transitional stage, the great house may lack romance, but on a summer night, when the shadows of the chestnut leaves cast their odd silhouettes upon its gleaming walls and its white roof-balustrades glitter against the starlit sky, the effect of the old manor, half-hidden among its trees, is magical and strikingly potent with suggestion, and the shades of its former occupants—the gouty general and his distinguished visitors—seem to walk again among the dense shadows under the chestnut-trees. . . .

There is no river trip in our country—and few anywhere—that can excel in beauty a voyage down the Hudson from Albany to New York.

So, as New York is to be the theatre of our next pilgrimage, let us take one of the big boats that make the trip so delightful and follow the historic stream from north to south, reviewing on our way its memories of the Revolution.

Though no battle of any great consequence was fought upon its shores, the Hudson was always considered an

* De Chastellux.

DOWN THE HUDSON

artery of vital importance by the Revolutionary commanders, for by means of it and its ferries, communications were maintained between New England and the Middle States. So its principal souvenirs form a tale of plot and counterplot, surprise and treason.

There is not much to interest us in the upper half of its course, though certainly one will enjoy the ever-changing prospect of the placid water, divided now and then by islands and framed in wooded hills, behind which the great purple silhouettes of the Catskills rise quite near and prominent to the westward. We also pass old Kingston, settled against the hills in its secluded bight—at one time the State capital, and later burned by the British on one of their forays. The only building of consequence that survived this fire is the stone house in which the State Legislature met after New York City was captured by the British, and in which, on the 30th of July, 1777, George Clinton was inaugurated first governor of the State.

Below Poughkeepsie the river widens and begins to take on that lake-like aspect that is so characteristic of all its lower course. The first of these lacustral openings is Newburgh Bay. Fishkill and Newburgh both lie upon it, and both towns hold their souvenirs of the closing chapters of the Revolution.

The Hasbrouck House, that is still plainly visible from the river at the south end of Newburgh, was Washington's principal headquarters during the last two years of the war. It stands on a green set out with obsolete cannon,

REVOLUTIONARY PILGRIMAGE

dating from various epochs, and seems to be specially guarded by a simple block of brownstone that marks the grave of Uzal Knapp, last survivor of Washington's life-guard, who died here in Newburgh at the age of ninety-nine.

At the northeast corner of the grounds rises a massive Tower of Victory, an Italianate structure adorned with bronzes, erected "in commemoration of the disbandment, under proclamation of the Continental Congress of October 18, 1783, of the armies by whose patriotic and military virtue our national independence and sovereignty were established." For it was here in Newburgh that the army was finally disbanded, and it was upon the lawn of this very Hasbrouck House that Washington took leave of his soldiers and subaltern officers before they returned to their homes.

In the Verplanck House, across the river in Fishkill, the officers met and organized, at General Knox's suggestion, the distinguished Society of the Cincinnati, that served to "perpetuate the mutual friendships formed" and that still contributes so much to keep alive the memory of our patriot forebears.

The interior of the Hasbrouck House—a very simple type of colonial dwelling—has a denuded air, for most of its relics and souvenirs have been transported to a museum that has recently been erected adjacent to it. But I like the effect of its bare, whitewashed rooms, with their thick reveals and low-studded ceiling beams, and the austere furnishings that suggest the simplicity

DOWN THE HUDSON

of camp life. The principal room is a large chamber that boasts seven doors and but a single window. Three of these doors lead to adjoining apartments—one to the dining-room, one to the office or sitting-room, and the third to a bedroom; while a fourth gives upon a little Dutch *stoep* that overlooks the Hudson, commanding an extensive view up and down the river.

But the eye quickly focusses upon the narrow gateway to the Highlands of the Hudson that stands guarded by Breakneck and Storm King, between which you catch a distant glimpse of West Point. From Newburgh the big day-boat rapidly covers the intervening stretch of water to this North Gate of the Highlands, and you enter at once the grand defile that is the crowning scenic glory of the river.

Most people prefer to see it on "a perfect day," when the heavens are blue and serene, and it certainly has its charms under these conditions. But I, for my voyage, would unquestionably select a day when the clouds hang low and heavy about the mountain-tops; when the deep purple shadows play over their surfaces, and occasional shafts of sunlight fitfully light a peak, a crag, or precipice, or project a beam across some stretch of glittering water, for to my mind the bold cliffs of the Highlands need these effects of light and shade to intensify their dramatic atmosphere and to suggest the dark tale—in many ways the most tragic of the Revolution—that took place among them and is indelibly interwoven with their souvenirs—the story of Arnold's treason.

REVOLUTIONARY PILGRIMAGE

The Hudson River at West Point

As we approach West Point we come to a sharp bend of the river that turns under the northern batteries, and see above us, soaring aloft, the great Victory Monument, framed by trees, with the beautiful outline of the new Post Chapel crowning the composition. On turning this bend we realize at once the strategic importance of West Point—always considered the key to the Hudson—and its great value to the army that held it.

At the time of the Revolution it was defended by an elaborate system of forts and redoubts, and here, at this very bend of the river, an enormous chain designed to impede navigation up and down stream stretched over

DOWN THE HUDSON

to Constitution Island. A few links of this formidable chain may still be seen up on the Post Parade—bits of a giant's handiwork, each weighing about a hundred and fifty pounds.

General Heath, who commanded West Point just after Arnold's treason, thus describes this chain:

"It was as long as the width of the river between West Point and Constitution Island, where it was fixed to great blocks on each side, and under the fire of batteries on both sides of the river. The links of the chain were probably 12 inches wide, and 18 inches long; the iron about 2 inches square. This heavy chain was buoyed up by very large logs of perhaps 16 or more feet long, the chain carried over them, and made fast to each by staples, to prevent their shifting; and there were a number of

Parts of the Great Chain which was Stretched across the Hudson

REVOLUTIONARY PILGRIMAGE

anchors dropped at distances with cables made fast to the chain to give it a greater stability. The short bend of the river at this place was much in favor of the chain's proving effectual; for a vessel, coming up the river with the fairest wind and strongest way, must lose them on changing her course to turn the point; and before she could get under any considerable way again, even if the wind was fair, she would be on the chain, and at the same time under a heavy shower of shot and shells." *

As we round Gee Point between the Chain Battery Walk and Constitution Island, a superb reach of the river opens out before us, broken mountain silhouettes lying one behind another, heavy and blue, then growing fainter and yet more faint as they recede into gray distances. On the right of the river, rising precipitously from the water's edge, tower the grim walls of West Point's battlemented buildings, stern, rugged structures, harmonizing well with their surroundings and with the purposes for which they were built.

On the wooded bank opposite, a mile or two below, once stood the Beverley Robinson House, whose name is still perpetuated in Beverley Dock—an old residence, built in 1750, and a landmark of the region until it was destroyed by fire in 1892. Historically it was of great interest, for in it took place the chief scenes in the story of Arnold's treason.

So, before we go further, let us briefly rehearse this dark tale, for, as we proceed down the river, we shall pass, one after another, the localities connected with it.

* Heath's "Memoirs."

DOWN THE HUDSON

In 1780 Benedict Arnold, then a major-general in the American army, was appointed commander of West Point, and, on coming to assume his new command, had taken up his quarters in the Beverley Robinson House. He had expressly solicited this post, for, even when he was making his request, he was contemplating his treasonous act and knew that the importance of West Point would enhance the price of his villainy. For many months he had been carrying on a correspondence, under the name of "Gustavus," with a "Mr. John Anderson, merchant," in New York, who was none other than Major John André, adjutant-general of the British army.

Finally, negotiations had proceeded to the point where André felt that a personal interview with Arnold was necessary. So, on the 18th of September, 1780, he rode up the Hudson to Dobbs Ferry, where he boarded the *Vulture*, a British sloop-of-war that lay at anchor off Teller's (Croton) Point.

A day or two later he was rowed across the river, and landed at the south end of Haverstraw Bay. Arnold, meanwhile, had come down the river in his barge, and at midnight the two men met in a bit of wood known as the Firs, not far from Haverstraw. Their conference lasted until dawn, when together they passed the American pickets and repaired to the house of Joshua Hett Smith, a Tory, who was actively aiding the plot.

While they were breakfasting at his house they heard a cannonade and, looking out of the window, could see that a party of Americans were firing at the *Vulture*. André

REVOLUTIONARY PILGRIMAGE

soon perceived, to his dismay, that the ship raised her anchor and dropped out of sight down-stream. He realized at once that, as he had no boat, his escape in that quarter was cut off. But Arnold provided him with a pass through the American lines, and Smith fitted him out with a change of clothes, so that he could doff the British uniform that he had worn under his cloak. This change of costume, however, together with the fact that he was within the American lines as a disguised British officer, definitely put him in the category of a spy.

Arnold now returned to the Beverley Robinson House, and André proceeded on horseback to King's Ferry, which he crossed and was riding at a brisk pace down the Albany Post Road to New York, when, just before he entered Tarrytown, he was stopped by a trio of militiamen—Paulding, Van Wart, and Williams. His answers did not satisfy them and, in spite of Arnold's pass, they searched him, finally finding in his stockings important papers with which Arnold had intrusted him, the blackest kind of evidence of the whole treasonous plot. Despite all proffered bribes they held him prisoner and marched him off toward West Point and General Washington.

Washington had been attending a conference in Hartford, and was expected to return to the Robinson House at any moment. Arnold was there awaiting him when a messenger arrived with a despatch telling of the capture of a "Mr. John Anderson," with important papers. Keeping his presence of mind, although he realized at

DOWN THE HUDSON

once what had happened, he hastily bade farewell to his wife, and, telling his officers that he was needed at West Point, he jumped into his eight-oared barge and was rowed swiftly down the river under the protection of a flag.

Washington duly arrived an hour or two later, and in a letter to the president of Congress, written the very next day, he thus relates what happened:

"ROBINSON'S HOUSE, IN THE HIGHLANDS
"September 26, 1780.
"SIR,
"I have the honor to inform Congress that I arrived here yesterday about twelve o'clock on my return from Hartford. Some hours previous to my arrival Major-General Arnold went from his quarters, which were this place, and, as it was supposed, over the river to the garrison at West Point, whither I proceeded myself to visit the post. I found General Arnold had not been there during the day; and on my return to his quarters he was still absent. In the mean time, a packet had arrived from Lieut.-Colonel Jameson, announcing the capture of a John Anderson, who was endeavoring to go to New York, with several interesting and important papers, all in the hand-writing of General Arnold. This was also accompanied with a letter from the prisoner, avowing himself to be Major John André, Adjutant-General of the British Army, relating the manner of his capture and endeavoring to show that he did not come under the description of a spy.

"From these circumstances, and information that the General seemed to be thrown into some degree of agitation on receiving a letter, a little while before he went

REVOLUTIONARY PILGRIMAGE

from his quarters, I was led to conclude immediately that he had heard of Major André's captivity and that he would, if possible, escape to the enemy, and accordingly took such measures as appeared the most probable to apprehend him. But he had embarked in a barge, and proceeded down the river, under a flag, to the *Vulture* ship of war which lay at some miles below Stony and Verplank's Points."

So Arnold reached the ship in safety, while André was brought a captive to the Robinson House. Washington refused to see him, and after being confined for a few days in old Fort Putnam, situated on a crag above West Point, he was sent for trial to Tappan, whither we shall follow him presently.

From the parapets of Fort Putnam one gains a splendid view of the Hudson Highlands. To the west lie the wild hills and deep ravines of Orange County, while to the east a superb panorama unfolds itself, from the North Gate of the Highlands to the South Gate—the river describing a majestic curve as it bends around Constitution Island. The old fort has been restored since I made the accompanying drawing, and its bomb-proof and vaulted barracks have been completely rebuilt. It loses some of its picturesqueness in consequence, but a few of its old cedars, dark, sinister, whipped by wind and weather, still cut their tragic silhouettes against the sky. Immediately below its parapets stands the new Post Chapel—an enduring monument to its gifted architects, Ralph Adams Cram and Bertram Goodhue—while, lower still, the broad

Old Fort Putnam, Showing the Magazines

DOWN THE HUDSON

green carpet of the Great Parade stretches out, with its trophies, statues, and the buildings of its War College.

As I sat upon the old walls thinking and gazing far out over this vast panorama, a sound of music suddenly arose in the still air, and I could hear the Post Band playing:

"And the Star-Spangled Banner in triumph shall wave
O'er the land of the free and the home of the brave."

What a thrill it gave me perched on those historic hillsides! How, despite treason and the plots of its enemies, Old Glory has triumphed, and how proudly it now waves its quadrupled constellation of stars from the tall flagstaff on the Great Parade! And, as if in consonance with this thought, the dark clouds that had been lowering about the mountains now drifted eastward, and the westering sun shot forth its rays from behind them, gilding the landscape with a great effulgence and throwing a gigantic rainbow—emblem of hope—upon the sombre masses of the disappearing thunder clouds.

Five miles below West Point an iron bridge on the west shore marks the mouth of Poplopen Creek. On the hill to the north of it you will notice a white flagpole. This is the site of Fort Montgomery, and to the south on another bluff used to stand Fort Clinton, both forts being very important defenses of the Highlands. Their effectiveness was increased by a giant chain, eighteen hundred feet long, similar to the one at West Point, that

REVOLUTIONARY PILGRIMAGE

stretched across the river between Fort Montgomery and Anthony's Nose, the steep pyramidal mountain opposite.

While Burgoyne was in the midst of his struggles in the north, Sir Henry Clinton made a diversion up the Hudson and delivered a cleverly planned attack on these two forts. He succeeded in deceiving General Putnam, who lay at Peekskill, as to his real objective, first landing his men on the east bank of the river, as if to threaten him, then transferring them by night across King's Ferry to the west bank, marching them around behind great Dunderberg so as to fall on both forts at once from their land approaches. Both were but poorly garrisoned and, after a short resistance, fell into his hands.

At a turn of the river below Fort Clinton you look between the crags of the Dunderberg and Anthony's Nose and obtain your first glimpse into Peekskill Bay, with the town of Peekskill sunning itself upon a hillside, resembling in many respects some pretty town on one of the Italian lakes. Another swing of the river, round the base of Thunder Mountain, and a longer reach of the Hudson is disclosed.

Stony Point closes this vista. Across the narrow passage between it and Verplanck's Point opposite, plied the all-important King's Ferry, one of the main lines of communication across the Hudson, and so often mentioned in reports of the movements of troops.

In June, 1779, Stony Point had been seized by the British, and its possession by them threatened to be a grave menace to Washington's communications. So he

DOWN THE HUDSON

intrusted General Wayne—"Mad Anthony," as he was called—with the difficult task of retaking it. As you pass it on the boat you will note that this point is a rocky promontory, surrounded on almost every side by water and only connected with the mainland by a narrow causeway.

General Wayne secretly led his troops by night to the head of this causeway. They were guided by a negro called Pompey—an ardent patriot, but who knew the British officers well enough to obtain from them the countersign, which, by a strange coincidence, that night was "The fort's our own." With the use of this password and the aid of darkness, Pompey came close to the first sentry on the causeway, and had him seized, gagged, and overpowered. The same tactics were used for the second sentry. Then the Americans stealthily crossed

Stony Point and the Medal Awarded to Anthony Wayne

REVOLUTIONARY PILGRIMAGE

the causeway, single file, and formed themselves in two columns with unloaded muskets and fixed bayonets. The two divisions took opposite sides of the hill, and charged up it with such rapidity that, before the garrison could recover from its surprise, they had met within the fort itself and carried it.

It was a brilliantly successful attack, and for it Congress awarded a medal to Anthony Wayne, "for his brave, prudent, and soldierly conduct." His report to Washington was laconic and characteristic:

STONEY POINT, 16th July, 1779,
2 o'clock A.M.
"DEAR GEN^L

"The fort and Garrison with Col^o Johnston are ours. Our officers and men behaved like men who are determined to be free.
"Yours most sincerely
"ANT^Y WAYNE."

As the boat passes King's Ferry there opens before you the broad expanse of Haverstraw Bay—a wide sheet of water framed by low-lying hills, with the Verdrietig Range, first precursors of the Palisades, off to the southwest. These shores of Haverstraw Bay bring us again to the story of Arnold's treason and the capture of Major André.

Down at its far end, off Teller's Point, the *Vulture* lay. From her André was rowed across the river and landed on the west bank, at the foot of the Long Clove. A few miles nearer to you his meeting with Arnold took place at midnight in the woods, at a locality known as "The

DOWN THE HUDSON

Firs," and at dawn on the 22d of September the two men proceeded together, past the American pickets, to Joshua Hett Smith's house, that still stands on a ridge known as Treason Hill, near West Haverstraw—a squarish stone structure which, when I last saw it, was not greatly changed in appearance since de Chastellux wrote this description of it:

"My thoughts were occupied with Arnold and his treason, when my road brought me to Smith's famous house, where he had his interview with André and formed his horrid plot. It was in this house they passed the night together, and where André changed his clothes. It was there that the liberty of America was bargained for and sold; and it was there that chance . . . prevented the crime. . . . Smith is still in prison, where the law protects him from justice. But his house seems to have experienced the only chastisement of which it was susceptible; it is punished by solitude; and is in fact so deserted, that there is not a single person to take care of it, although it is the mansion of a large farm."

The conspirators breakfasted together in the corner room at the southeast angle of the house, and it was while they were at breakfast that they heard the cannonade down the river, and that André, as I have stated, saw the *Vulture* drop down-stream and realized that his escape by means of her had been cut off.

So, in the light-blue surtout cloak that he had worn over his regimentals, but which now covered a coat "between crimson and claret," and with a civilian's round beaver hat upon his head, André set out later in

REVOLUTIONARY PILGRIMAGE

the day, with Smith as his guide, to make his way to New York by way of King's Ferry. They had crossed the river in safety and, with the aid of Arnold's pass, had proceeded almost to Tarrytown when Smith turned back, probably thinking that they had passed the last American lines.

It was just beyond this point, as we have seen, that André, riding alone, fell in with the three militiamen, and was taken prisoner.

The next and last of the lake-like reaches of the Hudson is the Tappan Zee, whose name is linked with the tragic end of André's story. For it was to Tappan, off in the hills to the west, that he was sent for trial before

Headquarters at Tappan from which the Order for André's Execution was Issued

DOWN THE HUDSON

a council composed of the principal officers of the American army, General Greene presiding.

His trial took place in the Dutch Reformed Church of the village, an edifice that has since disappeared but has been replaced by a larger one upon the same site. This is the church that appears at the head of the village street, depicted in my drawing (page 140)—a street that has changed but little in a hundred years.

When the board of officers had judged him guilty, "to be considered as a spy from the enemy," André was sent under close guard to a house near by, in this same village street—a substantial stone structure, still known as the '76 Stone House. It is now a tavern, and despite the addition of a "ballroom" at the back, has retained much of its old-time character, and certainly deserves the attention of one of our patriotic societies.

André's courage and deportment during his trial had greatly impressed his judges in his favor, and all wished that he might have been acquitted or exchanged for the traitor Arnold. But military law, then as now, was inflexible, and even his last touching appeal to Washington "to adapt the mode of my death to the feelings of a man of honor," and not to allow him "to die on a gibbet," had to be denied. So on the 2d of October, 1780, he was led forth to execution.

As he emerged from the old Stone House, "dressed in his royal regimentals and boots," walking arm in arm between Ensign Samuel Bowman and Captain John Hughes, two more officers stood upon the stoop and fell

REVOLUTIONARY PILGRIMAGE

in with him, one of them being John Van Dyk, who wrote the letter to which I allude in my visit to Washington's headquarters in Morristown. Five hundred troops were drawn up in the village street, and they, falling into a hollow square, accompanied the slow cortège as it took

'76 Stone House in which André was Imprisoned

its way toward the church, turned sharp to the west at the little triangular green and followed the road up the hill to the second turn beyond the present railroad-track.

Of this progress from the prison to the place of execution, Doctor Thacher has this to say:

"I was so near, during the solemn march to the fatal spot, as to observe every movement and to participate in every emotion the melancholy scene was calculated to produce. . . . The eyes of the immense multitude were fixed on him who, rising superior to the fears of death, appeared as if conscious of the dignified deportment he displayed. Not a murmur or a sigh ever escaped him,

DOWN THE HUDSON

and the civilities and attentions bestowed on him were politely acknowledged."

The road all the way was lined with soldiery, and all the American officers were in their places—all except Washington and his staff, whose absence André is said to have noted. Of the various versions of the final scene, Doctor Thacher's is usually quoted, but I prefer the less known one left us by Alexander Hamilton, because, though it gives us fewer material details, it contains such a fine estimate of André's charming character. It was written in the form of a letter to Colonel Laurens, and is given *in extenso* in the "Life of Alexander Hamilton," written by his son.

"Arrived at the fatal spot, he asked with some emotion, 'must I then die in this manner!' He was told it had been unavoidable. 'I am reconciled to my fate, (said he) but not to the mode.' Soon, however, recollecting himself, he added, 'it will be but a momentary pang;' and, springing upon the cart, performed the last offices for himself, with a composure that excited the admiration and melted the hearts of the beholders. Upon being told the final moment was at hand, and asked if he had anything to say, he answered, 'Nothing but to request you will witness to the world, that I die like a brave man.' Among the extraordinary circumstances that attended him, in the midst of his enemies, he died universally regretted and universally esteemed. . . .

"There was something singularly interesting in the character and fortunes of André. To an excellent understanding, well improved by education and travel, he

REVOLUTIONARY PILGRIMAGE

united a peculiar elegance of mind and manners, and the advantage of a pleasing person. It is said, he possessed a pretty taste for the fine arts, and had himself attained some proficiency in poetry, music and painting. His knowledge appeared without ostentation, and embellished by a diffidence that rarely accompanies so many talents and accomplishments which left you to suppose more than appeared.

Stone Marking the Place of André's Execution

"His sentiments were elevated and inspired esteem;—they had a softness that conciliated affection. . . . The character I have drawn of him, is drawn partly from what I saw of him myself, and partly from information."

Such was the man who died in the full promise of his youth. "His remains were placed in an ordinary coffin, and interred at the foot of the gallows; and the spot was consecrated by the tears of thousands." *

This spot, upon a hilltop above Tappan, is now marked by a block of granite surrounded by a circular iron railing. When last I visited it and stepped up to read the inscription, I found that, by a singular chance, I had come to the place upon the very anniversary of his death. So, as I looked about me at the surrounding hills and

---

* Doctor Thacher. André's remains were afterward removed to Westminster Abbey, where his final resting-place is marked by a handsome monument.

DOWN THE HUDSON

valleys, I seemed to behold Nature as André saw her with his dying look: the leaves just yellowing on the trees; the soft quiet of a day in early October; the blue mists hanging in the valley where the Sparkill meanders past Washington's headquarters, with a glimpse of the white Dutch church steeple nestled snugly among the trees of the village.

ABOUT NEW YORK

ABOUT NEW YORK

CONSIDERING that the great modern city of New York, like a giant octopus, growing bigger year by year, has reached out its tentacles and spread over the outlying country for many miles, defying every prediction and surpassing every dream of its founders, it seems a wonder indeed that anything at all remains among its gigantic edifices and close-built streets to recall the period of the American Revolution.

Yet such remains do exist and a visit to them, with a rehearsal of their souvenirs, will, I think, prove most interesting.

So let us begin our New York pilgrimage at the Battery, where Fort George (originally Fort Amsterdam), the outward and visible sign of military authority in Colonial days, used to stand upon the site of the present customhouse. It was a strong work, and its guns were supplemented by an important battery of artillery placed along the water-front to command the harbor—the battery that gave its name to the promenade.

In front of Fort George, on Bowling Green, stood a big equestrian statue of the King, George III, a cloaked figure, crowned and mounted on a prancing horse, and surrounded, in the year 1771, by the heavy iron railing brought out from England that still, despite all vicissitudes and changes in the neighborhood, fences in the

REVOLUTIONARY PILGRIMAGE

little triangular plot of grass. The ornamental supports for the lanterns are still in place, and the sharp iron palings and the posts that used to be surmounted with

Old Houses on State Street, New York City

heads, so clumsy in workmanship with their worn, hand-wrought appearance, contrast sharply with the finely finished, ornate bronze work on all the surrounding buildings.

ABOUT NEW YORK

From the town that centred round Bowling Green one main artery led north through the island and that was Broadway. Number One upon that thoroughfare, now a big office-building, bears a tablet stating that

> Here stood Kennedy House
> once Headquarters
> of Generals Washington and Lee.

General Charles Lee used it upon his arrival in the city at the beginning of the war while he was inspecting and putting in order its defenses. Washington occupied it as his headquarters during most of the troubled period of active operations which we shall soon follow in some detail. Lossing gives a picture of the old house that is reminiscent of some of those that still front the Battery on State Street—houses that afford an excellent idea of the fashionable residences of the Revolutionary period. The tablet might have added that Kennedy House, after the evacuation of New York by the Americans, became the headquarters of Sir Henry Clinton and of Sir Guy Carleton.

Now, if we walk up that narrow slit, walled in by gigantean structures—that

Tomb of Alexander Hamilton, Trinity Churchyard

REVOLUTIONARY PILGRIMAGE

wonder of the New World that is lower Broadway, we soon reach Trinity Church, in whose graveyard sleep many men and women of the Revolution. Near the south railing lies Alexander Hamilton, under a conspicuous tomb erected to the memory of

> The Patriot of Incorruptible Integrity
> The Soldier of Approved Valour
> The Statesman of Consummate Wisdom

as the epitaph records. In front of it is the plain slab that marks his wife's grave—"Eliza, daughter of Philip Schuyler"—whose girlhood home we have just visited at Albany, and to whose courtship I allude in my chapter devoted to Morristown.

In the north half of the cemetery, near the Broadway line, rises the so-called martyrs' monument, a tall Gothic memorial

> Sacred to the memory of
> Those brave and good men who died
> Whilst imprisoned in this city for their devotion to
> The Cause of Independence.

—the men who died in the Sugar House prison and were interred in Trinity Churchyard in nameless graves.

A few blocks farther up Broadway stands St. Paul's Chapel, now toned to a rich, smoky brown, recalling the London churches designed by Sir Christopher Wren and retaining more of its Colonial atmosphere than any other edifice in the city. It was finished about ten years prior to the Revolution and stood on the outskirts of the

ABOUT NEW YORK

city, fronting the river, with a lawn sloping down to the water, which at that time came up to Greenwich Street.

Under the Broadway portico is the monument erected in 1776, by order of Congress, to the memory of Major-General Richard Montgomery, who fell gloriously while charging the citadel at Quebec, killed just as he had called to his men: "Men of New York, you will not fear to follow where your general leads." In 1818 his remains were brought down from Canada and interred close by this monument.

During the British occupation many of the leading officers worshipped at St. Paul's, and on the day of his inauguration as first President of the United States, Washington went to it to attend divine service. Thereafter he attended it regularly and the double pew wherein he sat is

The Monument to Montgomery, St. Paul's Church

REVOLUTIONARY PILGRIMAGE

still to be seen in the left aisle, against the north wall of the church. Opposite it, in the right aisle, is the one occupied by the first American governor of New York, George Clinton.

To Fraunces' Tavern and its associations I allude in another chapter.

Now let us rehearse the story of the capture of New York by the British in 1776 and visit the places connected with that campaign.

When General Howe evacuated Boston in March, 1776, we saw him embark his army and set sail for Halifax. There he remained until the month of June, when he turned his attention to New York, his object being to capture the chief American seaport and make it the base of his future operations.

On the 28th of June four fleet frigates suddenly appeared off Sandy Hook, slipped through the Narrows, and dropped anchor in the outer harbor. On board of one of them, the *Greyhound*, was Howe himself, come ahead of his forces to confer with the royal governor, Tryon, who was awaiting him in the Lower Bay on one of the King's ships.

Washington's Pew, St. Paul's Church

On the following morn-

ABOUT NEW YORK

ing forty sail were sighted off the Hook, and within a few days a hundred and thirty men-of-war and transports lay anchored under the lee of Staten Island, where the Quarantine Station now is. They rapidly discharged their troops until the green hills of the island were whitened with their tents.

Washington had foreseen this probable move of Howe's and had done everything he could to prepare the city for it. He had carefully gone over the defenses and put them in the best order possible.

Map of Operations near New York City

There were four main strategic points to be guarded: King's Bridge, at the extreme north end of Manhattan Island; Fort George, at the Battery, whose guns, with those of Paulus Hook on the Jersey shore opposite, commanded the entrance to the Hudson River;

REVOLUTIONARY PILGRIMAGE

Governor's Island, that defended the mouth of the East River; and Brooklyn Heights, which overlook and command what was then New York City.

But a distance of fifteen miles separated King's Bridge from Brooklyn and two ferries were necessary to transport troops from Paulus Hook to the same locality. For these extensive lines of defense Washington disposed of scarcely twenty thousand men, many of them insufficiently armed and equipped, and many raw recruits.

A few days after the arrival of the British ships a messenger from Philadelphia brought tidings of the adoption of the Declaration of Independence. The threatening presence of the enemy's army down the bay and the hourly expectation of an attack had keyed the people of the city to a high tension. So that, when this news reached them, their patriotic enthusiasm knew no bounds.

At six in the evening, on the 9th of July, 1776, the Declaration was read at the head of the army drawn up on the common, where the present City Hall stands—a tablet on its southwest corner recording that fact. Then the populace, joined by a number of the soldiers, unable to control their feelings and not content with bonfires, tolling bells, and noise of all descriptions, flocked to Bowling Green, where stood the statue of the King, and, with shouts and jeers, pulled down the leaden effigy to melt it into bullets for the "cause of independence."

Only a day or two later, toward evening, a great booming of cannon from the fleet down the bay brought every

ABOUT NEW YORK

citizen to some point of vantage and every spy-glass in the city was fixed upon the British vessels. A great ship-of-the-line was seen standing grandly through the Narrows and, as she passed, she was greeted by every man-of-war with an admiral's salute. A flag flew at her peak and those of the watchers who knew cried out: "It's the admiral's ship; Lord Howe has come!"

Lord Richard, the admiral, who thus came to America to take command of the combined British fleets, was the brother of Sir William, the general, and these two were now to co-operate in putting down the rebellion in the colonies and in bringing them back to allegiance to the King. The admiral tried very honestly at first to accomplish this by peaceful means—pardons, treaties, and the like—but, of course, failed. Then his brother, the general, turned to sterner measures.

Besides the army that he had brought with him from Halifax, he had now been reinforced, in the month of August, by the arrival of Clinton's and Cornwallis's commands; by Commodore Hotham's fleet from England, bringing twenty-six hundred British troops and eighty-four hundred Hessians; and, lastly, by Sir Peter Parker's discomfited squadron from Charleston, thus swelling his effectives to twenty-five thousand men.

He now determined to transport the bulk of this formidable army from Staten to Long Island and there attack the Americans who were posted upon Brooklyn Heights in a line of intrenchments extending from Gowanus Cove to Wallabout Bay where the Brooklyn Navy

REVOLUTIONARY PILGRIMAGE

Yard now is. On the summit of the intervening hills, now Fort Greene Park, stood the main redoubt, then called Fort Putnam but since renamed Fort Greene.

The British landed in admirable order in the Narrows near Fort Hamilton and the Hessians were "transported

View from Old Fort Putnam (now Fort Greene), Brooklyn

to Gravesend Cove and made their landing with equal skill." A long range of hills crosses Long Island, extending from the Narrows toward Jamaica—the hills of Greenwood Cemetery, Prospect Park, Flatbush, and Cypress Hills. They are cut by four passes and Howe proceeded at once to threaten all four of them, sending one column, his left, under General Grant, along the bay to the vicinity of Gowanus Cove; de Heister with the Hessians, his centre, to occupy the two passes at Flat-

ABOUT NEW YORK

bush; and, at the last moment, Lord Percy, with the right wing, slipped silently by night far around by what is still known as the King's Highway, the road that passes Flatlands and leads to the Cypress Hills, returning behind them to take the American outposts in the rear.

Unfortunately, the American commander in Brooklyn, Nathanael Greene, who knew its defenses so well, was stricken with a raging fever a day or two before the battle, and Israel Putnam had been assigned to his place.

General Putnam's eyes seem to have been too intently fixed upon the very evident advance of the British left wing, so that when firing began in the direction of Gowanus Cove, before daylight on the 22d of August, he instantly ordered Lord Stirling, a fine active officer, "to stop the advance of the enemy" with two of the best American regiments—Haslet's Delawares and Smallwood's Marylanders. Stirling obeyed and by dawn was in contact with Grant's advancing column.

General Sullivan, who was in command of three important American outposts at the Flatbush Pass—Battle Pass, as the little valley in Prospect Park that I have drawn has come to be called—also at daybreak found the Hessians under de Heister in front of him, firing upon his positions and threatening an attack in force.

The firing near Gowanus Cove and the boom of de Heister's cannon were plainly audible in New York City, and Washington, hearing these guns, realized that a general action was on. He jumped into his barge, crossed

REVOLUTIONARY PILGRIMAGE

the East River, and galloped to the Brooklyn works just in time to witness the catastrophe that was there taking place.

Sullivan had maintained his position well, when the sudden thunder of Lord Percy's guns out on his left, on the Jamaica Road, told him he was outflanked and in serious danger of being cut off. He immediately ordered a retreat, but it was already too late. For as he retired he met, in his rear, the dragoons and light infantry and, at the same time, the Hessians charged upon his front. Caught thus between two fires, driven back and forth from one enemy to the other, the Americans fought gallantly and desperately. But numbers were against them. Some were trampled under the horses' hoofs; others furiously bayoneted by the hated Hessians, until the narrow pass became a terrible scene of slaughter. A few stragglers managed to cut their way through and escape, but nearly all were either killed or made prisoners; General Sullivan himself among the latter.

But this was not all; a worse disaster was impending. Washington, from his position on the heights, could see it coming, but was powerless to prevent it.

Stirling, who had been holding Grant's column in check, now also heard firing in his rear. He, too, thought he could retreat by fording Gowanus Creek, but upon retiring toward it he fell into Cornwallis and his grenadiers. No thought of surrender entered his head, however, and with his small army he boldly faced the enemy on both fronts. A fierce and desperate battle ensued,

Battle Pass, Prospect Park, Brooklyn

ABOUT NEW YORK

for the Marylanders were a game regiment, largely composed of young men of the best families of their State. Lord Stirling animated them with voice and example and they fought with such conspicuous gallantry and fire that Washington, watching them from his hilltop, wrung his hands in despair, exclaiming: "Good God! what brave fellows I must this day lose." But at last, pushed to desperation and seeing no hope of escape, Stirling surrendered.

In view of this defeat, Washington now fully expected that Howe would make an assault upon his main line of intrenchments, but the British general decided otherwise. Instead, he collected his men out of range of musket-shots and encamped for the night. It was an anxious night for the Americans, for everything portended a decisive battle on the morrow, and, in truth, when daylight did come it revealed the British army close at hand. The soldiers were already beginning to throw up intrenchments when a drenching rain drove them from their work.

Meanwhile reinforcements for the Americans had come over from New York: Shee's and Magaw's Pennsylvanians—fine, well-disciplined troops and well officered—and Colonel Glover's regiment of Marblehead fishermen, stalwart, hardy, amphibious men, whom we shall meet again on the banks of the Delaware.

On the morning of the 29th a dense fog overhung Long Island. But a reconnoitring party that rode out to Red Hook saw, through a rift, the British fleet bustling with activity and they feared that the ships might be

REVOLUTIONARY PILGRIMAGE

planning to sail up the East River and thus completely cut off the American army on the island. So they hastened back to Washington and reported what they had seen. A council of war was quickly convoked and it decided that a retreat was imperative and must be effected that very night.

Here, indeed, was a stupendous task—to ferry nine thousand men with their artillery and baggage over the East River, with its swirling tides and eddying currents, and to do this with such secrecy and in such silence that the enemy's pickets, only a quarter of a mile away, might suspect nothing of their movements.

Washington hastily requisitioned every boat that could be found and collected them on the Brooklyn side of the Fulton Ferry, placing them in charge of the men of Marblehead. A strong northeaster had been blowing all day accompanied by a heavy rain. The river was dark and angry, with a strong tide running. The militia regiments were first embarked but the wind was so high that even the Marblehead fishermen could not spread a close-reefed sail. So for three hours all boats were rowed with muffled oars.

But at midnight, as if by act of Providence, the tide turned, the wind dropped and veered to a gentle, favoring breeze; the barges could be loaded to the gunwale and their sails could be hoisted; and thus the retreat proceeded with celerity. General Mifflin, who, with the best troops, had remained up in the trenches till the last, now came down to the ferry with his covering party and

ABOUT NEW YORK

embarked. Washington, who had watched all this time at the point of embarkation, directing the movements of the troops, then crossed the river in the very last boat.

This retreat from Long Island remains one of the outstanding events of the war, one of Washington's great achievements, for by it he saved his army from inevitable disaster, rescuing it from the grip of a foe quite double its strength.

His stealthy departure was not discovered until dawn when, warned by reports, "Captain Montressor, aide-de-camp of General Howe, followed by a handful of men, climbed cautiously over the crest of the works and found them deserted." Howe's prey had escaped.

After the retreat from Long Island the army in New York was reorganized, but the Americans could scarcely hope to successfully defend both sides of Manhattan Island, whose long water-front was so exposed to attack. During the first days of September the British advanced up the Long Island side of the East River and threw outposts as far as Flushing. Their frigates succeeded in passing Governor's Island and ascended the East River to Newtown Inlet; so that the whole east shore of Manhattan was threatened.

Under this menace the Americans decided to evacuate the city, and, two weeks after the battle of Long Island, Washington began to remove the artillery and military stores to New Jersey. He was given little time to accomplish his purpose, however, for three British frigates ascended the Hudson and anchored near Bloomingdale.

REVOLUTIONARY PILGRIMAGE

On Saturday, the 14th of September, the bulk of the army marched out of the city and up to Harlem, leaving only General Putnam with about four thousand men to cover their retreat. The very next morning a heavy cannonading was heard in the East River. Many barges were seen to put out from Newtown Inlet and crossed, approximately at the East 34th Street Ferry to Kipp's Bay, under cover of the frigates, the "open flatboats filled with soldiers standing erect; their arms all glittering in the sunbeams."

Some militia was there to oppose their landing, but they broke and ran at the first sight of the redcoats, as Washington himself thus describes:

"At the first sound of firing, I rode with all possible dispatch towards the place of landing, when to my surprise and mortification, I found the troops that had been posted in the lines, retreating with the utmost precipitation. . . . I used every means in my power to rally and get them in order, but my attempts were fruitless and ineffectual, and on the appearance of a small party of the enemy, not more than sixty or seventy in number, their disorder increased, and they ran away without firing a shot."

This was one of the rare occasions upon which Washington lost his temper, and his rage at the cowardly militia was unbridled as he exclaimed: "Are these the men with whom I am to defend America?"

The British then marched unopposed across the island as far as the Inclenberg or Murray Hill and took up their

ABOUT NEW YORK

position upon the high ground that rises just above 34th Street, extending from Lexington to Sixth Avenues.

General Howe, with some of his officers, stopped for refreshments at the house of Robert Murray, a wealthy Quaker, whose residence gave its name to the hill. He happened to be away, but his wife set cakes and wine before the sybaritic British general and plied him so assiduously with good things that he remained quite a time in the house. This delay gave Putnam and his rearguard the needed opportunity to hasten forward and join the army up in Harlem. So it was generally asserted that Mrs. Murray saved Putnam's division of the army.

Washington now took up his quarters in the house of Colonel Roger Morris, that still stands on Washington Heights and is now better known as the Jumel Mansion.

Despite the fact that its surroundings are now disfigured by a great apartment-house, a huge water-tank, and several acres of car yards, its situation is still quite wonderful. As I sat with its genial and erudite curator on the little porch under

The Jumel Mansion

REVOLUTIONARY PILGRIMAGE

the big white portico, watching the cloud shadows play over the hills, I thought of the anxious hours that Washington must have passed up here, scanning the heights across the Harlem River for scouting-parties or watching the hills to the south where Earl Percy's troops lay encamped.

The handsome house is now maintained under the auspices of the Daughters of the American Revolution, and in its rooms is displayed a notable collection of Revolutionary relics of all descriptions: portraits, souvenirs, uniforms, arms and ammunition, besides furniture and old prints. There are, too, some of those curious andirons of Hessian soldiers, that were so popular, for the patriots loved to sit and toast their toes while they spat at the hated mercenaries who sizzled in reply.

Washington's council-chamber, as it is called, juts out at the back of the hall—a great drawing-room having windows on three sides and a fine chimneypiece at its far end. In the hall itself hangs Ercole's large portrait of Madame Jumel, now restored to its original position after many years of absence. But her story, fascinating as it is, does not belong to our quest, so we shall turn from thoughts of her to a rare old map that hangs in one of the rooms—a map of the "North Part of New York Island, exhibiting the Plan of Fort Washington, now Fort Knyphausen, with the rebel lines to the Southward which were forced by the troops under the command of Rt. Honble Earl Percy on the 16th of Nov^{r}., 1776."

The territory embraced in this map is the scene of our next field of operations, for I do not mean to burden the

ABOUT NEW YORK

reader with the minor battles that intervened between the evacuation of New York City and the capture of Fort Washington. The encouraging encounter on Harlem Heights; the engagements along the shore of the Sound; the battles at Chatterton Hill and White Plains were among these, but they ended with no material advantage to either side. Besides, little or no vestige of them remains in the now flourishing suburban towns of New Rochelle, White Plains, Mamaroneck, and Tuckahoe.

The last engagement took place at White Plains, and, after it, to obviate a more decisive battle, Washington retired to North Castle Heights about five miles above his last position. A day or two later Howe, to his surprise, turned about and left him.

"Yesterday morning the enemy made a sudden and unexpected movement from the several posts they had taken in our front. They broke up their whole encampments the preceding night and have advanced toward King's Bridge and the North River. The design of this manœuvre is a matter of much conjecture and speculation and cannot be accounted for with any degree of certainty. . . . I think it highly probable and almost certain that he (Howe) will make a descent with a part of his troops into Jersey, and as soon as I am satisfied that the present manœuvre is real, and not a feint, I shall use every means in my power to forward a part of our forces to counteract his design. I expect the enemy will bend their force against Fort Washington and invest it immediately. From some advices, it is an object that will attract their earliest attention." *

* Washington, in a letter to Congress.

REVOLUTIONARY PILGRIMAGE

Washington was right. The enemy did "bend their force against Fort Washington" and prepare to attack it.

The north end of Manhattan Island is a narrow strip of land, high, rocky, and precipitous in places. The Hudson River skirts it to the west; the Harlem River to the east; while its north end is separated from the mainland by the narrow but swirling rapids of Spuyten Duyvil Creek. At the time of the Revolution but one tie to the mainland existed—King's Bridge, in the locality that still retains that name.

The Americans had perfected quite an elaborate system of fortifications in this vicinity. On the height north of King's Bridge stood Fort Independence, supported by a number of redoubts designated by numerals. Upon Manhattan Island itself Cock Hill Fort commanded the mouth of Spuyten Duyvil Creek, and on the heights above it were Fort George and Fort Tryon. Still south of these the ground again rises, culminating at 183d Street in a bluff that overlooks both the Hudson and Harlem Rivers. Here, prior to the battle of Long Island, the Pennsylvania troops had built "a strong work, intended as a kind of citadel," which they named Fort Washington in honor of the commander-in-chief.

Major Graydon, who was captured with it, thus describes it in his "Memoirs":

"There were no barracks, or casemates, or fuel or water within the body of the place. It was an open construction, with ground at a short distance on the back of it equally high, if not higher; without a ditch of any

ABOUT NEW YORK

consequence, if there was a ditch at all; no outworks but an incipient one on the north not deserving the appellation, or any of those exterior multiplied obstacles and defenses that, so far as I can judge, could entitle it to the name of fortress in any degree capable of sustaining a siege. It required no parallels to approach it; the citadel was at once within reach of assailants."

About a mile to the south of it an inner line of intrenchments stretched across the island at 162d Street, just including the Morris Mansion, Washington's headquarters, within it. At 155th Street was a second line of intrenchments and at 145th Street an outer or first line, with batteries and outposts as far south as 128th Street, where the American defenses ended.

This part of the city should be of especial interest to New Yorkers, for upon it was fought the only battle in the city's history. Yet how many of its citizens, I wonder, have ever knowingly visited the site of Fort Washington?

Leaving Broadway at 181st Street, the nearest that is cut through, you climb quite a hill as you walk toward the river. Soon you reach Fort Washington Road, a broad avenue that leads to the north, and at the top of the hill you will find a monument, whose bronze tablet is thus inscribed:

This Memorial Marks the Site of
Fort Washington
Constructed by the Continental Troops
in the Summer of 1776.
Erected through the generosity of James Gordon Bennett
by the Empire State Society, Sons of the American Revolution,
1901.

REVOLUTIONARY PILGRIMAGE

From this memorial you gain an excellent idea of the terrain that the fortress commanded. The vicinity is not built over, but remains quite green and open, and its grassy slopes afford rendezvous for the mothers of the neighborhood and playgrounds for their children. To the east the land falls away abruptly to Broadway that lies far below you; to the north you overlook the slopes that bore Fort George and Fort Tryon; to the south lay the triple lines of the American defenses; while to the westward the precipitous bluffs overlook the Hudson.

Fort Washington, with Fort Lee opposite upon the Palisades, were supposed to command this North River, but, despite their cannon and the *chevaux-de-frise* that connected them, British ships could and did pass. This being the case, Washington was in favor of abandoning Fort Washington altogether, but his good judgment was overruled by some of his generals.

When Howe had turned his back on him at White Plains, Washington had marched his army to Tarrytown, crossed to the Jersey shore, and encamped near Hackensack, keeping in close touch, however, with the garrison he had left in Fort Washington under Colonel Magaw.

Howe now prepared to storm this last fortress remaining in American hands on the New York side of the Hudson. The Hessians, under Knyphausen, came down to Spuyten Duyvil and were ferried across to the lowlands northeast of Fort Washington. They were seen as day broke and cannonaded, but, splitting into two columns, they began to advance, Knyphausen leading the main

ABOUT NEW YORK

body by the present Kingsbridge Road, while Rall (of whom we shall see more at Trenton) directed his troops

Site of Fort Washington, Looking toward Fort Lee

against Fort Tryon, fighting, according to Cornwallis, "to the admiration of the entire British army." His soldiers were worthily matched, however, by the Marylanders, who held them at bay for several hours until

REVOLUTIONARY PILGRIMAGE

"at length they were obliged to submit to a superiority of numbers and retire under the cannon of the fort."

Meanwhile Lord Percy had been attacking the intrenchments to the south of the fort and Colonel Cadwalader, who commanded there, had been obliged to withdraw his men to the third or innermost line. Then the British succeeded in crossing the Harlem River at two points and took Cadwalader in the rear. He ordered a retreat, and his men, in much confusion, finally reached the fort. But there all was in disorder, the entire garrison being now crowded into a space intended for only one thousand men. A flag was sent in with a summons to surrender, and Colonel Magaw, completely surrounded and feeling further resistance futile, gave up the fort.

Thus fell Fort Washington, whose loss was one of the severest blows sustained by the patriots during the entire war. More than two thousand men, besides forty-three cannon and a large quantity of military stores, fell into the hands of the British. Greene, who had advised defending the fort, felt "mad, vexed, sick and sorry," and Washington wrote to Congress:

"The loss of such a number of officers and men, many of whom have been trained with more than usual attention, will, I fear, be severely felt; but when that of the arms and accoutrements is added, much more so; and must be a further incentive to procure as considerable a supply as possible for the new troops, as soon as it can be done."

IN THE JERSEYS

IN THE JERSEYS

I

TRENTON

AFTER the loss of Fort Washington, and Washington's retirement to the west bank of the Hudson, Cornwallis assumed command of the troops that were to pursue him and operate against him in New Jersey. So now we shall follow the two armies into that State.

General Greene was in command of Fort Lee, situated on the Palisades almost opposite Fort Washington and about where the Fort Lee Ferry still perpetuates its name. During the night of the 18th of November, 1776, five thousand British troops marched up the Hudson, crossed unseen, near Yonkers, and succeeded in dragging their cannon up the Palisades. Greene had expected no attack from that quarter and had placed no guard in that direction. So that he was taken completely by surprise and obliged to evacuate the fort in the greatest haste, saving his garrison but leaving most of his baggage and artillery behind him. Thus blow after blow fell upon the patriots.

Washington, "with the wretched remains of a broken army," succeeded in covering Greene's retreat, but then fell back across the Hackensack. The prospects were indeed gloomy and the British officers were writing home: "Lord Cornwallis is carrying all before him in the Jerseys; peace must soon be the consequence."

Too weak to stand and fight, Washington continued to retreat from point to point. His rear left Newark as the British advance entered it; he gained New Brunswick on the 28th, but on the 1st of December was obliged to move on, destroying the Raritan bridge behind him. Then, with a scant three thousand men, he fell back to Princeton and thence to Trenton.

He had ordered General Charles Lee (who was in the Highlands) to join him at all costs, but that officer, ambitious, jealous, and anxious for the chief command himself, would not co-operate, and claiming to be a "general detached to make an important diversion," led his troops off on his own account. On the 12th of December his forces hung upon the British flank at Vealtown—now fashionable Bernardsville (and I do not wonder that they changed the name)—and he himself was spending the night near by at Basking Ridge. Next morning, after a late breakfast, he had just finished a letter beginning, "My dear Gates—*Entre nous*, a certain great man is damnably deficient," when a party of British cavalry surrounded the house and summoned him to surrender. Within two minutes he came out, pale, unarmed, bareheaded, and begged the dragoons to spare his life. They seized him, and four minutes later hustled him off a prisoner.

IN THE JERSEYS

The patriots' only hope now centred in Washington, and that hope was a forlorn one indeed. His retreat to Trenton had covered a period of eighteen days, he hoping that winter, with its snows and impassable roads, would soon prove his ally and definitely impede his enemy.

But at Trenton, where he faced about with the Delaware behind him, he found that General Howe had joined Cornwallis with a new brigade. Before this strengthened foe he was forced to retreat again, beyond the river. This he accomplished just as the British arrived to see the last man over and to realize that he had secured every boat for seventy miles up and down the river.

But now only the waters of the Delaware lay between the British army and Philadelphia, where Congress was holding its sessions. So imminent did the danger seem that that body decided to adjourn to Baltimore; which it did. Howe, elated, returned to New York, and Cornwallis, also sure of success, prepared to embark for England to announce that the rebellion had been put down.

He left General Count von Donop in command of the line along the Delaware, with headquarters at Bordentown. The country soon felt the curse of his Hessian troops. These had been promised an opportunity to plunder and now they took it. I have before me a "Brief Narrative of the Ravages" about Princeton and Trenton—a long and pitiful tale of what we should now call "atrocities"—a first-hand document, to which I shall have occasion to refer again.

Von Donop gave to Colonel Rall (or Rahl, according to

REVOLUTIONARY PILGRIMAGE

the original German spelling) the command of the Hessians at Trenton. For twelve days this officer domineered the town, parading his troops through the streets with music, and spending his evenings drinking the best wines at the house of Abraham Hunt, at the corner of State and Warren Streets. When told that Washington might attack him, he cried, "Let them come; we will at them with the bayonet," believing, as did every one, that the broad Delaware with its floating ice was an insuperable barrier between them.

His troops were comfortably lodged in the town, for the most part in the two main streets—King and Queen, now Warren and Broad. His own grenadiers had their quarters in the jail, now a part of the Trenton Bank, and at the Blazing Star and Bull Head Taverns adjoining; the regiment von Lossberg, with some of the artillery, occupied the English church, now enlarged and modernized and called St. Michael's; while the von Knyphausen regiment occupied the Presbyterian church and the houses surrounding it. The yagers and Tories were down in the old barracks that we shall visit presently, and the British dragoons were quartered in the Quaker Meeting House, a quaint, gabled structure, still standing in Hanover Street. Thus, well housed and well fed, the Hessians went on with their preparations for a jolly German Christmas.

How different the picture across the river!

The winter began with bitter cold and the ragged Continentals were sleeping on the hillsides by the Dela-

IN THE JERSEYS

ware, without even a blanket to keep them warm. Destitute of every comfort and even of the barest necessities, without shelter of any kind, they lay upon the frosty ground. But, hungry and cold, like Spartan heroes their spirits were equal to the test.

The Point at Which Washington Crossed the Delaware River

These slopes by the Delaware have not changed much since then. In a few minutes you may go by train from Trenton out to Washington's Crossing, as the station is now called. A couple of modest inns stand by the river which is spanned by a bridge, whose wooden superstructure, since I drew it, has been replaced by one of iron. A long, narrow island divides the stream above it, and between this and the bridge was McKonkey's Ferry—the scene of Washington's Crossing of the Delaware.

REVOLUTIONARY PILGRIMAGE

On the New Jersey side of the river you will find a simple tablet bearing this inscription:

> This Tablet
> is erected by the Society of the Cincinnati
> in the State of New Jersey,
> to commemorate the Crossing of the Delaware River by
> General Washington and the Continental Army
> on Christmas night of
> Seventeen Hundred and Seventy Six.

On the opposite bank, the Pennsylvania shore, where the little village of Taylorsville sleeps under the trees, you will find a companion memorial:

> Near this spot
> WASHINGTON
> Crossed the Delaware
> on Christmas Night, 1776,
> The eve of the Battle of Trenton.

Upon the dedication of these two monuments in 1895, General William S. Stryker delivered the principal address, a copy of which he gave me when I met him some years ago in Trenton—an impressive personality and a striking face, attorney-general of the State, an ardent patriot, and the efficient president of the Trenton Battle Monument Association. I cannot do better, I feel, than quote from his oration, the scene preceding that Christmas eve of 1776:

"The night shadows were creeping over the woods on Jericho Hill and the road from Neeley's mill to Newtown.*

---
* Beyond Taylorsville, on the west bank of the Delaware.

IN THE JERSEYS

In the doorway of Samuel Merrick's house on that well-traveled road stood a general officer of Washington's army, listening to the distant ring of horses' hoofs on the frozen ground. A moment later, General Greene's expected guests drew rein before him and he saluted his commander-in-chief. General Washington was attended by an aide-de-camp, the gallant Colonel Baylor, and six Philadelphia troopers as a body guard. He had ridden over to be present on this Christmas eve at a council of war to which he had called his leading commanders. A few moments after the arrival of Washington and his guard, a little group of officers was seen dismounting in the dooryard of the old stone house, and the courtly Stirling, the best-dressed man in the army; the brave and determined New Hampshire General Sullivan and the foreign adventurer, de Fermoy,* were welcomed from the doorstep by General Greene. Then, at short intervals, came the experienced soldier, St. Clair,† and the equally skilled Stephen; the devoted Virginian, Mercer; ‡ Colonel Sargent of Massachusetts, and the sturdy mariner, Glover.**

"After preparing supper for General Greene and his compatriots, the Merrick family left the house to the exclusive use of the council. The meal had just been announced, when Colonel Stark,†† tall and straight as an Indian, and Colonel Knox, the artillerist, were admitted. The Reverend Doctor Alexander McWhorter, of Newark, pronounced grace at the supper of this important gathering of American military heroes. . . .

* Later, commander of Fort Independence, Ticonderoga.
† Whom we met at Ticonderoga.
‡ Killed soon after at Princeton.
** Commander of the men of Marblehead.
†† The hero of Bennington.

REVOLUTIONARY PILGRIMAGE

"The Commander-in-Chief laid before them his fully matured plan, so ingenious and yet so simple that all who read can grasp its military subtlety. To make the perilous crossing of the icy Delaware during the hours of darkness; to creep on the unwary Hessian foe in Trenton when Christmas wines and Christmas revelry had relaxed their customary vigilance and made a dull watch; to throw them into helpless confusion by the suddenness of the attack, and by striking from three sides at once—this was the plan of action upon which Washington had decided as a bold stroke to retrieve his country's fallen fortunes."

"Christmas day, at night, one hour before day," was the time set for the attack on Trenton.

Early Christmas morning Washington issued his orders for the march. Every detail had been carefully studied; and death was the penalty for quitting the ranks. The troops destined for the attack were paraded on the hill back of McKonkey's Ferry during the afternoon, and then moved toward the river. At dusk Washington and his staff arrived, and Colonel Knox, "with his stentorian voice," repeated the commands, which could be heard above the wind and the crunching of the ice.

"When the boats were shoved off from the Pennsylvania shore and had reached the swift current, the jagged cakes of ice struck them repeatedly and severely, and it was with the greatest difficulty that they could be properly handled. The wind was high, and at eleven o'clock the air was filled with blinding snow. Then again, as once before, over the East River after the battle of Long Is-

IN THE JERSEYS

land, and as he had promised at the council of war, Colonel John Glover and his magnificent Marblehead Regiment of sea-faring men did inestimable service in guiding the army over the dark and angry river."

It had been hoped that the crossing would be completed by midnight. But, as the Reverend Doctor Cooley tells us in a communication to the "State Gazette":

"It was between 3 and 4 o'clock in the morning before all the artillery and troops were over and ready to march. Many of the men were very destitute as regarded clothing. The present Mr. George Muirhead, of Hopewell, informed the writer that he had noticed men whose pantaloons were ragged and who had neither stockings nor shoes. The ground was covered with sleet, and snow was falling, although the day before there was no snow or only a little sprinkling on the ground. General Washington (who had sat in silence on a bee-hive, wrapt in his cloak, while his troops were crossing) as they were about to march, enjoined upon all profound silence during their march to Trenton and said to them '*I hope you will all fight like men.*'"

Then the ragged but glorious Continentals started on their nine-mile march. Their password was "Victory or death." In the black night, against a biting northeaster, they struggled up to the Bear Tavern, thence by the Old River Road, through the hickory woods to Birmingham, where they made a hasty breakfast. When told that the priming powder in the flint-locks was becoming damp, General Sullivan replied laconically: "Well, boys, we must fight them with the bayonet."

REVOLUTIONARY PILGRIMAGE

In Trenton the Hessians had retired heavy with their Christmas revels. They maintained six outposts: one on the Pennington Road; one on the Brunswick Road; two on the River Road; and two on the bridges down by Assanpink Creek.

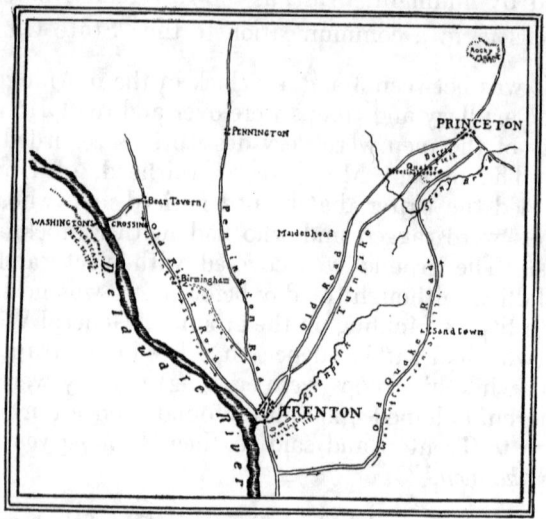

Map of Operations around Trenton and Princeton

At Birmingham Washington split his army in two divisions. One, under General Sullivan, was to follow the River Road; the other, under General Greene, to go by the Pennington Road, Washington himself accompanying the latter. This column was the first to come in contact with the Hessian pickets, who shouted, "Der Feind—Heraus! Heraus!" and fell back to spread the alarm. Three

IN THE JERSEYS

minutes later Sullivan's column struck the yager picket on the River Road and the Americans pushed into the town from both directions.

Rall's grenadiers came tumbling out of their quarters into King Street, while the von Lossberg regiment formed in the graveyard, still quaint and secluded, in the rear of the English church. Colonel Rall, when he heard all this commotion, threw up his window, opposite the English church, and, though still muddled with his wine, hurriedly dressed and, like the brave soldier that he was, threw himself upon his horse, galloped to the head of his regiment, and "started them on a run up King Street."

Meanwhile Washington had taken up his position on the high ground just back of where the monument now stands, from which point of vantage he could command a view of everything that was going on in the low-built village of that day. From this same point Captain Alexander Hamilton opened fire with his battery down King Street, while Captain Thomas Forrest trained his guns down Queen Street.

"Captain William Washington* and Lieutenant James Monroe,† perceiving that the enemy were endeavoring to form a battery in King Street, near where the feeder crosses the street, rushed forward with the advance guard, drove the artillerists from their guns and took from them two pieces which they were in the act of firing. These officers were both wounded in this successful enterprise." ‡

* The hero of the Cowpens.
† Afterward President of the United States.
‡ Reverend Doctor Cooley, in the "State Gazette."

REVOLUTIONARY PILGRIMAGE

Rall's regiment was pushed back upon the von Lossberg regiment. At each turn they met fresh Continentals. While Captain Forrest's guns created havoc among them, Mercer's brigade charged gallantly down Queen Street upon their broken ranks. Brave Rall, whom his superiors called the "Hessian Lion," seeing every avenue of escape being cut off, rose in his stirrups and shouted: "All who are my grenadiers, forward!" Just then he was struck by a bullet and fell from his horse in Queen Street, while the Continentals pushed his two disorganized regiments into an apple orchard that lay near the Friends' Meeting House, where, realizing that they were now surrounded by greatly superior numbers, they lowered their standards and grounded their guns, while the officers put their hats on the points of their swords.

General Stirling rode forward and Lieutenant-Colonel Scheffer, then senior officer of the Hessian troops, surrendered his sword and his command to him. Some of the Hessians and most of the British dragoons escaped over the Assanpink Creek; others were able to join von Donop as he retreated from Bordentown, and a few more reached General Leslie at Princeton, but nearly a thousand men remained prisoners of war, while six brass cannon and fifteen colors were also taken.

As one of his aide-de-camps rode up to him, Washington exclaimed exultantly: "This is a glorious day for our country, Major Wilkinson!" As indeed it was!

Later, "supported by a file of sergeants, Rall presented his sword to General Washington" and was taken to his

IN THE JERSEYS

headquarters (Stacy Potts), where he died of his wounds. He was buried, with a number of his Hessians, in the old Presbyterian churchyard on State Street, their graves being now covered by a portion of the new edifice.

Some of Trenton's Revolutionary landmarks have disappeared, others have been remodelled, but enough remain to distinguish the historic spots. To visit them you should begin down by the Delaware River, where, in the shadow of the gilded dome of the State House, stand the old barracks, to which I have alluded, and in which the yagers were quartered. Built in 1758, they are now being restored to their original condition and already contain an interesting little museum, due to the zeal of the Old Barracks Association, a group of patriotic women of the community.

You then walk over to Warren Street, and down to the Assanpink, which, though hemmed in by factories and mills, can still be seen—a brownish, busy stream, hastening to join the Delaware. Beyond it the highway, bordered by old houses, leads off toward Bordentown, where von Donop lay.

Now you follow up Warren Street (then King) toward the great monument that stands at its head. At the corner of State (then Second) Street stood the house of Abraham Hunt, where Rall spent most of his Christmas night drinking the rich merchant's good wine; and beyond, opposite Perry, where St. Mary's Cathedral now stands, were his headquarters, with the guard-house across the way.

REVOLUTIONARY PILGRIMAGE

At the end of Warren Street you reach the monument, placed where the American artillery stood to command both King and Queen Streets which here diverge. Beyond, to your left, stretches the Pennington Road, down which Washington came—then a country road but now a wide, paved street.

Upon the high ground where the commander-in-chief stood to direct his attack the tall granite column of the monument rises, surmounted by his figure in bronze, dressed as Trumbull painted him, one arm outstretched, pointing down King Street, directing the fire of Alexander Hamilton's battery; the other hand holding his field-glass. At the east side of the doorway in the base

Old King Street (now Warren Street), Trenton

IN THE JERSEYS

of the monument, his legs wide apart, stands a trooper of the Philadelphia Light Horse in his picturesque uniform, feeling the edge of his sword. At the west side a Continental soldier, a member of Colonel Glover's regiment, one of those "fishermen of Marblehead," to quote General Knox in his speech to the Massachusetts legislature, "alike at home upon land and water; alike ardent, patriotic, and unflinching whenever they unfurled the flag of their country"—the men who ferried the army over the icy Delaware.

Then, if you descend Queen Street, now Broad, you can picture, among the constructions still standing, the house before which Rall was mortally wounded as he tried to rally his men. Turning down Hanover Street, you come upon the old Quaker Meeting House, above mentioned, with its tablet:

The
Meeting House
was occupied by the
British
Light Dragoons
December, 1776.

Then, by crossing into State Street, you reach the Presbyterian church, in whose graveyard Rall and his Hessians lie buried.

And so our little Trenton pilgrimage is finished. We have seen all that is left to evoke that Christmas day of 1776 that meant so much to the patriots, turning for them the gloom of night into the bright hues of dawn—the day that wrung from Lord George Germaine, the British colonial minister, his bitter sentence, "All our hopes were blasted by the unhappy affair at Trenton"—the day that brought from the distinguished Italian historian, Carlo Botta, this eulogy: "All nations shared in the surprise of the Americans. All equally admired and applauded the prudence, the constancy, and noble intrepidity of General Washington. An unanimous voice proclaimed him the savior of his country; all extolled him as equal to the most celebrated commanders of antiquity. His name was in the mouth of all. All proclaimed him the Fabius of America."

II

PRINCETON

AFTER this signal success at Trenton, so inspiriting to the Americans, Washington led his little army triumphantly back, with their thousand prisoners and captured standards, to Newtown—a hard march indeed for the already wearied patriots, but their spirits were now buoyed up by the knowledge of work well done. After a few days' rest the commander-in-chief was back in Trenton, and by the first of the year was encamped upon the hills along the south side of the Assanpink beyond the bridge.

At the news from Trenton Cornwallis had cancelled his sailing for England, and by Howe's orders now returned to New Jersey with all speed to crush Washington. He took with him more than seven thousand of his best troops, he himself leading the advance. The situation again grew critical. Washington would not and could not retreat, for thus all the moral effect gained by his victory at Trenton would have been nullified. So he quietly awaited his enemy's coming.

As Cornwallis advanced down the old turnpike from Princeton (the road the trolley now follows) he was met at Five Mile Creek, near Maidenhead (now charming Lawrenceville, with its pretty homes and verdant golf-

REVOLUTIONARY PILGRIMAGE

links) by the fire of Colonel Hand's riflemen. When he reached Shebakunk Creek he had to bring up some cannon, so stiff was the resistance put up by Greene, who had advanced thus far and who was able to hold him in check

The Old Quaker Meeting House, near Princeton

just long enough to prevent him from attacking the main army that afternoon.

When Cornwallis found this out, he consoled himself by saying: "Never mind; I've got the old fox where I want him; I'll catch him in the morning."

That night set in cold and the wet ground froze so that the roads were good and hard. Washington had thought out his plan—a plan by which he might avoid a battle with superior numbers and yet not lose prestige by a retreat. His scouts had informed him that the British had

IN THE JERSEYS

no pickets on the Old Quaker Road that leads from Trenton to Princeton via Sandtown. So he determined to take that road, pass round his enemy, cut off his lines of communication, and, if possible, make a dash for the vast stores he had accumulated at Brunswick. A council of war heartily approved this audacious plan.

The camp-fires burned brightly; the sentries made their accustomed rounds so vigilantly that they completely deceived the British pickets only half a mile away. So the surprise and dismay of Cornwallis was complete when daybreak revealed an empty camp before him, his expected prey escaped, and heavy firing in his rear to tell him he had been outgeneralled.

For, as early as sunrise, the Americans were entering Princeton. They had advanced to the Stony Brook, had crossed it over the bridge that preceded the one that I have drawn, and had halted near an old Quaker Meeting

Stony Brook Bridge, near Princeton

REVOLUTIONARY PILGRIMAGE

House, built of field-stone, that still stands in a secluded nook down by the little river. Here Washington reformed his column, sending General Mercer with about five hundred men to destroy the bridge on the main turnpike, and thus impede Cornwallis's return.

This detachment quickly came in contact with two regiments of British that were just setting out to join Cornwallis. Mutually surprised, both forces played for position on some high ground centring round the farms of two brothers, William and Thomas Clark.

In the library of the University of Princeton I was shown a curious account of the battle that followed—a worn, frayed manuscript, stained with brown spots and broken into holes where it had been folded, and found among General Stryker's papers. The narrator's identity is not known, but he stood near enough to the battle to give us this eye-witness's account of it:

"As soon as it was light we saw the Regulars that was left at Princeton Marching toward Trenton and in about half a hour's time we saw them comeing back faster then they went; a Party of them came into our Field and laid down their Packs there and formed at the corner of our Garden about 60 yards from the door and then marcht away immediately to the field of Battle which was in William Clarks wheat field and Orchard Round about his house and how much further to the westard I know not. It was plain within sight of our door at about 400 Yards distance. . . .

"Before any Gun was heard a man was seen to fall and Immediately the Report and Smoke of a Gun was

IN THE JERSEYS

Seen and Heard. And the guns went of so quick and many together that they could not be numbered, we Presently went down into the Cellar to keep out of the Way of the Shot. . . . Almost as soon as the firing was over our house was filled and surrounded with Genl. Washington's Men, and he himself on horseback at the door. They brought in with them on their Shoulders two Wounded Regulars. . . . They was both Used very tenderly by the Rebels (as they call them). . . .

"As soon as the battle was over Genl. Mercer (who had his horse shot down under him, and then received several wounds by which in some days after he dyed) was carried into Thomas Clark's house with several other wounded men, And above Twenty was carried into William Clark's house. . . .

"Immediately after the Battle (as I said before) Genl. Washington's Men came into our house Though they were both hungry and thirsty some of them laughing out right, others smileing, and not a man among them but showed Joy in the Countenance. It really Animated my old blood with Love to those men that but a few minutes before had been Couragiously looking Death in the face in Releiving a part of their Country from the Barbarous Insults and Ravages of a bold and Dareing Enemy."

A crude but human picture certainly. To make it vivid you should go down to the battle-field itself and see the place as he saw it. On the way you pass stately Morven, the home of Richard Stockton, and used by Cornwallis as his headquarters. Then, beyond other handsome country houses, you reach the Pyne estate, where you turn from the main highway down the Old Post Road.

REVOLUTIONARY PILGRIMAGE

The "narrator" that I have just quoted stood about half-way down to the bridge. To his left occurred the first encounter between Mercer's troops, supported by Captain Neal's battery of two guns, and the two British regiments that were starting for Trenton but had turned back, as he describes, upon seeing the light flashing on the bayonets of the Americans. Both parties were surprised. The Americans got under cover of a rail fence in William Clark's orchard near his house. And, when the firing began behind it, our narrator went into his cellar!

After the third volley the British charged and the Americans retreated in disorder. Their officers, unwilling to yield, remained behind, trying to rally their men, and thus a number of these gallant men fell: Captain Neal, by his guns; Captain Fleming of the Virginians; Haslet, colonel of the Delaware regiment, and General Mercer himself, who, as the narrator recounts, "having had his horse shot down under him," was wounded, knocked down, bayonetted, and left for dead.

This last episode Trumbull has made the subject of his famous painting of the "Battle of Princeton," the precious sketches for which, in pen and *lavis*, hang in the University library, showing different elements of the composition shifted a number of times before the final arrangement was adopted.

A pile of cannon-balls on the battle-field now marks the spot where Mercer fell. Near it still stands the house of Thomas Clark, to which he was carried and in which he died.

IN THE JERSEYS

A flagpole and a little monument were erected here in 1897 by the Mercer Engine Company of Princeton. The tablet was unveiled by Master Hugh Mercer, great-

House and Room in Which General Mercer Died

great-grandson of the general, and the address upon this occasion was delivered by Professor Henry C. Cameron, of Princeton University, a close student of Princeton's history. Professor Cameron presented me with a copy of this speech and from it I quote the next episode—the climax of the battle.

REVOLUTIONARY PILGRIMAGE

As we have seen, the Americans were retreating in disorder when,

"upon hearing the fire, Washington sent the Pennsylvania militia and Moulder's battery to the assistance of Mercer. The flight of the Americans was stopped and the British pursuit arrested, but their artillery caused the militia to hesitate. Washington now appeared in person. comprehended the situation at a glance, and putting spurs to his horse, he dashed past the militia, galloped to the front of his wavering troops and with commanding voice cheered them on. . . .

"Washington seemed reckless of all danger; never was he in greater peril for he was between the lines. Reining up his horse with head to the enemy, he sat immovable, exposed to the fire of both armies and escape from death seemed impossible.

"His aid, Colonel Fitzgerald, who often told the story to one whom I remember in my boyhood, covered his eyes with his hat that he might not witness the death of his beloved chief. A roar of musketry follows, the gallant Hitchcock's Rhode Island regiment on the right and the 7th Virginia, with cheers, and other Continentals swing into line on the left, the enemy breaks and flies as the shout of victory arises from the American army. Washington's aid ventured to look, and, as the smoke of battle lifted, he beheld him safe; galloped to his side exclaiming, 'Thank God, your Excellency is safe,' and received the order, 'Away, my dear Colonel, bring up the men, the day is our own.'"

The British 55th made a last determined stand near Nassau Hall, but a few cannon-balls and superior num-

IN THE JERSEYS

bers finally dislodged them and they retreated toward New Brunswick.

Nassau Hall, around which still centre the University's traditions, fits, in essentials, the old descriptions of it. But you will admit that there have been changes in it and its surroundings since the days of the Revolution when you chance to read such an account as that given by a French traveller of distinction, Moreau de St. Méry, who wrote his "Voyage aux Etats-Unis d'Amérique," in the latter years of the eighteenth century.

He tells us that about eighty houses, some of them of brick, then bordered the road in Princeton.

Nassau Hall, Princeton

REVOLUTIONARY PILGRIMAGE

"On voit dans cette ville une église presbytérienne et un collège; ce dernier exige que nous nous arrêtions pour en parler, comme nous avons fait pour le visiter."

So he describes Old Nassau, giving its measurements correctly, but also telling us that the forecourt was dirty and full of the dung of animals that grazed there. In its dormitory were forty-two rooms, each for three students, and there were a chapel, a refectory, and a library of about two hundred volumes; while on the ground floor, opposite the principal door (just where it is to-day), was a large hall, "garnie de bancs."

On entering this hall one saw to the right a picture about eight feet high—a full-length portrait of General Washington. "Quoique la peinture de ce tableau ne soit pas sans merite, on peut néanmoins y critiquer trois choses." And he goes on to enumerate his three criticisms: first, Washington holds his hat in his hand while commanding in battle; second, Mercer scarcely seems to be suffering enough; and third, the aides-de-camp do not appear to be sufficiently concerned with their dying general.

The picture thus described is Charles Wilson Peale's well-known portrait of Washington that still hangs in this very hall. It has a curious history. In its place, in a handsome frame, prior to the battle of Princeton, hung a portrait of George III. One of the cannon-balls fired by the American troops in the brief engagement round Nassau Hall pierced the wall of the structure and took off the King's head. Washington, when he heard of this

IN THE JERSEYS

occurrence, wishing to make good the loss to the college, generously gave from his private purse the sum of two hundred and fifty dollars to help replace it. The board of trustees, not wanting another portrait of the King, commissioned Peale to paint the portrait that we now see hanging in the identical frame that once surrounded his Majesty's likeness.

I do not agree with all of M. de St. Méry's strictures, for I consider that the dying Mercer's head (said to have been painted from a brother who closely resembled the general) is an exceptionally able piece of painting, imprinted with a pathos and depth of suffering rarely seen in official portraiture. In the background one catches a glimpse of Nassau Hall itself, round which the battle rages.

While in the venerable shadow of Old Nassau I cannot refrain from giving an extract from the quaint diary of one of its students—a "campaign journal" as he calls it —in which he recounts the events immediately preceding the battle:

"On the 29th of November, 1776, New Jersey College, long the peaceful seat of science and haunt of the Muses, was visited with the melancholy tidings of the approach of the enemy.

"This alarmed our fears and gave us reason to believe we must soon bid adieu to our peaceful Departments and break off in the midst of our delightful studies; nor were we long held in suspense; our worthy President, deeply affected at the solemn scene entered the Hall, where the students were collected, and in a very affecting manner,

REVOLUTIONARY PILGRIMAGE

informed us of the improbability of continuing them longer in peace. . . . Solemnity and distress appeared on almost every countenance."

The president, to whom he alludes, was the Reverend Doctor John Witherspoon, whose grim portrait, with Bible in hand, still hangs in the hall. He was the only minister of the gospel in the Continental Congress, and when other of its members hesitated to sign the Declaration of Independence, he stepped forward courageously and said: "That noble instrument upon your table which secures immortality to its author, should be subscribed this very morning by every pen in this house. He who will not respond to its accents is unworthy the name of freeman."

Later on, in August, 1783, the Continental Congress held its sessions here in Old Nassau and summoned before it General George Washington to thank him officially upon the successful issue of the war in which he had "acted so conspicuous a part."

From that time until the following November Washington resided at Rocky Hill, a few miles distant, and, while there, wrote his "Farewell Orders," as they were called, but better known as his "Farewell Address to the Armies of the United States," which he dated "Rocky Hill, near Princeton, November 2, 1783." The white clapboarded house in which he then resided is still standing a few miles from the town. To visit it you take the Brunswick turnpike and follow the Old Post Road from Philadelphia to New York, over the very same

IN THE JERSEYS

route that the Americans took after the battle of Princeton.

Rocky Hill stands on an eminence just off this road, dominating a wide expanse of beautiful Jersey landscape, soft and green as a bit of rural England. The house is piously preserved as a museum, and the room, opening on the upper porch, in which the address was written, is still shown.

In January, 1777, well pleased with his successes at Trenton and Princeton, Washington pushed on to Pluckamin and thence to the high ground about Morristown, where he went into winter quarters until the following May.

III

MORRISTOWN

MORRISTOWN to-day is very well known as one of the most agreeable towns round about New York. Just too far from the metropolis to be called suburban, it possesses the handsome homes and extensive estates of a number of New Yorkers who, wishing to be sufficiently near the metropolis to enjoy its advantages, yet desire to live in the country and partake of the pleasures afforded by fine golf-links, riding to hounds, beagling, and other gentlemen's pastimes.

In Revolutionary days it centred round a green, placed where its three principal streets—Morris, Water, and South—converged and about which clustered most of its fifty-seven houses and its two hundred and fifty inhabitants. Its strategic position, perched as it is upon steep hillsides and dominated by Kemble Mountain, as well as the fine rich valleys about it that made provisioning more easy, twice made it Washington's choice for winter quarters.

We have just followed him hither for the first time in January, 1777. He, on that occasion, took up his headquarters in the old Arnold or Freeman Tavern that used to stand where the United States Hotel now fronts upon

IN THE JERSEYS

the main square. This first winter passed almost without incident. But as spring advanced the British tried to entice him down from his hillsides and lead him into a decisive battle. Instead of lending himself to their manœuvres, he threw out skirmishing parties and raised the Jersey militia to harass them as much as possible and with excellent results.

The Princeton student, whom I have before quoted, joined the Amwell militia and took part in many of these forays. In one of his later papers he thus describes what they did:

"The enemy had, some days before this, removed from Brunswick to Millstone, near the Court House and it was thought would make an attempt on Philadelphia. This roused the Militia of all the neighboring counties and they turned out with such spirit as will do them honor to the latest ages. Never did the Jerseys appear more universally unanimous to oppose the Enemy; they turned out Old and young, great and small, Rich and poor; Scarcely a man that could carry a musket was left at home. . . .

"The British then fled with greatest haste to Brunswick; but the Militia pursued them so closely and so warmly, that they made no stay there. On Sunday morning, June 22nd, they were driven out of the Town, and chased near to Amboy by the spirited Militia. . . . Thursday, June, 26, the enemy came out with their whole Body from Amboy and proceeded to Westfield, where they plundered and destroyed everything before them and distressed the Inhabitants in a manner before unheard of, but before they returned to Amboy numbers of them were cut off by part of our army, and some Militia. They returned to Amboy, and on Monday evening, June the 30th, 1777, they all left Amboy and went to Staten Island."

Thus were the Jerseys freed from the enemy, and thus did Washington, without a battle, again make himself master of the State. Thus "the British army, after having overrun victoriously the whole of New Jersey quite to the Delaware, and caused even the city of Philadelphia to tremble for its safety, found itself now restricted to the two posts of Brunswick and Amboy. Thus by an army almost reduced to extremity, Philadelphia was saved, Pennsylvania protected, New Jersey nearly recovered, and a vigorous and powerful army laid under the necessity of quitting all thoughts of acting offensively."*

The second time the American army wintered in Morristown was two years later. On that occasion they were better housed. Log huts were built, sixteen feet long and just high enough for a man to stand erect, and each provided with ten or twelve bunks. Washington had issued strict orders that "any hut not exactly conformable to the plan or the least out of line, should be pulled down and built again." The result was a model camp, so regular that a visitor narrates that "the encampments are exceedingly neat; the huts are all of a size and placed in more exact order than Philadelphia. You would be surprised to see how well built they are without nails."

There were about ten thousand men in the army that

* Botta.

IN THE JERSEYS

year. The park of artillery was nearest to town, lying upon the slope of a hill "along the present Mendham road just beyond the city limits where the road turns sharply to the left." Doctor Emory McClintock has carefully studied the topography of this camp and, in a paper read

Washington's Headquarters, Morristown

before the Washington Association of New Jersey, describes the location of each brigade around Kemble Mountain.

The summit of this high hill being visible from most of these encampments, as well as from headquarters, it was chosen as the camp alarm station with orders to fire its two guns at the first signal of an enemy's approach.

Washington's headquarters that winter were in the

house of Colonel Jacob Ford's widow, a fine mansion built of brick, covered over with planks, painted white, but not clapboarded, being laid edge to edge. It still stands but a short mile from the green out on the Newark turnpike. A refined and aristocratic air pervades it, set as it is upon broad lawns, quite free from neighboring houses. Its halls are spacious; its rooms large and finished with well-designed woodwork of the usual Colonial pattern. It is now arranged as a museum and is, I think, after Mount Vernon and the National Museum in Washington, the richest that I have seen in souvenirs and relics of our national hero.

The drawing-room is hung with portraits of him; behind it the room that he used as his office still contains his desk and other articles that belonged to the original Ford furniture. On the wall hangs Erskine's plan of the Morristown encampment, prepared under Washington's own direction. Adjoining this office was that of his chief secretary, Alexander Hamilton. These rooms lie to the left of the main hall; to its right are the dining-room and several smaller apartments, with the kitchen beyond—a kitchen sadly overfilled with a variety of ticketed utensils donated by patriotic women. The hall up-stairs is devoted to arms and uniforms.

The bedroom on the east front is the one that General Washington and his lady occupied during that winter. There are a few small objects in it that were there at the time and a fragment of the handsome carpet that he trod, framed and under glass, hangs upon the wall.

IN THE JERSEYS

But the articles that recall him most are those in a room across the hall: the clothes, sword, and accessories that he wore on the evening of his inauguration. The quiet suit, cut in the familiar pattern, is made of a finely woven ribbed silk, brownish gray in color and ornamented with large buttons covered to match. A knee-buckle, set with brilliants, and a pair of shoe-buckles of simpler pattern impart a touch of elegance to the costume. The dress sword is the one known as the Darke sword, because given him by his old friend, Major-General William Darke.

In the case with these articles are some of Martha Washington's slippers, one high-heeled pair, white; another, pale blue. Scattered throughout the house, with many articles of doubtful authenticity, are others of the highest historic interest, as, for example, the original letter written by Captain John Van Dyk concerning André's execution—to which I have referred in another chapter. You will find also finely tailored uniforms of British officers; the peaked hats of Hessian grenadiers; and knapsacks embellished with the familiar G. R. monogram, as well as numerous articles that once belonged to women of the period, such as shell combs, scarfs, an ear-trumpet that really is a trumpet, bonnets of leghorn and bonnets of silk, fans, rings, bracelets, and a curious sewing-bird that, screwed to a table, used to hold my lady's work within its beak.

Life here at the Morristown headquarters had its alarms that winter and its pleasures. The alarms were, for the most part, unnecessary, for no enemy came to

REVOLUTIONARY PILGRIMAGE

molest the army, but they were extremely annoying to the two ladies of the household, Mrs. Washington and Mrs. Ford, whose rooms, with the others, were invaded by the soldiers of Washington's life-guard, who threw up the windows, ready to repel any attack, while the ladies retired behind the curtains of their beds.

The life-guards, of whom there were two hundred and fifty, commanded by General Colfax, were quartered in log huts erected for them on the southeast lawn. Elijah Fisher, whose quaint "Journal" I quoted at Saratoga, was one of them and enjoyed his winter very much, for he says he "liked being there better than being in the Ridgment let them go where they would."

And certainly life had its diversions. Count Pulaski exercised his cavalry in the meadow below the house and gave exhibitions of daring Polish horsemanship that filled the young officers with envy. Here, too, presumably, "a young braggadocia of the army," anxious to emulate the Polish count's example, asked the privilege of breaking a spirited colt that Washington had just bought. His Excellency gave his consent and the young fellow mounted the horse, retaining his seat but a moment or two when his fiery mount threw up his heels, hurling his rider over his head and landing him in such ludicrous fashion that Washington "was so convulsed with laughter, that the tears ran down his cheeks."[*]

Distinguished visitors came and went. The new French minister, the Chevalier de Luzerne, was welcomed and

[*] Notes of the Reverend Mr. Tuttle. (Irving, " Life of Washington.")

IN THE JERSEYS

made a lengthy stay, numerous reviews and a handsome ball being given in his honor. Here occurred the funeral of his friend, Don Juan de Miralles, who died of a pulmonic fever and was buried in Spanish fashion with great pomp, Washington and his generals walking as chief mourners. Here, too, again to quote Elijah Fisher, "the Ingen chief come to Head Quarters to Congratelate with His Exelency and also Dined with him."

Another pleasing picture connected with that long winter is afforded by Alexander Hamilton's courtship. The house wherein it took place still stands just off the main road between headquarters and the town—a simple homestead that has now been moved so as to face a side street. It was the residence at that time of Doctor Jabez Campfield, and in it that winter dwelt the Surgeon-General, John Cochran. His wife was a sister of General Schuyler and the general's daughter Elizabeth, a charming girl of twenty-two, was visiting her aunt. Colonel Hamilton, who, as I have said, was Washington's chief secretary, met her often and became so interested in her that he spent most of his evenings in her society. So we can picture him, as he is described, returning to headquarters in the moonlight, his mind so full of romantic thoughts of her whom he had just left and was to marry in the following year, that he completely forgot the countersign. The sentry, obdurate, though he recognized his Excellency's aide-de-camp, refused to let him pass until a friend had prompted him and restored to his wandering thoughts the cabalistic word.

REVOLUTIONARY PILGRIMAGE

These were the lighter touches in a very sombre winter. In January the snow was from four to five feet deep and the cold intense. The sufferings of the ill-clothed troops were terrible. As usual, Washington's sympathy went out to his men and he tried in every way to alleviate their misery, but with little real success, as he thus writes to a friend: "We have had the virtue and patience of the army put to the severest trial. Sometimes it has been five or six days together without bread, at other times as many without meat and once or twice two or three days without either. . . . As an army they bore it with the most heroic patience; but sufferings like these, accompanied by the want of clothes, blankets, &c., will produce frequent desertions in all armies; and so it happened with us, though it did not excite a single mutiny."

ROUND ABOUT PHILADELPHIA

ROUND ABOUT PHILADELPHIA

I

CHADD'S FORD AND THE BRANDYWINE

OUR next visits will be paid to the historic localities in the vicinity of Philadelphia, whither the seat of war now shifted.

During the early half of 1777 Washington, as we have seen, had been able to free New Jersey from British forces and, as the summer ended, he was intently watching the movements of General Howe in New York. There lay the difficult problem. Would the British commander-in-chief ascend the Hudson to attempt to join Burgoyne or would he move south upon Philadelphia?

This city—the capital of the colonies—had been menaced once before just prior to the battle of Trenton and now, after a period of doubt, Howe decided to attack it again, as, to use his own words, the capture of Philadelphia seemed "the surest road to peace and the defeat of the regular rebel army."

So he embarked an imposing expedition early in July, and set sail from Sandy Hook on the 23d of that month, arriving off Cape Henlopen on the 30th. His intention had been to ascend Delaware Bay and disembark his army somewhere near Wilmington, but he found that

REVOLUTIONARY PILGRIMAGE

Washington had forestalled him by establishing a strong water-guard on the Delaware; by placing floating batteries in it; and by marching his main army down to Wilmington. In the face of such serious opposition, Howe realized that it would be impossible successfully to land his army.

So he was forced to put to sea again with his great fleet. His withdrawal perplexed Washington, for nothing was heard of him for some time. A council of officers had just unanimously decided that he had sailed for Charleston, when a message came from John Hancock, president of Congress, that "near two hundred of General Howe's fleet was at anchor in the Chesapeake Bay."

Washington, foreseeing the next move, was busy again. On the 22d of August he visited the defenses at Mud Island, Red Bank, and Billingsport, forts in the Delaware below Philadelphia, and, three days later, made "a Reconnoitre to the Head of Elk with a large party of Horse," as his account-book tells us.

The Head of Elk is at the extreme north end of the Chesapeake Bay. It is now known as Elkton, and lies on the main railway line between Philadelphia and Baltimore.

The British fleet sailed up the Chesapeake as far as Turkey Point, ten miles below the Head of Elk, and there disembarked the entire army, eighteen thousand strong. And a day or two later, this army was at the Head of Elk, only fifty-four miles from Philadelphia.

Washington was determined to oppose its further ad-

ROUND ABOUT PHILADELPHIA

vance, strong as it was. His own army only numbered about eleven thousand and many of these were raw recruits, but he considered that even a lost battle would be less dispiriting to the soldiers and the colonies than an

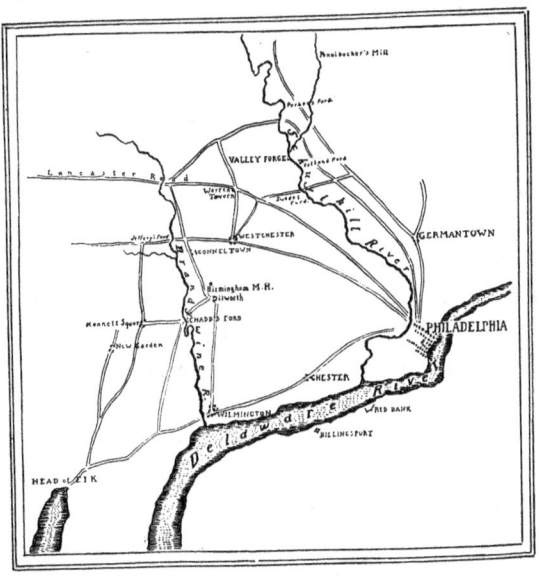

Map of Vicinity of Philadelphia

unopposed march of the British into Philadelphia. So on the 9th of September he took up a position, selected by General Greene, along the east bank of the Brandywine, a considerable stream that flows down to join the Delaware at Wilmington. Slight intrenchments were thrown up and Washington made his own headquarters in the village called Chadd's Ford.

REVOLUTIONARY PILGRIMAGE

I spent a summer in this village some years ago. Though the woods described in the Revolutionary accounts have largely disappeared, and are now replaced by open meadows and pasturelands, with here and there lines and clusters of handsome trees, many of the quaint old houses and mills yet remain as well as a number of those fine old stone barns that give such a distinctive note to the landscape—massive structures, usually placed on hill-slopes so that the wagons can drive into the upper story from the rear.

I stayed at a little inn kept by Quakers (many of the inhabitants hereabout are still Friends), and well kept, too, and in it, that season, were a group of New York artists out for their summer sketching.

Up the road, beyond Washington's headquarters, lived Howard Pyle, who had brought with him a special class of pupils from Wilmington and Philadelphia, several of whom now rank among our foremost illustrators. Mr. Pyle and I were both engaged upon illustrations for the same book and this was a bond between us which soon ripened into a good friendship. In his buggy he used to stop for me at the inn and we went sketching together up the valley of the Brandywine or over the hill toward the Birmingham Meeting House.

Those were delightful afternoons and the memory of them lingers as a precious reminiscence, for he was an exceptional man—stalwart and healthy and fine in mind as in body. He was, of course, as his work always showed, a very close student of the Revolutionary period, and his

ROUND ABOUT PHILADELPHIA

life was tinged with the flavor of that epoch. So, when I think of Chadd's Ford I love to recall his manly voice singing the martial ballads that he liked—the "British Grenadier," "Rule Britannia," and others of that ilk—

Washington's Headquarters, near Chadd's Ford

and his personality is closely linked in my mind with memories of the battle of the Brandywine, for our excursions together afford a vivid background for it.

As I have said, Washington took up his quarters at Chadd's Ford on the 9th of September.

REVOLUTIONARY PILGRIMAGE

That same afternoon General Knyphausen, with the Hessians, marched into New Garden and Kennett Square, on the opposite bank of the river, though a few miles distant from it. In this vicinity there were several fords along the Brandywine, by any one of which an army could pass: Chadd's, directly between the two hostile camps; Pyle's, below; Brinton's and others, above. On the following morning Cornwallis joined Kynphausen, accompanied by the commander-in-chief, General Howe. Thus, by the night of the 10th of September, the two armies lay watching each other. Washington thought he had picketed all the fords up and down the river, and so was facing only the possibility of a frontal attack.

Early on the morning of the 11th skirmishing began along the Brandywine, parties of Americans crossing and engaging the enemy, who drove them back. Knyphausen then brought up artillery and began bombarding the main American lines as if preparatory to a concentrated attack.

Meanwhile, unknown to Washington, Cornwallis, with General Howe himself and about five thousand troops, had made a long détour up the river, crossed its two feeders by small fords, and was even now coming down from Sconneltown by a road that led to the Birmingham Meeting House, in the rear of the American army. Though discovered at one time by an American patrol, this column had not been definitely located as it passed through the dense woods, and the surprise of its sudden appearance was complete. This surprise and the events that followed

ROUND ABOUT PHILADELPHIA

are graphically told in a statement by Joseph Townsend, a Quaker who lived up near Sconneltown and saw the battle that he thus describes:*

Lafayette's Headquarters, near Chadd's Ford

"At that time I resided at my father's, the place of my nativity, adjoining to the ground where West Chester now stands. . . . A majority of the inhabitants were of the Society of Friends, who could not consistently with their principles take any part in the war, and who generally believed it right to remain in their dwellings, and patiently submit to whatever suffering might be their lot. . . .

* "Bulletin of the Historical Society of Pennsylvania," vol. I, 1845–7.

REVOLUTIONARY PILGRIMAGE

"General Washington had his head quarters at Benjamin Rings' who resided near the east end of Chadd's ford, and General La Fayette was near at hand in the neighborhood.* They were frequently together, which afforded an opportunity to spectators to view them both at the same time. . . ."

He then describes the disposition of the two armies, as I have done, and the skirmishing on the morning of the 11th of September. Then, "possessed of curiosity and fond of new things," with his brother he rode "along side of the Brandywine for some distance, to discover the approach of the British army." But, seeing nothing, they went to a Friends' meeting up at Sconneltown and while there heard a disturbance outside.

"On our coming out of the house, and making some inquiry of what had happened, found it to be an alarm among some of the neighboring women, that the English army was coming, and that they murdered all before them, young and old. Some of us endeavored to quiet their fears by telling them it was not likely to be the case . . . and while we were reasoning with them, our eyes were caught on a sudden by the appearance of the army coming out of the woods into the fields belonging to Emmor Jefferis, on the west side of the creek above the fording place.† In a few minutes the fields were literally covered with them, and they were hastening towards us. Their arms and bayonets being raised,

* Both headquarters still stand quite close together on the main road. Lafayette had just been commissioned a volunteer major-general, and this was the first action in which he participated.
† Jeffery's Ford.

shone as bright as silver, there being a clear sky and the day exceedingly warm. Recollecting that there was no one at our dwelling, except some of our sisters, we concluded it advisable to return home as expeditiously as possible."

But the British changed their direction at Sconneltown and headed down toward the Birmingham Meeting House, so

"being disposed to have a better and a nearer view, we set out for the purpose and passing by the dwelling of Abel Boake, we soon met Sarah, his wife, who had been as curious as ourselves and had been among the soldiers as they marched along. . . . She encouraged our going amongst them, at the same time admiring their appearance and saying what fine looking fellows they were, and to use her own expression 'they were something like an army.'"

So the brothers went to have a nearer view and to talk to the officers, who seemed glad to see them—for, I suspect, the two had Tory leanings, as most of the Quakers did.

"They inquired what sort of a man Mr. Washington was. My brother had a knowledge of him by being with him at his quarters at Chadd's Ford, and replied that he was a stately, well-proportioned, fine-looking man, of great ability, firm and resolute, of a social disposition and was considered to be a good man.

"One of the officers then observed to me in some rapture 'you have got a hell of a fine country here, which we have found to be the case ever since we landed at the head of Elk.'

"The house we were in was elevated, so that on the first floor where we stood we had a pretty full view of the army as they progressed along; and while we were conversing together, my brother called on me to step to the door and see General Lord Cornwallis, who was passing by. He was on horseback, appeared tall and sat very erect. His rich scarlet clothing, loaded with gold lace, epaulets, etc., occasioned him to make a brilliant and martial appearance. . . . It may be observed that most or all of the officers who conversed with us, were of first rank, and were rather short, portly men, were well dressed and of genteel appearance, and did not look as if they had ever been exposed to any hardship; their skins being as white and delicate as is customary for females who were brought up in large cities or towns."

When the main action began, our friend retired to a hill, where

"in Samuel Osborn's field a number of my acquaintances were standing near a considerable number of persons on horseback and viewing them. . . . It appeared that those on horseback were some of the principal officers of the British army with their aids, who had collected together to consult respecting carrying on the engagement to the best advantage. Among them was General Howe. He was mounted on a large English horse much reduced in flesh, I suppose from being so long confined on board the fleet. . . . The general was a large portly man, of coarse features. He appeared to have lost his teeth, as his mouth had fallen in. As I stood alongside, I had a full opportunity of viewing him as he

ROUND ABOUT PHILADELPHIA

sat on horseback, and had to observe his large legs and boots, with flourishing spurs thereon.

"While the officers were in consultation, and we viewing them together with the smoke issuing from the cannon and musketry, we heard a tremendous roaring of

Birmingham Meeting House, near Chadd's Ford

cannon, and saw the volume of smoke arising therefrom at Chadd's Ford. General Knyphausen having discovered that the engagement was on with the front of Howe's army at the Meeting House, he immediately forced the troops under his command across the Brandywine, and the whole of General Washington's army in that station were routed from their breastworks. . . . From these circumstances General Washington concluded it prudent to effect a retreat which took place accordingly.

REVOLUTIONARY PILGRIMAGE

"While we remained on Osborne's hill, we had the opportunity of making many observations,—the engagement of both armies—the fields in front of us containing great heaps of blankets and baggage, thrown together to relieve the men for action—the regular march of the British army, consisting of horse and foot, artillery, baggage and provision wagons, arms and ammunition, together with a host of plunderers and rabble that accompanied the army. Almost the whole face of the country around appeared to be covered and alive with these objects. Their march continued about four hours.

"We remained on the hill for some time, and when the engagement appeared to be nearly over or at least that part of it which was in view, and the day being on the decline, we were about retiring; but as admiration and curiosity had been the order of the day, I proposed to some of my companions that we should go over the field of battle and take a view of the dead and wounded, as we might never have such another opportunity. Some of them consented, and others with some reluctance yielded. We hastened thither and awful was the scene to behold—such a number of fellow beings lying together severely wounded and some mortally—a few dead, but a small proportion of them considering the quantity of powder and ball that had been discharged. It was now time for the surgeons to exert themselves, and divers of them were busily employed. Some of the doors of the meeting house were torn off and the wounded carried thereon into the house to be occupied for a hospital. . . ."

This picturesque account very well describes the various episodes of the battle of the Brandywine. For it tells us how, while Knyphausen "kept the enemy

ROUND ABOUT PHILADELPHIA

amused during the day with cannon" down by Chadd's Ford, Cornwallis stole a march and, suddenly forming his troops up by the Birmingham Meeting House, fell upon Sullivan, who had been despatched at the last moment to oppose him there, defeated him and pushed him back; while Knyphausen, "having discovered that the engagement was on at the Meeting House," led his troops with a rush across the river and drove the Americans from their intrenchments. Caught thus between two armies, the wonder is that Washington was able to extricate himself at all and could effect his retreat with so little loss and in such good order.

In helping to cover this retreat, Lafayette, youthful, impetuous, desirous of proving himself worthy of his newly granted commission, was wounded in the leg at a spot upon the Dilworth Road now marked by a monument, appropriately inscribed.

The old Birmingham Meeting House still stands upon the hill above Chadd's Ford—still used by the Quakers for their meetings—a sturdy stone structure whose doors and window-shutters, now painted neat and white, remain perpetual reminders of the day when they were torn from their hinges to serve as litters for the British soldiers wounded in the battle of the Brandywine.

II

GERMANTOWN

AFTER the battle of the Brandywine, Washington retreated beyond the Schuylkill to Germantown; but as soon as his soldiers were somewhat refreshed he recrossed the river and again endeavored to stay Howe's advance upon Philadelphia. On the Lancaster Road, near the Warren Tavern, the two armies again confronted each other, but a sudden September deluge wet their powder and prevented the impending battle. The storm lasted all night and by morning Howe had slipped away toward Swedes' Ford, now Swedeland, opposite Conshohocken, a station we shall pass on the road to Valley Forge.

Washington crossed back by way of Parker's Ford, higher up the river, but again Howe changed his direction, made a feint up the Schuylkill toward Reading, and, when Washington had well started to save his Reading stores, Howe wheeled about, marched rapidly down the river, crossed it at the Fatland Ford, about where Port Kennedy now is, and pushed on to Philadelphia, which he entered on the 26th of September, 1777, having eluded Washington entirely.

Howe stationed his main army in Germantown, sending out detachments to reduce the forts at Billingsport

ROUND ABOUT PHILADELPHIA

and Fort Mercer on the Delaware below Philadelphia. These two expeditions weakened his effectives to such an extent that Washington, who meanwhile had received reinforcements from Peekskill, was emboldened to try another battle.

His base, at the time, was at Pennibecker's Mill, up the Skippack Creek. From this place he planned to descend by night and make a surprise attack upon the British who remained in Germantown, with their outposts extending as far up as Mount Airy. So, at seven in the evening of the 3d of October, the American army left camp, advancing upon Germantown in three divisions: Sullivan and Wayne leading the centre; Armstrong the right; and Greene the left. These last divisions took outer roads so as to flank the enemy and join the centre in Germantown itself.

At the time of the Revolution Germantown was a straggling settlement, ranged along a single street. To a certain extent it may so be described to-day, for its single main street, three miles or more in length, is only crossed by short thoroughfares. This long street follows the ridges of several hills up and down, so that no great part of its length can be seen at one time. It is still bordered by many of its old-time houses—a number of them historic and designated by tablets—whose dormer-windows, steep roofs, clapboarded fronts, and colonial doorways impart to it a decided flavor of other days.

It was down this main street that the principal action occurred in the battle of Germantown. The American

REVOLUTIONARY PILGRIMAGE

advanced brigade first came in contact with the pickets up at Mount Airy. These pickets were quickly supported by British light infantry, for the surprise had not been complete. Sullivan's troops now came up and the British retreated, fighting as they went. Even Colonel Musgrave, with the Fortieth, who pushed forward to the rescue, was not able to stem the tide and was obliged to fall back. The British retreat now became general, but when the retiring troops passed the great Chew house that stood near the street Colonel Musgrave flung himself, with five companies of his regiment, into the big stone mansion, barricaded the doors and windows, and from this improvised fortress fired upon the pursuing American column. The Americans hesitated, halted, and endeavored to dislodge Musgrave and his men. But the solid masonry of the stone house was like a single rock and their bullets bounded off its walls and fell harmless upon the ground. Even General Knox's cannon proved ineffective, and he, obeying a law of military tactics, would not advance and "leave an enemy in a fort in the rear."

An attempt was then made to set fire to the house. A brave young officer, Major White, one of General Sullivan's aides, ran in so close with a firebrand that the shots from the windows could not attain him. But a regular, slipping into the cellar, fired up from one of the grated windows and killed him. The stout oaken doors resisted all attack.

General Wayne's division, which had advanced far

ROUND ABOUT PHILADELPHIA

beyond the house in its pursuit of the British, now came back, and for a full hour the Americans laid siege to this annoying obstacle that upset all their preconceived plan of battle. For, the centre being thus delayed, the

The Chew House, Germantown

wings had pushed forward. Greene had met with notable success and had arrived, as ordered, in the vicinity of the Market House that used to stand where the Schoolhouse Lane crossed the main street. But, owing chiefly to the attack on the Chew house, as well as to the slowness of Armstrong's division, he was not supported by the arrival of the other parts of the American army.

REVOLUTIONARY PILGRIMAGE

The British, who had been thrown into the greatest disorder, now had time to reorganize their line. General Grey brought up the left wing and for two hours the battle raged up and down the street with the issue still in doubt.

The morning fog thickened and added to the confusion. Friend was mistaken for foe. At this critical moment Sullivan's division, feeling itself unsupported and hearing exaggerated rumors of reverses elsewhere, began to retreat. This retreat soon became general, and the "activity of a powerful and almost invisible enemy quickened that retreat."

Thus, what might well have been a victory was turned to a defeat—a defeat, however, that was not severe enough to discourage the American army nor seriously cripple it.

On the green at Germantown, near the spot where the old Market House used to stand, is a simple but dignified monument "erected by the Commonwealth of Pennsylvania," with a plan of the battle on one side, and on the other this extract from Washington's report to the president of Congress:

"Upon the whole it may be said that the day was unfortunate rather than injurious. We sustained no material loss. . . .

"The enemy are nothing the better by the event and our troops, who are not in the least disappointed by it, have gained what all young troops gain by being in actions."

ROUND ABOUT PHILADELPHIA

The last time I stood before this monument it was the centre of a pretty scene. As a local paper expressed it, "the descendants of the Colonial aristocracy of Germantown sold chickens, garden hats, and flowers for the sake of charity," for Vernon Park, as this green is now called, had been converted for the occasion into a huge May market, and in front of the old Wister mansion, with its statue of John Wister before it, "the very shrine of old Germantown families," booths had been erected, tea was being served, and young ladies, looking charming in chintzes and silks of colonial fashion, were vending flowers and favors for the benefit of a local charity. There were animals for the children to ride; there were music and a country store and attractions of all kinds as long as daylight lasted.

Toward evening I wandered up Germantown Avenue to the old Chew house. The stately and venerable mansion, called Cliveden, stands well back from the road on a lawn shaded by fine old trees. It was built in 1763 by Benjamin Chew, an eminent jurist, recorder of the city of Philadelphia, then attorney-general of Pennsylvania, and finally, in 1774, chief justice of its supreme court. His portrait in Independence Hall, copied from a miniature, shows a rather sour-faced man, thin, with large spectacles astride a stubborn nose of aristocratic pattern, aquiline, high-bridged, and full of character.

The chief justice remained "on the fence" at the beginning of the Revolution. He favored reform but not independence; wherefore, after refusing to indorse the

REVOLUTIONARY PILGRIMAGE

Declaration of Independence, he was put under arrest and sent to Fredericksburg, Virginia, which accounts for his absence during the battle.

One of his daughters, Peggy, was a heroine of the Mischianza, which I shall describe in my chapter on Philadelphia, and her love-affair with Major André forms a lighter touch in the British officer's story. His death, following so soon upon their violent flirtation, did not affect her too deeply, for she afterward married that stanch patriot and splendid gentleman Colonel John Eager Howard, hero of the Cowpens and donor of the land whereon the great Washington Monument now stands in his native city, Baltimore.

One has only to look at Cliveden's massive walls to realize what a fortress it could become, and how successfully it could withstand artillery of the calibre then in use. It is built of a very hard stone, granitic and thickly sprinkled with glittering particles that shine in the sun like mica. The stone is gray, the roofs slate-colored, and the doors and shutters white, giving the old demain an air of tranquil dignity, habited, like a gentleman, in quiet attire. On the lawns about it stand fragments of the statues that were battered and mutilated during the battle. Through one of the grated basement windows Major White was shot. Indeed the picture is still so complete and so unchanged that one can scarcely believe that a century and a half have passed since that memorable day in October, 1777.

Nor is this impression dispelled on entering the house.

ROUND ABOUT PHILADELPHIA

Mrs. Chew (the home has always remained in the Chew family) was at home on the afternoon I called, and graciously volunteered to take me about herself. From the main doorway I entered at once into a spacious hall, almost square and decorated with a triple arcade opposite the entrance. Through the three arches you perceive the stairs that lead to the second story. Old family portraits, a "silhouette" or two, several historic engravings, and the original furniture give the hall distinction.

A small room opens off at either side. Treasured in that to the left, Mrs. Chew drew my attention to the very pair of oaken doors that had so successfully resisted the American attack, battered and scarred, it is true, but not broken in by any device that could be brought to bear against them.

Behind these two rooms open two others, much larger than they—a dining-room and a drawing-room. In these also, woodwork, furniture, pictures are all in perfect accord with the general atmosphere of the house and form a rarely complete ensemble. My hostess, too, so simple and all in black, fitted admirably into the picture, especially as she stepped out into the sunlight when I was leaving and stood with her hand resting on one of the stone lions that guard the stairs—a perfect embodiment of quiet distinction.

III

VALLEY FORGE

WITH Washington's movements after Germantown—"the different and continual movements of the Army from the time of its march from Germantown till we hutted at Valley Forge, the 25th of Dec^r," to use his own words—we shall not concern ourselves here, for they constituted only a series of minor engagements of no great importance to the general narrative. So we shall follow him directly to his winter quarters on those hills beside the Schuylkill, where Isaac Potts operated his forge in the valley.

The army arrived there a few days before Christmas, and after their marches and countermarches, with no shoes on their feet, the soldiers hoped to find some repose, but were confronted instead with a new array of enemies—hunger and cold, pestilence and discouragement. For that year the army was indeed in dire straits; never before had it been so destitute. On the 23d of December Washington reports "two thousand, eight hundred and ninety-eight men were unfit for duty because barefoot and naked."

His officers as well as the Assembly of Pennsylvania had tried in vain to persuade him to risk all on the issue of one more decisive battle, but he, realizing only too

ROUND ABOUT PHILADELPHIA

well the condition and limitations of his poor, ragged troops, wisely adhered to his own plan and gave orders to build the winter huts on the hills of Valley Forge.

Do you know what Valley Forge looks like to-day? Have you ever visited this shrine "whereon our patriotism should delight to pile its highest and most venerated monument"?

If so, you know that it is now a State Park, laid out with wide, smooth roads and decorated with a profusion of monuments, both great and small. When I first visited it, some fifteen years ago, it was still an uncultivated tract of land, dotted here and there with farms and crossed here and there with country roads, while the remains of its old intrenchments could still be seen, half hidden by a sturdy growth of trees. Now these intrenchments are even better defined and, in places, planted with blossoming laurel, while broad asphalt roads lead to imposing monuments and statues.

I wonder which is the right impression. The motorist, the hurried tourist, the caravans of curious that visit it from Philadelphia in huge, sightseeing buses will, of course, prefer it as it is to-day. But the pedestrian, the poet, the dreamer of dreams, and the lover of "atmosphere" will sigh for the Valley Forge of years ago.

And truly, given its traditions and pathetic associations, it scarcely seems the place for pompous equestrian statues, columns, and triumphal arches. Markers to designate the placement of the various encampments—well and good, and the more of them the better; but to

REVOLUTIONARY PILGRIMAGE

destroy the solemnity of these cheerless hills by bronzes and marble monuments seems to me irrelevant and of questionable taste. It is only too evident that the motives that prompted the erection of these memorials were of the best; the advice of a more enlightened park commission might have directed their activities toward a better result.

Valley Forge is but an hour from Philadelphia by the railroad. The train follows all the way along the Schuylkill, which, at first, through the outer industrial districts of the city, is harnessed by mills and factories, but later flows free and placid between well-wooded hills.

Beyond East Falls we crossed the Wissahickon, whose banks afford the favorite drive from Germantown; and beyond Norristown we passed to the west bank of the river and soon after drew up at the station of Valley Forge—a station whose long colonnades suggested the crowds that at times arrive here.

Luckily, the morning of my last visit I was almost the only passenger to alight, so I wandered off quite by myself. The railway-station stands very near the house known as the Washington Headquarters. In it, prior to the Revolution, dwelt Isaac Potts, who operated a forge up the creek that here flows into the Schuylkill—the Valley Creek, as it was called, whence the name Valley Forge.

During the "hutting" of the troops Washington insisted upon sharing their hardships by remaining with them in his marquee up on the slope of Mount Joy.

ROUND ABOUT PHILADELPHIA

But when the soldiers were securely under shelter in their log huts he took up his headquarters in this stout little Potts house, substantially built of field stone, with solid doors and window-shutters. He added a log cabin "to

The Old Potts House at Valley Forge

dine in, which has made our quarters much more tolerable than they were at first," as Mrs. Washington, who joined him later, writes to a friend.

And truly it was a small house for the commanding general of an army—with but two little rooms on the ground floor and two above, with a few steps leading down to a kitchen and to the dining-room to which she alludes. It is now kept in perfect repair; its old woodwork and panelling have been scraped and freshly painted, and it has been appropriately furnished in excellent taste by the Norristown Chapter of the Daughters of the American Revolution.

In the field near by the life-guard was quartered, and beyond lay General McIntosh's brigade. The main encampments, however, were much farther away, over on the other slope of Mount Joy.

To visit these various camps you should follow up the Valley Creek, a sombre and romantic stream that on dark days runs so silently and so stealthily under the overhanging branches that it recalls some tragic vale in Dante.

Beyond the site of the forge and the spring, you reach a covered bridge, at which you turn to the left up the hill and soon come upon General Knox's quarters—a farm now owned by Senator Knox. From this point begins the long succession of encampments, each division marked by one or more monuments. The first of these is a monument to unknown soldiers; then one to Baron von Steuben, taking the form of a portrait statue erected by the German-American Alliance in 1915. Beyond it a reconstruction of one of the log huts designates the site of the camp hospital. On the hill above you catch a glimpse of Fort Washington.

The first troops along this line were those of Scott's and Woodford's brigades; then came the Pennsylvanians under General Anthony Wayne. A great equestrian statue of this general here dominates the landscape, the

ROUND ABOUT PHILADELPHIA

gallant Pennsylvanian turning in his saddle to gaze far out across the broad Chester valley, here revealed for a great distance, as if eagerly scanning its undulations in quest of an approaching enemy. The intrenchments that protected his division are still plainly visible in the woods that skirt the road.

General Poor's command came next and completed this first salient of intrenchments, for here the brow of the hill deflects and, turning sharply backward, forms a second line nearer to the Schuylkill. The road turns with it and passes, on the highest ground, a massive arch erected by the United States Government—the Washington Memorial Arch, as it is called—inscribed with Washington's own tribute to his men written in a letter to Governor Clinton: "Naked and starving as they are, we can not enough admire the incomparable patience and fidelity of the soldiery." And surely every man who passed that winter in Valley Forge, with its wretched sicknesses and high mortality, its hunger and its cold, was a patriot of whom his descendants may well be proud.

Beyond the arch a plinth with a widely curving seat serves as Massachusetts' tribute to her soldiers who occupied this position under Glover and Learned. Patterson's, Weedon's, and Muhlenberg's divisions came next, stretching from here down to the Schuylkill, where they were flanked by a redoubt.

Instead of following this line, you should now return to the arch and take the Old Gulch Road, that leads back through the valley toward Washington's Headquarters.

REVOLUTIONARY PILGRIMAGE

Down in the hollow, you find the Camp School built in 1705. Though still furnished with its old desks and benches ranged along the wall, and with the pegs for the children's hats and coats, it is now a diminutive museum, presided over by an aged veteran who triumphantly points out, gathered about it, various trophies in the shape of captured cannon.

From the Camp School you may ascend Mount Joy and see the main redoubt, called Fort Washington, whose parapets, now restored and set out with artillery, command a splendid panorama of all the surrounding country. Hence another line of intrenchments leads down to the Star Redoubt, that overlooked the Schuylkill and the temporary bridge. We are now again near Washington's Headquarters, and have completed our circuit of the Revolutionary camp-ground.

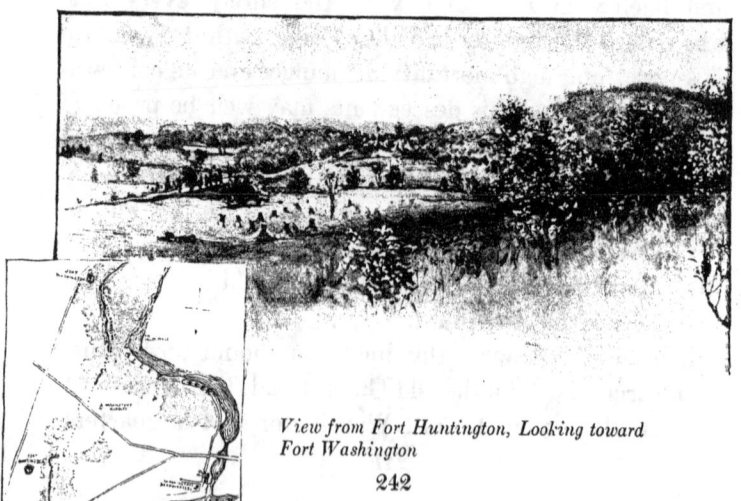

View from Fort Huntington, Looking toward Fort Washington

ROUND ABOUT PHILADELPHIA

There are many more markers and monuments than I have noted, but such is the main topography of the camp at Valley Forge, whose hills are filled with memories of the ardent patriots who passed that dreary winter there, sleeping in the rude log huts on bunks of straw—when they could get it—for even straw was a difficult thing to obtain and many died for the lack of it. "Unprovided with this, or materials to raise them from the cold and wet earth, sickness and mortality have spread through their quarters in an astonishing degree. Nothing can equal their sufferings, except the patience and fortitude with which the faithful part of the army endure it." *

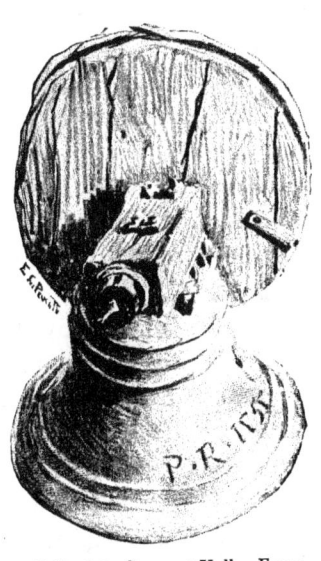

Bell Used in Camp at Valley Forge

This winter at Valley Forge was probably the most trying of Washington's life. The sufferings of his soldiers touched him deeply and he endeavored in every way to alleviate their distress. But the winter was a bitter and a gloomy one and tried his fortitude to the utmost. Isaac Potts relates that one day while wandering in the woods near his forge he heard a voice.

* Report of the Committee of Arrangement of Congress.

REVOLUTIONARY PILGRIMAGE

Silently advancing, he saw a horse tied to a tree, and near it his venerated guest, kneeling upon the ground, his eyes filled with tears, praying. Awed as if he had intruded upon some holy scene, Potts quietly withdrew and made his way back to his forge. This is the Washington that we must remember in our times of trouble —not only the successful general and able President but the man who knew how to face adversity and grapple with it.

To add to his troubles, the "Conway cabal" came to a climax in the middle of that winter. General Conway, a schemer, by political intrigue and pressure upon Congress, had tried to have Washington superseded as commander-in-chief by Horatio Gates, whose brilliant capture of Burgoyne and his army (through no particular merit of his own) he contrasted with Washington's ill success at the Brandywine and Germantown. Washington boldly faced his critics, quietly winning most of them over, so that Conway, in dudgeon, resigned his commission as inspector-general of the army. To his astonishment, this resignation was accepted, and the Baron von Steuben, who had just arrived in America, was appointed in his place.

Von Steuben quickly became the man of the hour. "Officers and men alike were placed under the rigid training of this veteran martinet . . . ; and the effects of his stern discipline and exacting drill were of permanent value." *

* Colonel Henry B. Carrington, "Battles of the Revolution."

ROUND ABOUT PHILADELPHIA

Here is a soldier's estimate of this patriot army, written by one of its enemies, Captain Johann Heinrichs of the Hessian Yager Corps, among whose letters to his brother I find the following, dated Philadelphia, January 18, 1778:

"Nor is their standing army to be despised . . . as they are, per se, a brave nation, which bravery is surprisingly enhanced by the enthusiasm, engendered by falsehood and vagaries, which are drilled into them, so that it but requires time and good leadership to make them formidable. . . .

"The enemy is encamped in huts in Wilmington and Valley Forge, and Washington and Stirling have wagered as to who had the best huts erected. . . . Our army x.y.z. strong, lies in Philadelphia, which is fortified by eleven redoubts and one outpost; we are supplied with all that is necessary and superfluous. Assemblies, Concerts, Comedies, Clubs and the like make us forget there is any war, save that it is a capital joke."

There are the two pictures. The ragged, shivering Continentals, their feet wrapped in rags, borrowing from each other the blankets in which they were to mount guard—cold, hungry, but filled with patriotism, "their bravery surprisingly enhanced by the enthusiasm engendered by falsehood and vagaries," but benefiting by "good leadership to make them formidable"; while the British army was weakening itself in a life of indolence and pleasure in snug Philadelphia, "supplied with all that is necessary and superfluous," so that war was a "capital joke."

REVOLUTIONARY PILGRIMAGE

But when the icy barriers broke and spring was in the air a ray of hope dawned for the patriots—a gleam of encouragement shot from across the sea. *La Sensible*, frigate, toward the first of May, anchored in Falmouth Harbor, Maine, and a French herald stepped ashore to announce an armed alliance between his country and the United States.

The news reached Valley Forge soon after, and one May morning the ragged Continentals, their uniforms patched and mended, were drawn up on parade. The treaty of alliance was read from the head of the army; the chaplains of each regiment advanced to the front of their men and led them as "in solemn silence, the army at Valley Forge united in thanksgiving to Almighty God that he had given them one friend on earth."

Then, at a signal, thirteen cannon were fired, followed by a running fire of musketry up and down the line, and the whole army shouted: "Long live the King of France!" Again the thirteen cannon, again the rattle of musketry; then the cry: "Long live the friendly European Powers!" A third and last discharge, and a mighty shout: "The American States!"

PHILADELPHIA

PHILADELPHIA

AS a contrast to this picture of Valley Forge it is now my purpose to follow the British into Philadelphia and depict some of the "Assemblies, Concerts, Comedies, and Clubs" of which our Yager captain speaks—the gayeties of that winter when officers and soldiers alike were welcomed and indulgently petted by the rich Tories and neutral Quakers of the city.

But before we do this let us for a moment take a retrospective glance at the city, so as to see it as it then appeared, and awake some of its memories.

At the time of the Revolution Philadelphia was just beginning to grow into the plan that William Penn had laid out for it. He had conceived that it would some day centre, as it now does, where its two principal streets, Broad and Market, cross each other. But, owing to the commercial facilities of the Delaware River, the buildings, in colonial days, had all followed "along the Delaware for the convenience of being near the warehouses and shipping. Front Street, which is parallel with the river, is near three miles long, and out of it open upwards of two hundred quays, forming so many vistas terminated by vessels of different sizes."*

Market Street, then called High Street, was considered of great breadth and length, and "would be," ac-

* De Chastellux, "Travels in North America."

cording to a resident, "one of the finest streets in the world, were it not for the market situated in the middle of it; but the upper part is occupied by the houses of opulent citizens and will in time become truly noble."

As I have said, the thickly populated section still centred along the Delaware water-front, so that it is down in that section of the city that we still find all the landmarks of the days of the Revolution.

One of the most interesting reminders of this period stands near the foot of Chestnut Street, between Third and Fourth, in a narrow alley that opens between two modern buildings, widening behind them into a sort of square. Upon this little quadrangle faces Carpenter's Hall, quite shut off from all the world nowadays by the tall structures that surround it. Its façade of red brick diapered with glazed black headers, its pediment, its three arched windows above and simple but well-proportioned door below, flanked on either side by a shuttered window, all retain their original character intact.

Yet this modest building, so humble, so retiring, so shyly tucked away from the bustle and traffic about it, was, so to speak, the birthplace of our nation. For in it, just prior to the Revolution, the first assemblage of delegates from the American colonies convened to discuss their grievances against the mother country.

To this Congress came such men as the two Adamses and Robert Treat Paine from Massachusetts; Eliphalet Dyer, Roger Sherman, and Silas Deane from Connecticut; John Jay, Isaac Low, and Philip Livingston from New

PHILADELPHIA

York; Thomas Mifflin, Edward Biddle, and John Dickinson from Pennsylvania; Henry Middleton, the Rutledges, and Christopher Gadsden from South Carolina; while Virginia sent her favorite sons—Peyton Randolph, Richard Henry Lee, George Washington, Patrick Henry, Benjamin Harrison, Edmund Pendleton, and Richard Bland.

On the 5th of September, 1774, these delegates met in Carpenter's Hall. The assembly-room, as we see it to-day, remains quite as these fathers of our country beheld it—a large, bare chamber, buff in color, whose only architectural embellishments are the two Ionic columns that form a sort of screen before the alcove opposite the entrance door. The walls are hung with the souvenirs

The Assembly Room, Carpenter's Hall

REVOLUTIONARY PILGRIMAGE

and photographs that form the precious heritage of the Carpenters' Company, that still uses the building as its headquarters. Some of the original Windsor chairs stand behind a railing and the speaker's desk has been placed just where it used to stand when this first Continental Congress convened.

So the picture can become quite vivid if you sit quietly in a corner and call it to mind.

There, at the speaker's table, sat Peyton Randolph of Virginia, then in his fiftieth year, with Charles Thomson of Pennsylvania, the secretary, beside him—a "meagre figure, with hollow eye and white hair that did not fall quite so low as his ears." Ranged round the walls in their straight Windsor chairs sat the other fifty-three delegates—the best men that the colonies had to give, "a collection of the greatest men upon this continent in point of abilities, virtues, and fortunes," as John Adams expressed it.

The first sitting was occupied with routine and the presentation of credentials. At the second sitting came a pause. What was to be done? Who would open that grave debate? No one seemed disposed to start so momentous a discussion. Then a quiet-looking, serious member arose, dressed in sober black, wearing an unpowdered wig, with, perhaps, his spectacles thrown up upon his forehead, as Sully afterward painted him—so simple a figure, so unostentatious, that the question rose to every lip: "Who is he?" And the word went round, "Patrick Henry of Virginia"—he who had electrified the entire

PHILADELPHIA

country a few months before with his ringing words: "Give me liberty or give me death!"

Deliberately he began to recite the wrongs inflicted upon the colonies; deliberately he declared all government dissolved and that a new one should be formed. He discussed the representation of each colony in the Continental Congress, allotting to each delegates in proportion to its population, and he concluded by declaring that all boundaries were now effaced: "The distinctions between Virginians, Pennsylvanians, New Yorkers and New Englanders are no more. I am not a Virginian, but an American."

The discussion was now begun; various members spoke, and John Jay, dissenting from Patrick Henry's conclusions, exclaimed: "I cannot yet think that we came to frame an American constitution, instead of endeavoring to correct the faults in an old one. The measure of arbitrary power is not full, and it must run over before we undertake to frame a new constitution."

On the 7th of September news of serious clashes between General Gage and the people of Boston reached the Congress, as it opened its session with prayer. The Reverend Mr. Duché read the Psalter for that day, a part of which happened to be the thirty-fifth Psalm of David, and John Adams wrote his wife: "It seemed as if Heaven had ordained that Psalm to be read that morning." These are a portion of its strangely prophetic words:

"Plead my cause, O Lord, with them that strive with me; and fight thou against them that fight against me.

REVOLUTIONARY PILGRIMAGE

... Take hold of shield and buckler, and stand up for mine help. Draw out also the spear and stop the way against them that persecute me.

"Who is like unto thee, which deliverest the poor from him that is too strong for him; yea, the poor and needy from him that spoileth him?"

Then the minister, unexpectedly to everybody, launched into an extemporaneous prayer "for the Congress, for the province of Massachusetts Bay, and especially for the town of Boston." "I must confess, I never heard a better prayer or one so well pronounced," says Adams. Members of all denominations joined in it fervently, but Bishop White, who was present, tells us that George Washington was the only member to kneel.

But a short way farther up Chestnut Street stands Independence Hall—the old State House—historically, at least, the most interesting and evocative building in the city. Little by little, during recent years, it has undergone a thorough restoration, so that it now stands quite as the old prints depict it in Revolutionary times. I present the drawing that I made of it some years ago. The central or main building remains as it is shown, but since then the end pavilions have been restored to their simpler form, the small domes have been removed, and the arcades between them and the main building replaced. As it now stands the edifice is a splendid example of our sturdy colonial architecture, typical of the stanch simplicity of the men who built it.

Upon entering you find yourself at once in a spacious

PHILADELPHIA

hall, whose fluted columns, panels, and cornices, vigorous in detail and simple in design, accord well with the spirit of the age in which they were built—honest, devoid of

Independence Hall, Chestnut Street Front

needless ornament, with no unnecessary carving or gilding. Such was the good taste of the epoch.

Through an archway opposite you catch a glimpse of the old Liberty Bell, whose voice proclaimed to the waiting multitude the ratification of the Declaration of Independence. The arch to the right gives access to the supreme-court room, with its bench for the justices still

REVOLUTIONARY PILGRIMAGE

in place and their serene faces, honestly painted, looking down from the walls. The arch to the left leads into the Declaration Chamber, as it is now called.

Like the remainder of the building, this is in simple but excellent taste, dignified yet free from ostentation. Pilasters divide its walls into large equal compartments; spacious windows, both front and rear, give upon the street and upon the park that lies behind the building. A handsome crystal lustre is the room's only luxury.

The original speaker's chair, with his desk and his inkwell, stands upon a dais at the far end of the room. Over the desk hangs a facsimile of the immortal document that was signed upon it. During the momentous sessions of the summer of 1776 this chair was occupied by John Hancock of Boston—then a vigorous young man of forty, in appearance as Copley painted him, his fine, firm features framed in an uncurled wig and white neckcloth. Beside him, at the secretary's desk, sat Charles Thomson, whom we have already met in Carpenter's Hall. The other delegates were seated in leather chairs, about twenty of which are still ranged around the walls marked with the names of the men who occupied them.

On the 2d of July, 1776, the Continental Congress, convened in this room with forty-nine members present, voted, without a dissenting voice, "that these united colonies are, and of right ought to be, free and independent states; that they are absolved from all allegiance to the British crown, and that all political connection between them and the state of Great Britain is, and ought to be,

PHILADELPHIA

dissolved." Two days later it ratified the Declaration of Independence.

The precious original document is preserved among the

Room in Which the Declaration of Independence was Signed

archives of the State Department in Washington, badly faded owing to a mishap in making a copy of it.

In this same State Department library I found the original draft of the Declaration in Thomas Jefferson's own handwriting, clear and manful as his firm words and thoughts. It shows some slight alterations and revisions, made when it was submitted to two of the other members of the committee, Benjamin Franklin and John Adams, whose interlineations are thus plainly

View of Independence Hall from the Park Side

marked: =Dr. Franklin's handwriting; *Mr. Adams's handwriting.

In this library also is a letter written by Thomas Jefferson that will interest us in this connection. It lies in a case beside his writing-case and is dated "Monticello, Sept. 16, '25." In answer to an inquiry he replies:

PHILADELPHIA

"At the time of writing that instrument (the Declaration of Independence) I lodged in the house of a Mr. Graaf, a new brick house three stories high of which I rented the second floor consisting of parlour, bed-room ready furnished; in that parlour I wrote habitually and in it wrote this paper particularly. . . . The proprietor Graaf, was a young man, son of a German and then newly married. I think he was a bricklayer and that his house was on the south side of Market Street probably between Seventh and Eighth."

The news of the ratification of the Declaration of Independence was announced to the people, as I have said, by the ringing of the bell in the State House steeple. This historic Liberty Bell—the bell so portentously inscribed with a line from the Scriptures, "Proclaim liberty throughout all the land, unto all the inhabitants thereof"—is now placed at the back of the hallway in the stair-well. Now no longer does it swing aloft, but, cracked and voiceless in its ripe old age, reposes comfortably and peacefully on solid ground.

Stairway in Independence Hall

REVOLUTIONARY PILGRIMAGE

The main stairs lead you up to the banquet-hall, that extends across the entire front of the building. In its day it saw many notable gatherings, such as a dinner of three hundred covers given by leading citizens to celebrate the repeal of the Stamp Act, and another to welcome the delegates to the First Continental Congress. In rooms adjoining hang portraits of many of the gentlemen who banqueted at its tables, or sat in deliberation in the rooms below—patriots, merchants, bankers, jurists, and the generals whose campaigns we have been following: Greene, Gates, Lincoln, and Knox; handsome Anthony Wayne, courtly Schuyler, blue-eyed, ruddy Daniel Morgan; and the Southerners: bold Marion, the Pinckneys of Charleston, and Colonel William Washington, whose exploits we shall review later on; while from still another group look down the foreign officers—Lafayette, Rochambeau, de Grasse, Steuben, Pulaski, and Kosciusko—who aided us to success.

Philadelphia is particularly rich in these historic portraits. Over in the rooms of the Historical Society of Pennsylvania hangs another fine collection of them—pictures of even higher artistic merit than those in Independence Hall. In cases there are also many interesting mementos of Revolutionary days, such as Franklin's punch-keg, Robert Morris's strong box, beautifully bound in brass (but, oh, how small for a multimillionaire!), rare prints, and books rarer still, and in a corner of the gallery cork models of some of the historic houses that have disappeared: the old court-house, squatting on its stout arcades;

PHILADELPHIA

"Loxley's House," that used to stand in South Second Street and in which dwelt brave Lydia Darrach, who apprised Washington of the intended attack at Whitemarsh; the famous "Slate Roof House," once occupied by William Penn; and General Howe's headquarters that used to stand in High Street (now Market) near Sixth.

Philadelphia still retains one old house that is the object of many a pious pilgrimage—a little two-story affair about fifteen feet wide, with but a single dormer in its roof—squeezed in between a number of structures of more recent date down on Arch Street, near the river. Well-authenticated tradition has it that here Betsy Ross made the first American flag.

The Betsy Ross House

Up to the first day of January, 1776, there had been no regular emblem for the revolted colonies. Upon that New Year's Day a flag of thirteen stripes—the "rebellious stripes"—but still retaining the British union in its corner, was unfurled

REVOLUTIONARY PILGRIMAGE

at the head of the newly organized Continental Army at Cambridge; but it was not until June 14, 1777, that Congress took definite action and resolved "that the flag of the thirteen United States be thirteen stripes alternate red and white; that the Union be thirteen stars, white in a blue field, representing a new constellation."

Betsy's husband, George Ross, was a lawyer, a signer of the Declaration, and a member of this Congress, and tradition depicts him and his wife receiving George Washington and Robert Morris in the little back room of the "Betsy Ross house," near the old fireplace with its blue tiles, to show them the first flag made according to the terms of this resolution.

In an up-stairs room of the Jumel Mansion in New York (see page 165) hangs a patched piece of *toile de Jouy*, or printed calico, stamped with a curious allegory, presumably of French fabrication and closely tied to the design of this first American flag, perhaps a precursor of it. My attention was called to it by the curator, who shares this opinion. As is usual in such prints, the design is made by two scenes used alternately. One depicts Washington, standing in a chariot beside a figure bearing Mercury's wand and showing upon her shield the inscription, "American Independence, 1776." The chariot is drawn by leopards led by Indian boys blowing trumpets, from which depend two flags—one the Serpent Flag of Maryland, the other a flag of thirteen stripes. The second scene shows Franklin, accompanied by Liberty, bearing an inscription, "Where Liberty dwells, there is

PHILADELPHIA

my country," and guided toward a Temple of Fame by a figure of War, whose shield is painted with thirteen stars, the "new constellation." Thus, in the union of the two scenes the original Stars and Stripes appear.

There is another picture closely wedded to Franklin and his family that I wish now to present—also a French interpretation, written for us by the Marquis de Chastellux, who was taken about in Philadelphia, toward the close of the Revolution, to see its people and its sights.

"First we began by visiting Mrs. Bache. She merits all the anxiety we had to see her, for she is the daughter of Mr. Franklin. Simple in her manners, like her respectable father, she possesses his benevolence. She conducted us into a room filled with work, lately finished by the ladies of Philadelphia. This work consisted neither of embroidered tambour waistcoats, nor network edgings, nor of gold and silver brocade—it was a quantity of shirts for the soldiers of Pennsylvania. The ladies bought the linen from their private purses, and took a pleasure in cutting them out and sewing them themselves. On each shirt was the name of the married or unmarried lady who made it, and they amounted to twenty two hundred."*

Does this sound like a picture of a century or more ago or one of yesterday?

During the British occupation (and this brings us back to the main thread of our narrative) Benjamin Franklin's house, that stood in a court off High Street, was occupied by Major, then Captain, André, whose tragic fate we have

* "Travels in North America."

REVOLUTIONARY PILGRIMAGE

witnessed at Tappan. He was a brilliant officer, a charming gentleman and a dilettante, expressing himself with facility and felicity in all the arts. Franklin's daughter, the Mrs. Bache above referred to, writes to her father in Paris after André's departure:

"I found your house and furniture, upon my return to town in much better order than I had reason to expect from the hands of such a rapacious crew. They stole and carried off with them some of your musical instruments, viz., a Welsh harp, a ball harp, a set of tuned bells which were in a box, a viol-da-gamba, all the spare armonica glasses and one or two spare cases. Your armonica* is safe. They took likewise the few books that were left behind, the chief of which were Temple's schoolbooks and the History of the Arts and Sciences in French which is a great loss to the public. Some of your electric apparatus is missing; also a Captain André took with him a picture of you which hung in the dining room."

Artistic robbers, certainly, these pilferers who stole harps and violins, rare books and historic portraits—thieves of refinement!

Not all the inhabitants of Philadelphia fared as well, for the British officers were indeed a "rapacious crew." General Howe "seized and kept for his own use, Mary Pemberton's coach and horses in which he used to ride

---

* These old musical instruments, first introduced by Benjamin Franklin, are to be seen in museums, and I have heard them played on several occasions. Kindly Miss Custis played a set of these "musical glasses" for me in her home in Williamsburg, tuning them with water to the right note, and then playing them by passing the wet finger round the edges.

PHILADELPHIA

about town." * The officers, quartered upon the inhabitants, spent their days in gambling and other equally profitable pastimes, and their nights at entertainments. "By a proportionate tax on the pay and allowances of each officer, a house was opened for daily resort and weekly balls, with a gaming-table and a room devoted to the players of chess." Three times a week plays were enacted by the officers, and Major André and Captain Delancey were the chief scene-painters, the former's waterfall curtain remaining in the Southwark Theatre until that building was torn down. The younger officers, following the example of some of the older ones, played for heavy stakes and openly gave way to their vices, two of them impudently advertising in a paper for "a young woman, to act in capacity of housekeeper. Extravagant wages will be given and no character required."

With the spring came news of Sir William Howe's recall to England. As "he was much beloved by his officers and soldiers for his generosity and affability," his departure was viewed as nothing short of a calamity. So a great fête was planned as a testimonial of this devotion of the army to its general—a festival the most elaborate that America had witnessed up to that time, whose extravagance was severely criticised by both Whigs and Tories and did much to alienate sympathy from the British cause.

Major André, who took a prominent part in its organization, wrote a long description of it to a friend

* Watson's "Annals of Philadelphia."

REVOLUTIONARY PILGRIMAGE

in England, and his letter was published in the "London Annual Register," in 1778. It is too long to quote *in extenso*, but I shall append some of the salient passages of this, his description of the "Mischianza," or Italian medley, as it was called.

"A grand regatta [on the Delaware] began the entertainment. It consisted of three divisions. In the first was the Ferret galley, with Sir William and Lord Howe, Sir Henry Clinton,* the officers of their suites and some ladies. The Cornwallis galley brought up the rear, having on board General Knyphausen and his suite, three British generals and a party of ladies. On each quarter of these galleys, and forming their division, were five flat boats, lined with green cloth, and filled with ladies and gentlemen. In front of the whole were three flat boats with a band of music in each. Six barges rowed about each flank, to keep off the swarm of boats that crossed the river from side to side. The galleys were dressed out in a variety of colors and streamers. In the stream opposite the center of the city, the *Fanny*, armed ship, magnificently decorated, was placed at anchor, and at some distance ahead lay his majesty's ship *Roebuck*, with the admiral's flag hoisted at the fore-topmast head. The transport-ships, extending in a line the whole length of the town, appeared with colors flying, and crowded with spectators, exhibiting the most picturesque and enlivening scene the eye could desire."

This water pageant started at the foot of Vine Street, passing southward, "keeping time to the music that led

* Who had just been appointed to succeed General Howe as commander-in-chief.

PHILADELPHIA

the fleet," to the foot of Market Street, and there halted while the bands played "God Save the King" and cheers were given. The guests then landed "a little to the southward of the town, fronting a building," the old Wharton Mansion that stood well back from the river, between which and it stretched a stately garden.

"The company as they disembarked arranged themselves in line of procession and advanced through an avenue formed by two files of grenadiers, and a line of light horse supporting each file. This avenue led to a square lawn, lined with troops and properly prepared for the exhibition of a tilt and tournament according to the customs and ordinance of ancient chivalry. . . . Two pavilions received the ladies while the gentlemen arranged themselves in convenient order at each side.

"On the front seat of each pavilion were placed seven of the principal young ladies of the country, dressed in Turkish habits and wearing in their turbans the favors of the knights who were to contend in their honor."

The knights then entered in two companies, those of the Blended Rose and those of the Burning Mountain. Among the former was André himself, appearing in honor of Miss Peggy Chew, and with him was Lieutenant Sloper, who appeared in honor of Miss Margaret Shippen, who afterward married Benedict Arnold.

After the tournament, with its splintering of lances and encounters with swords, a passage was opened and the company proceeded toward the house through two triumphal arches, erected in honor of the two brothers, the general and the admiral, along an avenue lined with

REVOLUTIONARY PILGRIMAGE

troops, and enlivened with "the colors of all the army planted at proper distances." They then entered the house, where refreshments were served, the "windows were thrown open and a magnificent bouquet of rockets began the fireworks." These included wonderful devices, designed by Captain Montressor, chief engineer. The arches were illuminated, and Fame appeared on top of one of them and blew from her trumpet the inscription, "Leurs Lauriers sont Immortels."

"At twelve supper was announced, and large folding doors, hitherto artfully concealed, being suddenly thrown open, disclosed a magnificent saloon of two hundred and ten feet by forty, and twenty two feet in height, with three alcoves on each side, which served for sideboards. . . . Fifty six large pier-glasses, ornamented with green silk artificial flowers and ribbons; a hundred branches with three lights in each; eighteen lustres, each with twenty four lights, suspended from the ceiling; three hundred wax tapers disposed along the supper tables; 430 covers; 1,200 dishes, twenty four black slaves in Oriental dresses, with silver collars and bracelets, arranged in two lines, and bending to the ground as the general and admiral approached the saloon; all these, forming together the most brilliant assemblage of gay objects, and appearing at once as we entered by an easy descent, exhibited a coup d'œil beyond description magnificent. . . . After supper we returned to the ball-room and continued to dance till four o'clock.

"Such, my friend, is a description, though a faint one, of the most splendid entertainment, I believe, ever given by an army to their general. . . ."

PHILADELPHIA

Truly, a fête to be remembered and talked about, especially in those simple colonial times! But the "Mischianza" was the Belshazzar's feast of the British. Soon after it General Howe boarded his brother's flagship, the *Eagle*, and later sailed for England.

It then became known that the home government had resolved upon the evacuation of Philadelphia as a military necessity, for reinforcements sufficiently large to hold it could not be sent. The Tories of the city were dismayed at the news and, not daring to face their irate patriot neighbors after their winter revels with the British officers, packed up their belongings and prepared to flee with the army and go as exiles to New York.

At three in the morning of the 18th of June, a warm summer night, Sir Henry Clinton began to move his army across the Delaware, and by ten in the morning his entire force of seventeen thousand men was safely over on the New Jersey shore. He marched by way of Mount Holly and Crosswicks to Allentown, where, fearing danger in crossing the Raritan River, he decided to proceed by way of Monmouth to Sandy Hook and thence to New York.

Washington had been watching him and, despite adverse criticism among his generals, started in pursuit, crossing the Delaware above Trenton and marching via Princeton to Englishtown, where he overtook him and gave battle at Monmouth, an inconclusive action whose episodes we shall not follow here.

CAMPAIGNS IN THE CAROLINAS

CAMPAIGNS IN THE CAROLINAS

I

CHARLESTON

INSTEAD of remaining inactive in New York during the winter of 1779–80 the new British commander-in-chief, Sir Henry Clinton, decided to sail for the South, for, says Colonel Tarleton, who accompanied him, "the richness of the country, its vicinity to Georgia (a loyalist state) and its distance from General Washington, pointed out the advantages and facility of its conquest."

So transportation was provided for eighty-five hundred men, and these were convoyed by a proud fleet under Admiral Arbuthnot. New York harbor was safely cleared on the day after Christmas, and for a while, despite the season of the year, favorable weather was encountered. But then a series of storms set in, and the ships were separated and buffeted at sea during the entire month of January. While they are beating about in the Atlantic let us hasten ahead of them and look at the city for which they were bound.

Charleston, to my mind, retains more of the atmosphere of Revolutionary days than any other of our larger cities. Its old-fashioned main street; its narrow thoroughfares neatly paved with brick; its homesteads, shut behind high walls, many of them still occupied by descendants of the old colonial families, give it an air of distinction—an aspect quite different from that of the bustling cities of the North; while its fragrant Old World gardens, overgrown with honeysuckle and jasmine and rippling with the notes of the mocking-bird and the purple grackle, lend to it a particular charm rare indeed in the newer American communities.

Along the Battery and in the neighboring streets—King, Broad, and Tradd—many of the old houses are still furnished as they were a century ago. Upon a recent visit I went to one of them—the Pringle House, perhaps the most perfect of them all—to see the present-day descendant of the family that has always occupied it—an elderly lady of quite another age, fitting perfectly into her surroundings, enhancing by her presence the dignified old rooms panelled in wood, the handsome English furniture and the family portraits that look down from the walls, beginning with Miles Bruton, builder of the house, and his daughter, the heroic Rebecca Motte, and progressing through a succession of jurists and statesmen and ladies in panniers to men in the black neckcloths and broadcloth coats of our grandfathers.

In one of the rooms a friend, who was taking me about, and who had occupied this particular apartment for twenty-one years, led me over to the chimneypiece and, pointing to a slab of black marble fitted in under the mantel-shelf, asked what I saw there. At first I could detect nothing at all, but on getting in a certain light I

CAMPAIGNS IN THE CAROLINAS

could discern, quite plainly, a full-rigged frigate under sail, scratched with a diamond, like a sgraffitto, upon the polished surface. Again my companion asked: "And what more can you see?" Then I made out the profile of a British officer in powdered wig and regimentals, and

The Pringle House, Charleston

my friend explained: "We call him Sir Henry Clinton; you know this house was headquarters during the British occupation."

With this rare companion and several others I explored the nooks and corners of the old city (and that is a long story), and at the Southern Club listened to its history told by the men who know it best.

One afternoon we motored out to St. James Goosecreek to see the old church and the Middleton estates near by.

REVOLUTIONARY PILGRIMAGE

St. James' was built in 1713. It still stands quite alone in the pine-woods, in a most romantic spot, with ancient slate gravestones set about it and trees, pendent with moss, shading its old brick walls. Inside, too, the church has never changed. The white pilasters, the balcony with the hatchments of the Izards, the wall tombs that date back to the building of the church, the pews with their high wainscots—all are as they ever have been, even to the great carved lion and unicorn that still hold the royal arms of England over the high altar.

The sight of this coat of arms, so surprising to find, recalled to my mind one of Garden's anecdotes, an incident that happened during the early days of the Revolution in this very church. The minister,

St. Michael's Church

"the Reverend Mr. Ellington, in the course of service, praying, 'That it may please thee to bless and preserve his most gracious Majesty, our Sovereign Lord King George,' a dead silence ensued and, instead of the usual response, 'We beseech thee to hear us, good Lord' a murmuring voice pronounced, 'Good Lord, deliver us.'"

In the very heart of Charleston, where Broad Street intersects Meeting,

CAMPAIGNS IN THE CAROLINAS

stands St. Michael's, perhaps the most successful and imposing colonial church in our country. Its chimes, that have pealed over the city and regulated its life for a cen-

Statue of William Pitt, Charleston

tury and a half; its old pews inscribed with the same names they have borne for many generations; its organ, now played, I am told, by a descendant of its maker—John Snetzler fecit, Londini, 1767, as he signs himself upon it; the brass chandelier with its forty-odd lights, are all there to attest its antiquity as well as the good

REVOLUTIONARY PILGRIMAGE

taste of its builders, while its spire is still, as it ever has been,

> "The guardian beacon of our coast
> The seaman's hope when waves are wild."

Almost within its shadow, in a green square across the way, stands a curious relic of the past—a marble statue of the elder Pitt draped as a Roman and armless as the Venus of Milo. Its pedestal bears this inscription:

> In grateful memory
> of his services to his country in general
> and to America in particular
> The Commons House of Assembly
> of South Carolina
> unanimously voted
> this statue
> of
> The Right Honorable William Pitt, Esqr
> who
> gloriously exerted himself
> in defending the freedom of Americans
> the true sons of England
> by promoting a repeal
> of the Stamp Act
> in the year 1766.
> Time shall sooner destroy this mark of their esteem
> Than erase from their minds their just sense of his patriotic
> virtues.

This statue originally stood at the intersection of the two main streets—Broad and Meeting. Its right arm was carried off by a cannon-ball during the siege of 1780; later it was pulled down and consigned to oblivion (Time having destroyed their just sense of his virtues); then it was resurrected and placed before the Orphanage, and finally, in 1881, it was moved back again near its original situation. It remains one of the few statues dating from colonial times that I know of in our country.

At the outbreak of the Revolution, the Charlestonians quickly sided with the patriot cause. On the day following the skirmish at Lexington, some of the citizens seized all the powder in the city. In September, 1775, Colonel William Moultrie drove the garrison from Sullivan's Island and took possession of the fort at the mouth of the harbor. The British governor, Lord William Campbell, fled from his mansion, still standing down in Meeting Street, and went on board of one of the King's ships that lay in the harbor.

In March, 1776, intelligence reached the city that a British fleet, under Sir Peter Parker, was under way to attack it. Colonel Moultrie, in all haste, started to build a new fort on Sullivan's Island, and this was but half finished when Parker's ships dropped anchor to the north of Charleston bar. Divided counsels among the British commanders, coupled with adverse weather conditions, prevented an attack until somewhat later.

This gave the patriots an opportunity to work, which they embraced with feverish activity. The city's defenses were strengthened, while Moultrie energetically pushed work on his fort, at that time called Fort Sullivan, but

REVOLUTIONARY PILGRIMAGE

ever since known, from its gallant defender, as Fort Moultrie. It was a square with bastions at each corner, made of palmetto logs strongly reinforced with sand.

Before we watch the battle that ensued, one of the most spectacular of the war, let us take a look at the topography of Charleston Harbor. To the right of the

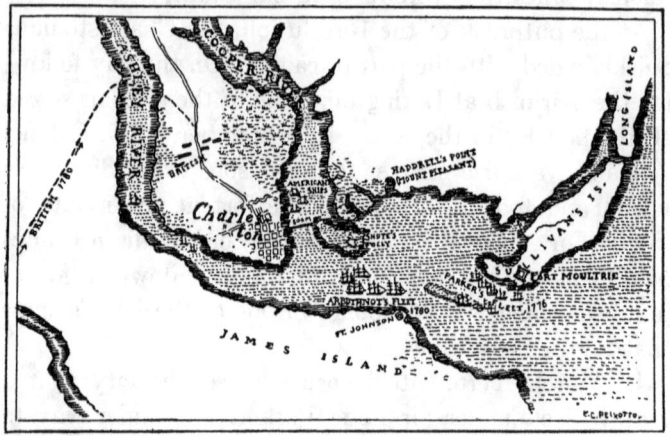

Charleston Harbor

entrance is a sandy island grown over with thickets and clumps of palmettos; this has always been known as Sullivan's Island. Beyond it, to the north, lies a larger island, then called Long Island but now known as the Isle of Palms. On the opposite side of the entrance is a large tract of land called James Island. Between it and Sullivan's, quite in the entrance itself, lies an islet whereon stands Fort Sumter (also fraught with memories, but of

CAMPAIGNS IN THE CAROLINAS

another period), which forms the only visible part of a long shoal known as the Middle Shoal. Between this shoal and Fort Moultrie is the only channel deep enough to admit large ships, so that this fortress is really the key to the harbor.

Now let us take the ferry to Mount Pleasant. If we do this in the cool of a summer morning we shall find children in throngs, with their mothers and nursemaids, going for a day's outing on the beach at the Isle of Palms. As we follow the channel round the end of Shute's Folly, we enjoy a series of fine retrospects of the old city strung along its wharfs, its slender church spires—St. Michael's, St. Phillip's, and others—still maintaining their ascendency over the temples of Mammon that now overtop and dwarf the steeples of most of our American cities. There, too, stands the old Exchange or Custom House (where the Provincial Congress met in 1774, "setting up the first independent government in America," as its tablet records), covered with pink stucco, its colonnade facing the water-front and overlooking the bay, just as Leitch depicts it in his engraving of the city made in 1780.

From Mount Pleasant the Isle of Palms trolley took me through the village and along the shore to a long viaduct built across the channel that separates Sullivan's Island from the mainland at the very point where General Lee ordered Moultrie to build a bridge by which he might retreat in case of a disaster. This order Moultrie ignored, for, says he in his "Memoirs": "I never was

REVOLUTIONARY PILGRIMAGE

uneasy on not having a retreat, because I never imagined the enemy could force me to that necessity."

I now found myself upon the island, long, low, and sandy, and to-day sparsely built over with summer resorts and homes, set in Southern-looking gardens. But the principal buildings are still the barracks and quarters that cluster round Fort Moultrie. Brick bastions now replace those of palmetto logs, but the emplacement is the same. New batteries with up-to-date guns have been built along the shore beyond, but the sentries still watch the sea as Moultrie did on that cloudless June morning of '76.

His observant eye, on the 28th, assured him that the expected attack was coming, and he quickly made his preparations. Says he in his "Memoirs":

Fort Moultrie

CAMPAIGNS IN THE CAROLINAS

"I hurried back to the fort as soon as possible. When I got there I found that the ships were already under sail. I immediately ordered the long roll to beat and officers and men to their posts, when the ships came sailing up, as if in confidence of victory. We had scarcely manned our guns. They were soon abreast of the fort, let go their anchors and began their attack most furiously."

This was near eleven o'clock. First came the *Solebay* of twenty-eight guns, then the big *Experiment* of fifty; next the *Bristol*, the flag-ship, with the commodore, Sir Peter Parker, and the royal governor of South Carolina, Lord William Campbell, on board; and last the *Active* of twenty-eight guns. Following this first division of larger ships, came a second squadron of frigates: the *Sphinx*, *Actæon*, and *Syren*, which were ordered to pass around the big ships and enfilade the fort. Then a mortar-ship, the *Thunder Bomb*, took up her position off the east bastion and prepared to throw her shells.

To oppose this formidable array Moultrie disposed of but four hundred and thirty-five men, officers included. He had made a flag—there being no official emblem of the colony—with a field of blue and a crescent in the upper dexter corner, and this floated proudly on the flagpole of the fort. Word was passed round: "Mind the fifty-gun ships; mind the commodore!"

When the first terrific broadside from the fleet was hurled into the fort, the shots embedded themselves in the tough palmetto logs as in a sponge, or struck into the shifting sand, inflicting little or no damage. Broadside followed broadside, and the *Thunder Bomb*

REVOLUTIONARY PILGRIMAGE

"threw her shells in good direction and most of them fell within the fort, but we had a morass in the middle that swallowed them up instantly and those that fell in the sand, in and about the fort were immediately buried, so that very few bursted among us." *

These broadsides were answered by a slow and deliberate fire from the fort, each shot crashing into the ships' timbers with telling effect. In the early afternoon the flag-ship *Bristol* swung about with her stern squarely to the fort, and was raked from stern to stem, every man on her quarter-deck being put out of action—all except the "Commodore who stood alone—a spectacle of intrepidity and firmness which has seldom been equaled, never exceeded." Forty of her crew were killed, seventy-two wounded; her hull was struck seventy times, and her rigging cut to pieces.

Inside the fort equal gallantry was displayed. The men, in the torrid June noonday, fought half naked through the long hours. A shot carried away the flag-pole, and the people in the city, watching through their spy-glasses, thought the fort had surrendered.

"Sergeant Jasper perceiving that the flag had fallen without the fort, jumped through one of the embrasures and brought it up through heavy fire; fixed it upon a sponge staff and planted it upon the ramparts again."†

---

* Moultrie's "Memoirs."

† In White Point Gardens, at the Battery in Charleston, Jasper's statue stands upon a tall pedestal, his flag clutched in one hand, the other pointing across the bay to the scene of his dashing exploit. On the back of the pedestal are his words: "Don't let us fight without a flag."

CAMPAIGNS IN THE CAROLINAS

Meanwhile the three frigates had tried to make their way round and take the fort upon its unfinished flank. But luckily all three went aground on the Middle Shoal, and night found them stuck fast there. Next morning, the people of Charleston strained their eyes to see the result. There still lay the three ships, but at high tide two got off, the *Sphinx* losing her bowsprit as she fouled the *Syren*. But the *Actæon* stuck fast, and her crew, setting fire to her, abandoned her where she lay. A party of Americans boarded her then, pointed her guns toward the retiring fleet, and fired a few farewell shots at Sir Peter Parker's ships as they sailed out of the harbor discomfited.

How vivid the scene became to me as I lay upon the sand by the bastions of old Fort Moultrie! There, just before me, the four gallant British ships lay, with cables sprung, within four hundred yards of the fort. Beyond them a long, white line of foam marked the bar. There, off toward Fort Sumter, on the Middle Ground, the three frigates went ashore, and there the *Actæon* stuck fast. Off to the right the city strung its houses, filled on that occasion with beating hearts and straining eyes. The morning vapors parted and a stray shaft of sunlight lighted St. Michael's spire,

"The seaman's hope when waves are wild."

So, disastrously, ended the first British attempt to take Charleston. For three years thereafter the city enjoyed comparative peace and quiet, though her sons

REVOLUTIONARY PILGRIMAGE

went north in great numbers to do their share in battling for freedom. Charleston remained the principal patriot rendezvous in the South, organizing her resources and doing her best to aid and equip the Northern armies with arms and clothing.

Then General Prévost, the British commander in Georgia, determined to try an expedition into South Carolina. He appeared before Charleston in May, 1779. A hasty defense had been organized and the authorities temporized long enough to permit the return of General Lincoln with the main American army in the South. Prévost was forced to retire, so that his invasion was little more than an unsuccessful raid.

Now, as we have seen, at the beginning of 1780 Sir Henry Clinton embarked his expedition at New York and set out to subjugate the South, his fleet finally gathering in Edisto Inlet, below Charleston, by the 11th of February.

Charleston, meanwhile, had been preparing to receive him. The intrenchments across the Neck were strengthened; Fort Moultrie, the works at Haddrell's Point (Mount Pleasant), and the batteries along the city front were put in order. But the troops to man them were so few that at first General Lincoln, the American commander, thought of evacuating the city and saving his army. But, assured of reinforcements, he finally decided to defend it as best he might.

The British landed on John's Island, crossed to James Island, and marched up the Ashley River to the west of

CAMPAIGNS IN THE CAROLINAS

the town where they prepared to cross to the Neck.* About the same time, Admiral Arbuthnot entered the harbor with his fleet, succeeding in sailing them past Fort Moultrie with comparatively little loss. His galleys now ascended the Ashley, and under the protection of their guns the British crossed the river. The few American vessels in the harbor retired behind the boom that stretched across the mouth of the Cooper River and there were sunk to prevent the British from ascending that stream.

But the city was now almost surrounded. Across the Neck, to the north, extended the British lines. The fleet lay out in the harbor within cannon-shot of the town. And now Cornwallis arrived with three thousand fresh troops, seized Haddrell's Point, and the investment was complete.

The British batteries opened fire and maintained a continuous cannonade from land and sea. Day after day this went on. The situation became desperate. Clinton demanded a surrender, but would promise no conditions. On the 8th of May a truce was asked and granted, but Lincoln refused the terms offered. So that night, after a forty days' siege, the British batteries opened anew with redoubled fury. Two hundred cannon poured their shot into the city; flames leaped from burning buildings; the third parallel was completed, and there seemed no further hope of successful resistance. That night, says gallant Moultrie,

"It appeared as if the stars were tumbling down. The fire was incessant almost the whole night; cannon

---
*See map, page 280.

REVOLUTIONARY PILGRIMAGE

balls whizzing and shells hissing continually among us; ammunition chests and temporary magazines blowing up; great guns bursting and wounded men groaning along the lines; it was a dreadful night."

Human nature could endure no more. Lincoln was forced to capitulate, and not only give up the city but surrender his entire army under very severe terms.

II

THROUGH SOUTH CAROLINA

THE fall of Charleston seemed, for a time, to put an end to all resistance in South Carolina. Sir Henry Clinton wrote to Lord Germaine: "There are few men in South Carolina who are not either our prisoners or in arms with us." Emboldened by this seeming situation, he issued a drastic proclamation declaring that any man in the province who did not take up arms for the King would be treated as a rebel. Thus, all those who had expected to remain passive and neutral saw themselves suddenly constrained to bear arms against the cause they really held at heart, and this they could not make up their minds to do.

Clinton returned to New York, intrusting Lord Cornwallis with the command of the army in the South, with orders to overrun both Carolinas, starting at Charleston and gradually working northward, leaving all the country in his rear in complete, if unwilling, subjection to the King.

But partisan bands began to form all over the State, gathering under the leadership of men who soon became famous. Sumter assembled recruits between the Broad and Catawba Rivers in the north; Pickens and Clarke upon the Saluda and Savannah in the south; while Marion, "the fearless and faultless," in the swamps of

REVOLUTIONARY PILGRIMAGE

the Pee Dee and the Santee, and even at the very gates of Charleston itself, collected his matchless horsemen—"Marion's Men," as they were called—whose exploits form the theme of many a song and story.

To traverse the Carolinas and see the haunts of these men was the object of my next pilgrimage; and as I did so I proposed to trail Cornwallis upon his long march northward toward Virginia and the Chesapeake.

So one bright Monday morning I left Charleston, regretfully, and took train for the "up-country." Though the sky was clear, it had rained during the night, and the observation platform of the "Carolina Special" proved a very agreeable spot, dustless and, as the train is not a fast one, affording an excellent opportunity for seeing the country.

As far as Summerville (as its name implies, a resort for Charlestonians) and even beyond, to Branchville, where the Atlanta line diverges, there is nothing of particular interest to see, except, perhaps, some typical Southern scenes about the depots: a big, fat mammy rounding up her numerous progeny; a "yaller gal" driving a cow hitched to a buggy; a lusty negro leading his faithful mule to his work in the fields.

Beyond Branchville we turned due north and soon reached Fort Motte—a place that holds its associations of the Revolution. Here, in the latter days of the war, dwelt Rebecca Motte (whose name I have already mentioned) in a great country house that the British had seized and converted into a fortress. Lee and Marion

CAMPAIGNS IN THE CAROLINAS

came along with their men and prepared to attack this outpost, but its garrison resisted so bravely that there seemed no way to dislodge them. Then, says Garden in his "Anecdotes":

Map of Campaigns in the Carolinas, Showing Cornwallis's March from Charleston to Virginia

"Lieutenant-Colonel Lee informed Mrs. Motte that, in order to accomplish the immediate surrender of the British garrison, occupying her elegant mansion, its destruction was indispensable. She instantly replied: 'the sacrifice of my property is nothing and I shall view its destruction with delight, if it shall in any degree contribute to the good of my country.'" *

* "Anecdotes of the American Revolution," by Alexander Garden.

REVOLUTIONARY PILGRIMAGE

So she placed in Marion's hands a bow with some arrows that, with lighted ends, were soon winging their way to the roof of the house. Its dry shingles promptly took fire and, with roaring flames all about them, the garrison was soon forced to surrender.

Just beyond Fort Motte I first perceived the Congaree, which, joining the Wateree down below, forms the Santee—all three taking their names from the Cherokee tribes that once dwelt along them. All three are intimately connected with the partisan warfare of the Revolution, their cane-brakes and evergreen forests—natural hiding-places for these roving bands, whence they could issue at will and to which they could retire with perfect safety—having been the favorite haunts of Sumter, the "Game Cock," and Marion, the "Swamp Fox," as the British called them.

What perfect retreats they were—these Carolina swamps! As we proceeded we traversed miles of them, sometimes crossing long wooden trestles shut in by dense masses of rich foliage—pines, oaks, maples, from which hung festoons and garlands of vines and creepers, while mighty cypresses towered aloft draped with swaying beards and wisps of moss. At other times we passed ponds whose mirror-like surfaces were starred with hundreds of white lilies. Then again, through the dense foliage, I could dimly discern sombre depths, where pools of tarnished, brownish water could be faintly seen, stagnant, bristling with "cypress-knees," dank and humid.

Brilliant scarlet tanagers and modest gray mocking-

CAMPAIGNS IN THE CAROLINAS

birds flitted in obscure shadows, in which, according to an old writer, "Fire-flies carry their Lanthorns in their Tails and on dark nights enlighten them with their golden spangles."

Such were the haunts of Marion's Men; such were their hiding-places.

> "Our band is few, but true and tried,
>   Our leader frank and bold;
> The British soldier trembles
>   When Marion's name is told.
> Our fortress is the good green wood,
>   Our tent the cypress tree;
> We know the forest round us,
>   As seamen know the sea.
> We know its walls of thorny vines,
>   Its glades of reedy grass;
> Its safe and silent islands
>   Within the dark morass.
>
> "Well knows the fair and friendly moon
>   The band that Marion leads—
> The glitter of their rifles,
>   The scampering of their steeds.
> 'Tis life to guide the fiery barb
>   Across the moonlight plain;
> 'Tis life to feel the night wind
>   That lifts his tossing mane.
> A moment in the British camp
>   A moment—and away
> Back to the pathless forest,
>   Before the peep of day." *

* William Cullen Bryant, "Song of Marion's Men."

REVOLUTIONARY PILGRIMAGE

Somewhere in the vicinity of one of these dusky swamps Garden places this amusing story of Colonel Horry, one of Marion's Men, who, with a detachment, was ordered to await the approach of a British scouting-party and entrap them in an ambuscade. They duly fell into his hands, when, at the critical moment,

"from a dreadful impediment in his speech by which he was afflicted, he could not articulate the word 'fire.' In vain he made the attempt—it was *fi, fi, fi, fi*—but he could get no further. At length, irritated almost to madness, he exclaimed '*Shoot*, damn you,—*shoot*—you know very well what I would say—*shoot, shoot* and be damn'd to you!'"

At Kingsville, if you have a day or two to spare, you can make a détour and by taking a branch line go over to Camden, the scene of one of the disasters of the war.

When Cornwallis started northward from Charleston, he made his first headquarters at Camden. He had thus far encountered no organized resistance. But de Kalb had brought troops from the North and these, joining reinforcements that were on their way to the relief of Charleston but had turned back upon hearing of its surrender, now constituted quite an army.

Unfortunately, Congress appointed General Gates, "the conqueror of Burgoyne," to the command of this army of the South. He joined it at Hillsboro, in North Carolina, and despite the July heat marched it directly over the pine-barrens, by the shortest route, to Camden,

CAMPAIGNS IN THE CAROLINAS

"sure of victory and of the dispersion of the British army." The troops arrived sick and worn out, and the result was to be foreseen.

The armies came together in the early morning, mutually surprised, and at the first shock of battle the green American militia, with no competent leader, "fled like a torrent," as Gates himself declares—and he fled with them. Only de Kalb and his Continentals maintained their positions, fighting gallantly until de Kalb himself was killed and his troops, opposed by vastly superior numbers, were forced to give in.

Gates himself was the first to arrive at Charlotte, sixty miles in the rear. He was presently relieved of his command by the Congress that had just appointed him and summoned before a court of inquiry. Thus ended the military career of this incompetent schemer, who at one time had almost succeeded in having himself placed at the head of the American army.

By this disaster at Camden the American army of the South was again reduced to a mere shadow. The defeated militia had returned to their homes; the Continentals had marched

Cornwallis's Headquarters at Camden, S. C.

REVOLUTIONARY PILGRIMAGE

north again; so that it looked as if Cornwallis would now proceed, as an unopposed conqueror, through both the Carolinas.

Fortunately, at this critical juncture Congress appointed Nathanael Greene, a resolute and efficient commander, to reorganize the Southern army. This, in spite of disheartening obstacles, he proceeded to do, and how skilfully he did it we shall see at Guilford Court House.

Meanwhile we shall resume our journey via Columbia, the pretty capital of South Carolina, to Spartanburg, a thriving town situated in the cotton belt on the main line of the Southern Railway.

This city affords a very convenient starting-point from which to visit two of the most important battle-fields of the Carolinas, King's Mountain and the Cowpens. In search of information, just after my arrival, I hunted up an aged veteran, who was able to give me some advice and who suggested that I see Mr. John Cleveland, a descendant of the Colonel Cleveland who took such a prominent part in the battle of King's Mountain. With this gentleman, who proved most kind and hospitable, I passed a pleasant and instructive evening.

The following morning I boarded an early train going north, soon crossed the Pacolet—so often mentioned in this "up-country" warfare—passed, for the time being, the station called Cowpens, and then traversed a fine upland district of rolling hills, handsomely wooded and only partially cultivated. Then, after crossing the Broad River, the Blue Ridge Mountains (well named upon this

CAMPAIGNS IN THE CAROLINAS

bright, fresh morning) came into view along the north horizon, while to the south, every now and then, my eye caught a jagged silhouette, vaguely suggesting a couchant lion, long and low, that I knew from descriptions must be King's Mountain. The main range lies in North Carolina, but this last spur, the scene of the battle, lies just a mile and a half below the boundary—that is, in South Carolina.

After the battle of Camden, as I have said, the "Palmetto State" appeared to be completely in Cornwallis's power. Nevertheless he was wary and wished to make his victory secure. He himself set out for Charlotte to subjugate North Carolina, but he despatched Major Ferguson with a body of regulars and the King's American Regiment—Tories under Captain Abraham de Peyster, of New York—to recruit the loyalists and break up the partisan bands that were making forays in the region, and especially to disperse the Mountain Men, as the frontiersmen from over the Blue Ridge were called.

Ferguson was a coarse and cruel officer and allowed his troops undue license. They plundered and committed outrages wherever they went, and left behind them a train of resentment and a spirit of vengeance of the fiercest description. He finally, with his ranks swelled by loyalists to more than a thousand men, took up his position in all security, as he thought, upon this dominating spur of King's Mountain.

But the train of vengeance he had kindled behind him began to bear its fruit. From all directions men col-

REVOLUTIONARY PILGRIMAGE

lected: incensed Virginians under Campbell; Carolinians under Cleveland, Shelby, and Sevier—undisciplined troops, to be sure, but hardy and brave; regiments without a general; men without a commissary to feed them or a surgeon to dress their wounds, but all smarting under the wrongs inflicted upon themselves or their families by Ferguson's Tories and Tarleton's hated cavalry. It was a veritable man-hunt that they organized.

And, as an old local doggerel puts it,

"On the top of King's Mountain the old rogue they found
And like brave heroes, his camp did surround."

On his hilltop, a hundred feet above his assailants, Ferguson felt secure. But the patriot leaders determined to attack him from every side at once. Colonel Campbell with the Virginians took up his position to the south; then, in the order named, came the commands of Sevier, MacDowell, Winston, and Cleveland, extending round the mountain to the east, and ending with Colonel Shelby's men to the north. Campbell, who seems to have assumed command, gave the signal at the right moment by yelling, at the top of his voice, in true Virginia style: "Here they are, boys. Shoot like hell and fight like devils."

The Indian war-whoop rang out, and the battle was on. Up the hill the Americans clambered from all sides, the British charging down upon them with fixed bay-

CAMPAIGNS IN THE CAROLINAS

onets. But, hiding behind trees and rocks, taking advantage of every bit of cover, these hardy hunter-mountaineers fired with deadly aim. As they continued to ascend and the coil grew tighter, Ferguson dashed about, blowing his shrill whistle to encourage and incite his men. Mounting from rock to rock and tree to tree, the Americans pressed on, and all the while the British ranks grew thinner. Finally, the patriots pushed their way to the very top of the mountain and the British stood surrounded.

Two white flags went up, but Ferguson cut them down with his sword, shouting: "I'll never surrender to such banditti." He gallantly tried to cut his way out, but, recognized by the hunting-shirt he wore over his uniform, he was shot and fell from his horse unconscious. Then ensued a terrible scene, for the Americans, infuriated by recent outrages and by the memory of Tarleton's barbarity at Waxhaws, still shot down the British soldiers who held aloft white tokens of surrender, so that it was with the greatest difficulty that their officers could finally restrain them and prevent a literal "no quarter." The battle lasted less than an hour, but not one of the enemy escaped.

In its effect upon the people the battle of King's Mountain was as electrifying as Bennington or Trenton. It changed the entire aspect of the war in the South. It roused and stirred the patriots of both the Carolinas and new regiments quickly sprang into being. As Jefferson expressed it, it "was the joyful annunciation of that

REVOLUTIONARY PILGRIMAGE

turn of the tide of success which terminated the Revolutionary War with the seal of independence."

The site of this memorable engagement is marked with two monuments—one quite old; the other made of blocks of granite laid in tiers and bearing this inscription:

> In memory of
> The Patriotic Americans
> who participated
> in the Battle of
> King's Mountain
> This monument is erected
> by their
> Grateful Descendants.

It was fought on the 7th of October, 1780. News of it first reached Cornwallis as he lay at Charlotte, and it was the first sting of the hornets. Hitherto he had proceeded as a victor; now his troubles were to begin. Such a blow was it, indeed, that he fell back to Winnsboro, in South Carolina; while Greene advanced to Charlotte and took up his headquarters in the town Cornwallis had just deserted.

From these headquarters he issued an order appointing Daniel Morgan to the command of a special corps to operate in the Catawba region and along the border between the two Carolinas, "to protect the country, spirit up the people and annoy the enemy."

Thus, the beginning of 1781 found Cornwallis at Winnsboro, Greene at Charlotte, and Morgan on the

CAMPAIGNS IN THE CAROLINAS

Pacolet, near its junction with the Broad. Cornwallis determined first to strike at Morgan, and then to fall upon Greene himself. So he detached Colonel Tarleton, with his famous and hated cavalry legion and a portion of the Seventy-First Regiment supported by two cannon, to hunt out Morgan and crush him.

Tarleton found him upon the Pacolet and crowded him over Thicketty Mountain to a place known as the Cowpens, a locality that took its name from the fact that it was once a tract of grazing land, the old grants designating it as "Hannah's Cowpens."

This pursuit took them through the very country that I now traversed on my return from King's Mountain to Spartanburg. First I crossed the Broad River, then the station of Thicketty recalled the position of Thicketty Mountain, and soon after I arrived at Cowpens.

The battle-field lies several miles from the station, and except for its topography presents no special objects of interest. For no monuments mark it, for reasons that I shall explain presently, yet the place is hallowed by memories of one of the gallant actions of the war. The field of battle is rather open country, sparsely wooded, and a little more thickly choked with shrubbery than in the days of the Revolution. Then it was clear enough to allow the evolutions of cavalry and, in this engagement, cavalry was a decisive factor.

Morgan took up his position with his back to the Broad River, which also passed around his left flank, so that in case of defeat it was quite impossible to retreat. He thus explains this strange choice of terrain, for he deliberately placed himself in this position.

"As to covering my wings, I knew my adversary, and was perfectly sure I should have nothing but downright fighting. As to retreat, it was the very thing I wished to cut off all hope of. I would have thanked Tarleton had he surrounded me with his cavalry. . . . When men are forced to fight, they will sell their lives dearly; and I knew that the dread of Tarleton's cavalry would give due weight to the protection of my bayonets and keep my troops from breaking."

This field that he chose was quite level, with but two slight elevations, the first low, the second, nearer the river, high enough to screen cavalry. Behind this one, Morgan placed Colonel William Washington's troopers. On the smaller hillock he formed his best troops under Colonel John Eager Howard, and in front of them he spread two separate skirmish lines of militia. Having thus disposed his command at dawn on the 7th of January, 1781, he told his men to "ease their joints" until the enemy came in sight.

Tarleton left his encampment at three in the morning, hoping to surprise Morgan, but upon his arrival after a long march he found the little American army prepared for him and looking calmly on while he formed his line of battle only four hundred yards away.

After a preliminary skirmish Colonel Tarleton marched his infantry steadily forward in serried ranks to smash the skirmish lines of militia. These stood their ground

CAMPAIGNS IN THE CAROLINAS

well and, when the redcoats had advanced to within fifty yards, poured a deadly fire into their ranks, and then retreated behind the main line of Continentals stationed upon the first low hill.

The British, with a shout, now quickened their advance, which, however, was attended with some confusion. Tarleton lengthened his line, and Howard, seeing this, realized the danger to his right flank. Washington's cavalry had already emerged from behind the hill and were swinging ahead to engage the British dragoons when their commander, as he advanced, could see the confusion in the enemy's ranks; so he sent a hasty message back to Morgan: "They are coming like a mob; give them a fire and I'll charge them."

At Morgan's command the Continentals, who had begun to falter on their hilltop, now stiffened their line, and, delivering a death-dealing volley into the shouting ranks of the on-coming enemy, charged back at them with their bayonets. "The effect was immediate and conclusive." The British ranks broke; the men fell upon their knees and gave in. "Exertions to make them advance were useless. . . . Neither threats nor promises could avail." *

Colonel Washington, with his cavalry, was impetuously pursuing Tarleton's fleeing legion, when, riding far ahead of his men, he suddenly found himself confronted by Tarleton himself with two of his officers. A fierce hand-to-hand encounter ensued. Washington was aided in par-

* Tarleton, "Campaigns of 1780 and 1781."

rying the rain of blows only by a youth of fourteen, and his sword, striking that of one of Tarleton's officers, broke off short. He would, in all probability, have lost his life had not Sergeant-Major Perry come up in the nick of time to ward off the next blow.

Washington had wounded Tarleton in the hand and had himself received a pistol-bullet in the knee. This sharp and bitter encounter forms the background for another of Garden's anecdotes anent the repartee of American ladies.

"The haughty Tarleton, vaunting his feats of gallantry to the disparagement of the Officers of the Continental Cavalry, said to a lady at Wilmington 'I have a very earnest desire to see your far-famed hero, Colonel Washington.' 'Your wish, Colonel, might have been fully gratified,' she promptly replied, 'had you ventured to look behind you after the battle of the Cowpens.'

"It was in this battle that Washington had wounded Tarleton in the hand, which gave rise to a still more *pointed* retort. Conversing with Mrs. Wiley Jones, Colonel Tarleton observed—'You appear to think very highly of Colonel Washington, and yet I have been told that he is so ignorant a fellow, that he can hardly *write* his own name.' 'It may be the case,' she readily replied 'but no man better than yourself, Colonel, can testify, that he knows how to *make his mark.*'"

After this victory at the Cowpens Morgan sent off six hundred prisoners to Virginia—a very heartening success for the Americans. Congress awarded him a gold medal

CAMPAIGNS IN THE CAROLINAS

and a silver one each to Colonel Howard and Colonel Washington.

The last-named officer's widow (whose home still stands facing the Battery in Charleston) presented the scarlet banner that his squadron carried that day to the Washington Light Infantry. This military organization of Charleston, named in her husband's honor, still has this prized flag in its possession, and consequently has taken a particular interest in the battle of the Cowpens. In 1856 it journeyed all the way from Charleston to the battle-field, in those days a hundred miles from any railway.

Monument to Daniel Morgan, Spartanburg

With appropriate exercises a shaft was erected, topped by a gilded eagle—the first monument, I believe, to mark any Southern Revolutionary battle-ground. But vandals and relic-hunters (a curse upon them!) carried away the memorial, bit by bit, so that nothing now remains of it. When a new monument was projected it was thus

REVOLUTIONARY PILGRIMAGE

deemed wiser to erect it in the town of Spartanburg itself, near by.

There it now stands in the principal square, a sturdy shaft, simply inscribed and surmounted by a fine bronze figure, modelled by J. Q. A. Ward, of Daniel Morgan, who is supposed to be looking off toward the battle-field. In a letter to the committee the sculptor thus describes the peculiar costume that he has portrayed:

"The coat or tunic was a fringed hunting-shirt adopted from the Indian costume and much worn by the frontiersmen of that time. The fringed leggins and mocassins belonged to the same costume which was used by Morgan's Riflemen.

"The cap, a peculiar one of fur, with a cluster of pine leaves as a sort of pompon, was loaned me by a gentleman of Charleston through the kindness of the Hon. Wm. A. Courtenay (then Mayor). This was an original cap preserved from the Revolutionary War. . . . Of course the manner of wearing the hair, the cravat and ruffled shirt-front are all in the mode of the time."

The morning after my visit to the scene of these two victories at the Cowpens and King's Mountain I left Spartanburg to proceed northward, for I was now to follow the two main armies, Cornwallis's and Greene's, that were manœuvring to confront each other.

III

GUILFORD COURT HOUSE

IT was not until two months later, however, on the 15th of March, 1781, that these hostile armies finally stood face to face. Greene had played for time, meanwhile, and had received important reinforcements of militia, until he now felt strong enough to confront Cornwallis's veterans. So, choosing a locality north of Salisbury, he drew up his battle-lines round Guilford Court House, a settlement situated at a crossroads near the present town of Greensboro, in North Carolina.

The main line of the Southern Railway approximately follows the line the Americans took on their march northward after the battle of the Cowpens. How many travellers, riding luxuriously nowadays over this line on their way north from Asheville and other resorts of the Blue Ridge country, or from Miami and Palm Beach in the winter, realize that they are following the weary footsteps of the patriots who marched and countermarched over this same territory to fight the bitter Carolina battles?

From Spartanburg I now trailed them, stopping en route at Charlotte, for, though now a busy, modern-

REVOLUTIONARY PILGRIMAGE

looking town set in a pretty pastoral country, Charlotte has its place in Revolutionary annals.

To it, you remember, Gates retreated after the defeat at Camden, and in it Cornwallis made his headquarters for a considerable time prior to King's Mountain; but he found its patriotic inhabitants so inimical, so irritating, that he dubbed the place the "Hornet's Nest" when he left it for Winnsboro. That the people liked the name, and that they remember it still, is evidenced by the fact that the local baseball-team calls itself the Hornets.

On the occasion of my last visit the town was all agog with excitement. The President of the United States was to arrive within a few days to deliver an address, then particularly pertinent, upon the one hundred and forty-first anniversary of the signing of the Mecklenburg* Declaration of Independence, which document, prepared by a convention of patriots known as the Mecklenburg Committee, declared themselves and the "American Colonies" free and independent of Great Britain on the 31st of May, 1775, or more than a year before the Jeffersonian Declaration. In front of the court-house a monument commemorates this fact, now well authenticated.

Beyond Charlotte I soon reached Salisbury, and then crossed the Yadkin near the spot where Greene crossed it while its waters were rising, Cornwallis following as soon as the flood had sufficiently subsided.

Greensboro lies just a little farther north—a thriving

*The county in which Charlotte is situated.

CAMPAIGNS IN THE CAROLINAS

town in the centre of a tobacco and cotton growing district. There, in the busy main street, I quickly found a motor to take me out to the Guilford battle-field, a few miles distant, the scene of a struggle that did so much to determine the final issue of the Revolution.

My first impression of this historic spot was one of extreme annoyance. A group of patriotic citizens, animated by the very best intentions, acquired the battleground some years ago. They have since decorated it lavishly with granite tents, boulders, pyramids and triumphal arches until it now resembles a suburban cemetery. The patriotism that inspired the great effort involved is not questioned; the good taste is. Bronze figures of Clio and statues of former presidents of the Battle Ground Company—no matter how public-spirited these citizens may have been—seem sadly out of place upon this historic field. I wish to except from this general criticism the great equestrian statue of Nathanael Greene that has recently been unveiled. Had it stood alone, dominating the landscape, the impression would have been noble and effective. Upon the other hand, the markers designating the positions of troops are most useful to the visitor, being, to my mind, the best means of marking the Revolutionary battle-fields.

To follow the various phases of the battle of Guilford Court House, you should first take your place beside the sign-board that marks the position of Singleton's artillery. His guns occupied a piece of rising ground, pointing their noses down the highroad that leads from Salisbury. On

REVOLUTIONARY PILGRIMAGE

either side of his two cannon stretched the first skirmish-line of North Carolina militia, with "Light Horse Harry" Lee's cavalry on one flank and Colonel William Washington's upon the other. The militia were protected by a ditch and fence that ran along where a row of maples now stands.

Up the road before you came Tarleton's cavalry in column, leading the van of the British army. When in sight of the Americans they halted, and the steady ranks of the regulars began to deploy and take position at each side of them until their lines were as long as those of the Americans. Then, says Tarleton, "a sharp conflict ensued between the advanced parties of the two armies. In the onset, the fire of the Americans was heavy and the charge of their cavalry was spirited."

But the weight of the British soon forced back this first skirmish-line and disclosed a second line, the Virginians, also at each side of the road, three hundred yards behind, stationed where the railroad-track crosses the Salisbury road near the two great stone arches. These troops stood their ground well, for Morgan, knowing the temper of these raw recruits, had suggested to Greene to "put the militia in the centre with some picked troops in their rear, with orders to shoot down the first man that runs." After a splendid resistance this line also gave way and sought cover in the surrounding woods.

And now the British guards and grenadiers advanced across a gully against the American main line—the Continentals, posted on rising ground to the left of the road,

CAMPAIGNS IN THE CAROLINAS

where a shaft of pinkish stone marks their position. Behind them ran the road to Reedy Fork, and at its junction with the main road we have been following stood the court-house that gave its name to the battle, its emplacement still plainly visible and marked with a tablet.

The Battle-field at Guilford Court House

Two fierce charges by the regulars were gallantly repulsed by the Continentals, who even forced the redcoats back again across the ravine. "At this period," says Tarleton, "the event of the action was doubtful and victory alternately presided over either army." But the British were able to bring up additional forces into this main action and could be no longer resisted. Greene, perceiving this, ordered a retreat, and his troops retired, keeping their lines intact. "Earl Cornwallis," says Tarleton, "did not think it advisable for the British cavalry to charge the enemy, who were retreating in good order."

The British had fought with extraordinary dash and bravery, but had met such determined resistance that a full third of their number were killed or wounded during the two hours of this desperate encounter. Cornwallis held the field, but, as with Burgoyne after the first battle of Saratoga, "the British had the name, the Americans the good consequences of victory." Fox declared in the House of Commons: "Another such victory would ruin the British army."

Greene fell back twelve miles and expected Cornwallis to pursue him. But Cornwallis, realizing his precarious position, with his weakened army far from the sea and reinforcements, having cared for his wounded as best he might, crossed Deep River. Greene followed him, still expecting another battle. But Cornwallis suddenly turned about again, recrossed the river, and with all despatch set out by the main road via Fayetteville to Wilmington, where, near Cape Fear, the British ships lay.

Seeing his enemy thus turning from him, Greene turned about also and started south upon his campaign that was to win back the Carolinas to the patriot cause, thus fulfilling the lines of an old ditty that used to be popular at the end of the war and was sung to the tune of "Yankee Doodle":

CAMPAIGNS IN THE CAROLINAS

> "Cornwallis led a country dance;
> The like was never seen, sir;
> Much retrograde and much advance
> And all with General Greene, sir.
> They rambled up and rambled down,
> Joined hands, and off they ran, sir;
> Our General Greene to old Charlestown,
> And the Earl to Wilmington, sir."

But the earl did not even venture to remain long in Wilmington, for, as he wrote to Sir Henry Clinton in New York:

"I could not remain at Wilmington lest General Greene should succeed against Lord Rawdon (in South Carolina) and by returning to North Carolina, have it in his power to cut off every means of saving my small corps, except that disgraceful one of an embarkation, with the loss of cavalry and every horse in the army."

And in a later despatch he adds:

"I can not help expressing my wishes that the Chesapeake may become the seat of war, even (if necessary) at the expense of abandoning New York. Until Virginia is in a measure subdued, our hold on the Carolinas must be difficult."

So for Virginia he set forth, and thither we shall now follow him and witness the last dramatic act of the war.

THROUGH VIRGINIA

THROUGH VIRGINIA

I

WILLIAMSBURG

WHEN Cornwallis entered Virginia he took the main road direct to Petersburg, crossed the James River at Westover, and proceeded to Richmond. Meanwhile, apprised of his coming, Washington despatched Lafayette with about twelve hundred men to oppose him as best he could. Cornwallis received reinforcements, and Lafayette, before this strengthened enemy, was obliged to retire to northern Virginia. But here he was joined by some troops from Pennsylvania and thus was able to take the field again.

Cornwallis then turned south, staying at Elk Hill for a time, while Tarleton made an unsuccessful raid to the west in an attempt to capture Jefferson and the Virginia Assembly, then in session at Charlottesville. Upon Tarleton's return Cornwallis set out for Williamsburg, at which place he arrived about the middle of June, 1781.

During all this time Lafayette had been hanging upon his flanks, harassing his every movement; and this young man of twenty-three had proved himself so swift and active, yet so prudent and wary, that not once could Cornwallis catch him off his guard or take him at a disad-

REVOLUTIONARY PILGRIMAGE

vantage. His army, too, increased all the time, for his "youth and generosity, courage and prudence were his spells of persuasion," and the young Virginia gentry flocked to his banner.

So Lafayette's dream of battling for the freedom of mankind was now really coming true—a dream that had obsessed him from his boyhood and become tangible when, at a banquet at Metz, he first heard of the shots fired at Lexington and Concord. Thenceforward, heart and soul, he was won to the American cause, and was anxious to stake his life, his fortune, and his future happiness upon its issue. In return he received the love and admiration of the American people. "It is no trifling compliment to say, that, next to the Commander-in-Chief, and the intrepid Greene, no general stood higher in public favor, or more constantly commanded the admiration of the army than La Fayette."*

After a brief stay in Williamsburg Cornwallis again crossed the James River and proceeded to Portsmouth, while Lafayette took up his quarters in the old Virginia capital.

For, until two years previous, Williamsburg had been the capital of the province. In 1779, however, the seat of government had been transferred to Richmond, and this was a serious blow to the proud little town—a gentlemanly community that would not barter and trade— and a blow from which it has never wholly recovered, for Williamsburg has ever since remained a somnolent

* Garden's "Anecdotes."

THROUGH VIRGINIA

place, without commerce, without prosperity, but retaining for these very reasons the glamour of respectability and ancient lineage, its old houses being haunted with

The Home of the President of William and Mary College, Williamsburg

memories of some of the nation's most distinguished personages.

A single street traverses it from end to end—a broad, level thoroughfare, still unpaved and dusty, and just a mile in length—Duke of Gloucester Street, as it is called, named for the heir apparent when William and Mary sat upon the throne of England.

William and Mary College, named, when it was built, for the sovereigns, the second oldest institution of learn-

REVOLUTIONARY PILGRIMAGE

ing in our country, stands at one end of this street, while at the other used to stand the State Capitol, until it was destroyed by fire many years ago. The venerable college still holds its sessions, and prepares its graduates for life's struggles, as it has done for two hundred and twenty odd years. Among its presidents and chancellors have been such men as Washington and Madison; among its students it has enrolled three Presidents of the United States, as well as a great number of eminent jurists, patriots, and statesmen.

Its old brick buildings recall some ancient English seat of learning, which effect is heightened by the noble trees that arch their branches overhead to shade the quadrangle, whose focal point is a marble monument, erected just prior to the Revolution, to the memory of

The
Right Honourable
Norbonne Berkeley
Baron de Botetourt
His Majesty's
Late Lieutenant and
Governor General of the
Colony and Dominion
of Virginia

as the inscription upon it records, adding: "America! Behold your friend!" The sight of this figure, richly robed and heavily cloaked, brought to my mind a rare old print called "The Alternative of Williamsburg"—a

THROUGH VIRGINIA

crude engraving depicting a group of men writing the "Resolves of Congress" upon a barrel-head, while this very statue looks down upon them.

At about the middle of Duke of Gloucester Street opens the Court Green, an extensive common named for

Bruton Church and the George Wythe House

the old colonial court-house that still stands upon it. Near by rises Bruton Church, one of the most ancient in our land, pervaded with an atmosphere of rare distinction, for the tombs in its churchyard are graven with illustrious names, while its pews bear the name-plates of the great sons of Virginia, many of whom have been among its vestrymen—Custises, Randolphs, Tylers, Wallers, and Blairs. The governor's seat is still in place, and of a

REVOLUTIONARY PILGRIMAGE

Sunday, I am told, the students of William and Mary occupy the gallery.

Adjoining it stands the old George Wythe house, which Washington made his headquarters while in Williamsburg, now toned by wind and weather to a faded pinkish brown. It is the present home of a genial gentleman, who, when we visited the old Virginia capital some years since, was living upon the James River, a few miles away, in historic Carter's Grove, one of those handsome country houses—the pride of the State—whose lawns and terraces overlook the river.

At that time I visited "The Grove," and made the accompanying drawing of its hall and staircase, whose rail still bears the scars said to have been made by the sabres of Tarleton's cavalrymen. Most of the houses in Williamsburg have their stories. During that earlier stay we visited almost all of them, each haunted with memories, and some with well-authenticated ghosts. Each held its prized possessions: a sketch of Washington, made at a dinner-party by Latrobe's facile pencil; a portrait of Mary Cary, Washington's reputed first love; a set of historic china or a rare musical instrument.

In one I saw this letter framed upon the wall: "General Washington presents his compliments to Colonel Tucker and requests the favor of his company at dinner tomorrow, 3 P. M." Above this invitation hung a portrait, Gilbert Stuart's masterly presentment of John Randolph of Roanoke, an ancestor of the family, then a

THROUGH VIRGINIA

young man of thirty. In another, scratched upon a window-pane, these cabalistic words were pointed out to me: "1796, Nov. 23, Ah, fatal day!" What stories lurk behind these fragments of forgotten history—vague, intangible, yet so teeming with suggestion!

Hall in Carter's Grove

Other houses have a more definite history. Near the site of the old Capitol stands the home of Peyton Randolph, the man whom we have seen presiding over that momentous assembly, the first Continental Congress, and whose head, when he was speaker of the House of Burgesses of Virginia, was framed in that strange high-backed chair that I saw in the State Capitol at Richmond. Bassett Hall was long the residence of the Tylers; while in a house nearer the inn lived William Wirt, first chan-

REVOLUTIONARY PILGRIMAGE

cellor of Virginia. Such are the memories that cling about the old town.

At the outbreak of the Revolution Williamsburg became a perfect hotbed of rebellion. Its royal governor, Lord Dunmore, having seized the powder stored in the Powder Horn—a queer, octagonal structure that still faces the court-house—Patrick Henry, with the patriots at his back, demanded its surrender; the community flew to arms and Dunmore escaped to his ships. Early in 1776 the Virginia Convention met in Williamsburg and instructed its delegates in Congress to vote for independence, and on the 29th of June the State formally declared itself free and independent, and elected Patrick Henry its first governor.

Williamsburg was then the headquarters of the Virginia militia, and in the orderly book of its commander, General Lewis, I came upon these quaint instructions regarding *tenue* and dress of officers and men—regulations that governed the Virginia riflemen, whose exploits we have witnessed on many a field—the men whom the British dubbed derisively "shirtmen," because of the hunting-shirts described.

"It is recommended to the Colonels to make their men appear as uniform as possible in their Dress, that their Hatts shall be cut, all cocked in Fassion, that their Hair be likewise cut exactly the same length. When the Regiment are under Arms, the Officers to appear in their Hunting shirts; the Officers as well as men to die their shirts in an uniform manner. These attentials may ap-

THROUGH VIRGINIA

pear Trivial, but they are in fact of considerable importance, as they tend to give what is call'd Esprit de Corps, without which Regiments never grow to Reputation.

"R.O. The Captains of the 6th Battalion, together with the other Officers, are immediately to provide themselves with hunting shirts, short and fringed; the men's shirts to be short and plain, the Sergeants' shirts to have small white cuffs and plain; the Drummers' shirts to be with dark cuffs. Both Officers and Soldiers to have Hatts cut around and Bound with black; the Brims of their Hatts to be 2 inches deep and Cocked on one side with a Button & Loop & Cockades, which is to be worn on the left."

Many of these were the Culpepper Men, who bore upon their banner a rattlesnake, with the device: "Don't tread on me," and ugly antagonists they were for any foe, these Virginia riflemen.

Such was the town, such were the people and the soldiery to whom Lafayette came in the month of June, 1781. And from Williamsburg he continued to watch his enemy.

Cornwallis remained at Portsmouth, where he was always assured of a retreat through the Carolinas, until he received orders from Sir Henry Clinton to proceed at once across Hampton Roads to Yorktown and co-operate with the British fleet when it should arrive from New York. So, on the 1st of August, against his own good judgment, Cornwallis began to transport his army up the York River to Yorktown, where his entire forces were concentrated by the 22d.

REVOLUTIONARY PILGRIMAGE

Lafayette's spirits now rose and he began to foresee the happy issue that terminated this Virginia campaign, for he thus wrote to Washington:

"In the present state of affairs, my dear general, I hope you will come yourself to Virginia. Lord Cornwallis must be attacked with pretty great apparatus; but, when the French fleet takes possession of the [Chesapeake] Bay and rivers, and we form a land force superior to his, his army must sooner or later be forced to surrender. I heartily thank you for having ordered me to Virginia; it is to your goodness that I am indebted for the most beautiful prospect which I may ever behold."

On the 30th of August his spirits rose higher still, for a great French fleet, under the Comte de Grasse, arrived in Hampton Roads. Five days later more than three thousand troops landed from this fleet and joined the Americans at Williamsburg.

Now came Washington's opportunity. He had been feigning an attack on New York, taking the greatest pains to deceive and bewilder his enemy so as to cover his real purpose, which was to hasten to Virginia at the proper moment with his best troops and aid Lafayette in the capture of Cornwallis at Yorktown. And so successfully did he mislead Sir Henry Clinton that, even when he crossed the Hudson, with two thousand Americans and four thousand French soldiers supplied by De Barras's fleet at Newport, the British commander still thought his real objective was New York.

Then, suddenly and expeditiously, when it was already

THROUGH VIRGINIA

too late for Clinton to act, this combined army set out via Trenton and Philadelphia on their way to the South. The American troops marched through the capital on the 2d of September and were given a tremendous ovation, and on the following day the French soldiers passed through, the combined forces then proceeding rapidly to the Head of Elk, where they embarked for Virginia under convoy of the French fleet.

Meanwhile, with his officers, Washington had ridden down by way of Mount Vernon, his first visit to his home in six years. There, on the 10th of September, he entertained the French commanders, de Rochambeau and de Chastellux, and on the 14th he reached Williamsburg, in time to congratulate his dear Lafayette on his twenty-fourth birthday.

All was now excitement and bustle in the allied camp. The northern army was arriving and the French officers were vying with each other in politenesses and harmony of action. What a brilliant scene there must have been around the old George Wythe house, where Washington was quartered! How the Palace Green before it and the Court Green beyond must have glittered with the brilliant uniforms of the French King's soldiers! How the music must have echoed up and down Duke of Gloucester Street as the allied forces assembled, arriving, regiment by regiment, from their landing-place on the James River! By the 25th of September twelve thousand men were quartered in and about the town.

Washington, Rochambeau, and the general officers now

REVOLUTIONARY PILGRIMAGE

visited the French admiral on board his flagship, the *Ville de Paris*, and perfected their plans for the siege. On the 28th the entire allied army marched out of Williamsburg and went to take up its position close about the fortifications that the British had thrown up around Yorktown.

II

YORKTOWN

SO to Yorktown let us now proceed by way of the country that Josiah Quincy so enthusiastically described when he visited it in 1773:

"Excellent farms and large cleared tracts of land, well fenced and tilled, are all around me. Peach trees seem to be of spontaneous growth in these Provinces . . . and, intermingled with many small pine trees of exquisite verdure, form a prospect to the eye most delightful and charming."

To me it seemed equally pleasing, as we motored one May morning not long ago, with the white hawthorn blooming by the wayside, the birds singing in the pine woods, and the negro cabins alive with pickaninnies playing in the doorways, over clay roads and sand roads until we crossed the backbone of the narrow peninsula and caught a glimpse of the York River, stretching broad and blue to Gloucester Point directly opposite.

At the time of the Revolution Yorktown was, as it is now, a village built upon a bluff, occupying the highest ground below Richmond on either the York or James Rivers. For this reason it had strategic value and Cornwallis had been improving its natural advantages by intrenching his position as skilfully as possible. On his

REVOLUTIONARY PILGRIMAGE

right lay a creek and swamp, while his front was protected by a long ravine so that his main intrenchments faced the southeast, where he had also placed his principal redoubts.

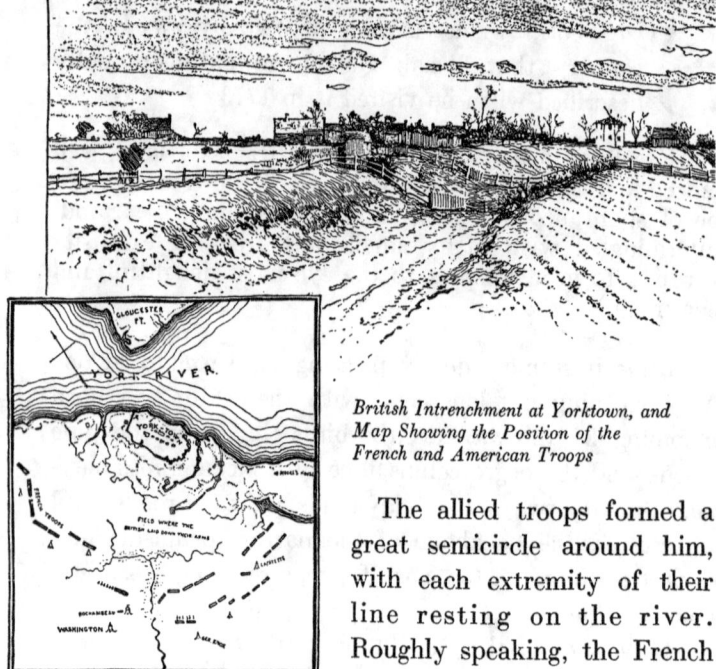

British Intrenchment at Yorktown, and Map Showing the Position of the French and American Troops

The allied troops formed a great semicircle around him, with each extremity of their line resting on the river. Roughly speaking, the French troops held the left half of the line, and the Americans the right, the massed artillery being placed at the point of junction just in front of Washington's headquarters.

It did not take long for Cornwallis to discover that,

THROUGH VIRGINIA

despite his strong intrenchments, he was in a very critical position. On the 11th of October he sent the following despatch to Sir Henry Clinton:

"I have only to report that nothing but a direct move to York River, which includes a successful naval action, can save me. The enemy made their first parallel on the night of the sixth, at a distance of six hundred yards, and have perfected it and constructed places of arms and batteries with great regularity and caution. On the evening of the ninth, their batteries opened and have since continued firing without intermission, with about forty cannon, mostly heavy, and sixteen mortars, from eight to sixteen inches. We have lost seventy men, and many of our works are considerably damaged; and in such works, in disadvantageous ground, against so powerful an attack, one can not hope to make a very long resistance."

He thus reports the further progress of the siege:

"October 12th, 7 P. M. Last night the enemy made their parallel at the distance of three hundred yards. We continue to lose men very fast.

"October 15th. Last evening the enemy carried my two advanced redoubts by storm and during the night have included them in their second parallel. My situation has become very critical. We dare not show a gun to their old batteries and I expect that their new ones will open to-morrow morning. . . .

"A little before day broke, on the evening of the 16th, I ordered a sortie of about 350 men under Lieut.-Col. Abercrombie to attack two batteries which appeared to be in the greatest forwardness and to spike the guns. . . .

REVOLUTIONARY PILGRIMAGE

This action proved of little public advantage, for the cannon having been spiked in a hurry, were soon rendered fit for service again."

He then relates in some detail his attempt to pass his army under cover of the night across the river to Gloucester Point and thus effect a retreat. But this plan failed, for, just as a greater part of the guards had been ferried over,

"the weather, from being moderate and calm, changed to a most violent storm of wind and rain and drove all of the boats, some of which had troops on board, down the river."

Thus his last hope vanished.

"Our works in the meanwhile were going to ruin. We at that time could not fire a single gun, only one eight inch, and a little more than one hundred cohorn shells remained. . . . I therefore proposed to capitulate." *

Washington willingly acquiesced in Cornwallis's proposal, and commissioners were appointed to draw up terms of surrender—the Vicomte de Noailles and Colonel Laurens representing the allies; Colonel Dundas and Major Ross the British. They promptly met that same afternoon—the 17th of October—in a house known as the Moore House, that still stands down by the York River, about a mile and a half below Yorktown—a one-story dwelling, to which an inappropriate mansard roof has been added.

* Cornwallis's despatches to Sir Henry Clinton.

York River, Seen from the Inner British Works and Looking toward Gloucester Point

THROUGH VIRGINIA

As you drive to it you pass the remains of the "two advanced redoubts" mentioned by Cornwallis in his despatch of October 15—the little forts that were carried in friendly rivalry by details from the allied armies. The redoubt nearest the river was assigned to

The Moore House

the American troops under Colonel Alexander Hamilton; the other to French troops under the Baron de Viomenil.

The Americans carried their redoubt easily, after a brilliant charge that did not meet very serious opposition, but the French faced a more difficult problem, for the work they were to carry was the better fortified of the two. Its abatis and the palisades of its glacis held them in check so long that when they had cleared these

REVOLUTIONARY PILGRIMAGE

obstructions they had already lost many men. But, undaunted, they threw themselves into the ditch, scaled the parapet, and, leaping like tigers into the redoubt itself, succeeded in carrying it at the point of the bayonet. Washington cited both columns for bravery in general orders, and the French King restored to his regiment, known as le Gatinois, its old and honored name, "Royale Auvergne sans tache."

Yorktown village of to-day contains some two or three score houses—a few less perhaps than it did at the time of the Revolution—a number of them being of the rustic type so often seen along English byways. The old brick custom-house still stands, while the most notable among its ancient residences is the handsome house that was built by "Scotch Tom" Nelson and that, at the

Principal Street in Yorktown, Showing Monument Commemorating the Surrender

THROUGH VIRGINIA

Governor Nelson's Home

time of the siege, was the home of Thomas Nelson, then governor of Virginia and commander of the State militia.

When the American artillery began to bombard the town this stanch patriot signalled out his own house to the gunners as an excellent target for their aim. Its old brick walls still bear witness to the accuracy of their marksmanship. The box hedges of its garden have now grown so tall that one may stand within their shadow, and by its doorway there is a laurel-tree said to have

REVOLUTIONARY PILGRIMAGE

been planted by Lafayette. When I last visited it the house was being carefully "restored" for a new owner—a gentleman from Illinois.

Immediately after Cornwallis's surrender Congress resolved that a marble column be erected at Yorktown, "ornamented with emblems of the alliance between the United States and his most Christian Majesty, and inscribed with a succinct narrative of the surrender of Earl Cornwallis." It took just a century to carry this decree into effect, for the monument that now stands upon a hill beyond the town—a tall marble column topped with a figure of Peace—was not dedicated until the centennial celebration of the surrender. It has now become a well-known landmark, visible far and wide, up and down the river.

Beyond it, by following a road that passes remains of old intrenchments—links between the first and second parallels—you reach a national cemetery, quiet and peaceful, the simple, numbered headstones of "its silent army" stretching in long perspectives under the dappled shadows of pine-trees. Near one of its walls, but just outside it, a plain obelisk, entangled in wild underbrush, marks the field whereon the British laid down their arms.

The ceremony was an imposing one, and as you stand upon this historic field you can readily call it to mind.

Along the right side of the Hampton road that crosses the little plain the American troops, nine thousand in number, were drawn up in line, with General Washington upon his white horse at their head. Along the left side

THROUGH VIRGINIA

were the seven thousand French troops under the command of the Comte de Rochambeau. Each line was about a mile in length. A great crowd, gathered from all the surrounding country, stood silently in the background expectantly awaiting the appearance of Cornwallis's soldiers.

The British troops were then seen issuing from their trenches, their colors cased as stipulated in the terms of surrender, their drums beating a British march. A French chaplain, the Abbé Robin, tells us that

"We were all surprised at the good condition of the English troops as well as their cleanliness of dress. To account for their good appearance, Cornwallis had opened all the stores (about to be surrendered) to the soldiers before the capitulation took place. Each had a complete new suit, but all their finery seemed to humble them the more, when contrasted with the miserable appearance of the Americans."

All looked for Cornwallis, but in vain. In his place Major-General O'Hara rode up to General Washington and explained his commander's absence owing to an indisposition. He was referred to General Lincoln, to whom he tendered Cornwallis's sword. Then twenty-eight British captains advanced, bearing the twenty-eight regimental standards. Opposite them, at six paces' distance, stood a like number of American sergeants. Ensign Wilson, the youngest commissioned officer in the American army, had been appointed to conduct this ceremony, and he ordered the British captains to advance two paces and deliver the flags to the sergeants. But the captains hesitated, unwilling to surrender their flags to non-commissioned officers. Colonel Hamilton, who was officer of the day, rode up, heard their grievance, and ordered each in turn to hand his furled banner to Ensign Wilson, who handed it to the designated sergeant. Finally the soldiers marched up and laid down their arms, some throwing them angrily upon the ground as if to render them useless.

Cornwallis's absence on this occasion has been much criticised. It can be condoned, however, when we think of all he had been through and when we consider this, his loyal tribute to his captors:

"The treatment, in general, that we have received from the enemy since our surrender, has been perfectly good and proper; but the kindness and attention that has been shown us by the French officers in particular, their delicate sensibility of our situation, their generous and pressing offers of money, both public and private, to any amount, has really gone beyond what I can possibly describe, and will, I hope, make an impression on the breast of every British officer, whenever the fortune of war should put any of them in our power."

The surrender at Yorktown virtually put an end to the war. There was desultory fighting long after it but no general engagements. Yet, it seems to me, our pilgrimage would be incomplete without one or two more visits.

III

HAMPTON ROADS

FROM Yorktown we went on to Old Point Comfort. Captain John Smith is said to have given the place its refreshing name upon his arrival after his long and tedious voyage, and it applies just as well to-day as ever it did, for the big rambling hotel is a veritable haven of refuge for the weary traveller, who, as he sits upon its broad verandas facing the wide waters of Hampton Roads, may dream, as he watches the leviathans of our modern navy in the offing, grim and gray, of days gone by when Howe's two hundred sail came standing in between the capes, transporting the British army on its way to Philadelphia. He may also, in imagination, behold de Grasse's gallant ships—the proudest fleet that, up to that time, had ever sailed American waters—come grandly into the Chesapeake to co-operate with Lafayette and cut Cornwallis from the sea.

And, as he looks upon the surrounding shores, he may summon many other memories from the past. Up the James River, not far away, stand the ruins of Jamestown, so called by Captain John Smith in honor of his sovereign, while yonder capes that guard the entrance to the Roads were named for the royal princes Henry and Charles, and the nomenclature of all the adjacent counties—to cite them at random—Princess Anne, Isle of

REVOLUTIONARY PILGRIMAGE

Wight, Warwick, Sussex, Surrey, Prince George, King William, King and Queen, Gloucester, revives memories of the days of royal rule.

Down toward the south, sheltered on the Elizabeth River, lies old Gosport Navy Yard, now become one of our most important naval stations. In busy Norfolk opposite stands St. Paul's, on the site of a "Chapel of Ease" built in 1641. The present "Borough Church" is but a century younger and still bears embedded in its wall a cannon-ball fired from Lord Dunmore's ships when he, the last royal governor of the province, bombarded the town in 1776. The noble overarching trees that shade this venerable church, its ivy-covered walls, its fountain, and the old headstones of its graveyard compose a veritable picture of rustic England and arrest every passer-by in Church Street.

In Hampton still stands St. John's, with tombs about it that date back to the first years of the eighteenth century. As I was wandering among them one afternoon, reading the quaint epitaphs, an elderly man approached and, pointing to one of them, asked: "Do you see anything peculiar about that inscription?" At first I could perceive nothing extraordinary in the simple statement, but, upon a second look, I noticed the date of death, November 31, 1770. "And a queer year it must have been," chuckled the gray old man, who turned out to be quite a character, a descendant of one of the committee that purchased the land upon which the church was built in 1727.

THROUGH VIRGINIA

At Fortress Monroe, in Trophy Circle, are gathered a number of captured cannon—one taken from Burgoyne at Saratoga; others from Cornwallis at Yorktown. The old fort itself, with its moated walls and deep embrasures, tells of a day also gone by, and recalls the epoch of another event that added historic lustre to Hampton Roads— the deadly duel between the *Monitor* and *Merrimac*.

Even to-day these waters are making history, for when I was last there the *Eitel Friedrich* and the *Appam*—sea rover, captured prize, privateer—were lying in the harbor and the *Deutschland*, first merchant submarine to cross the Atlantic, came in but a few weeks later; while the British cargo-boats, entering in ballast and departing laden above the water-line, were all painted battleship gray to elude the ever-watchful periscopes.

Such are a few of the memories that linger round Hampton Roads. Reveille in the morning, taps at evening, parades and guard-mount, with the military balls on Saturday nights, give to Old Point Comfort a martial atmosphere rarely found to-day in this our peace-loving nation.

When our visit was ended we boarded one of the steamers that ply up Chesapeake Bay to Baltimore or Washington. Next morning, very early, I awoke just in time to see Mount Vernon perched high upon a bluff above me, and presently our friends were greeting us in Washington.

MOUNT VERNON

MOUNT VERNON

HAVING followed, as I had set out to do, the principal campaigns of the Revolution and visited the historic sites connected with them, I now was ready for my last pilgrimage—to the home of him who had presided over this great drama, its chief actor, the man by whose guiding hand the American armies had finally been led to victory.

On the 4th of December, 1783, Washington had bade farewell to his officers in the "Long Room" on the second floor of Fraunces' Tavern, that still stands at the corner of Broad and Pearl Streets in New York City (now restored and maintained by the Sons of the Revolution), and had gone to the water-front, crossed in a barge to New Jersey, and proceeded to Annapolis, where he resigned his commission as commander-in-chief of the American army before Congress there assembled. And by the following Christmas eve he had returned once more to his beloved Mount Vernon, a plain country gentleman, to take up his old life again.

So my especial object in visiting his home upon the Potomac on this occasion—which was not my first visit, nor, I hope, will it be my last—was to picture this Virginia gentleman, this retired general, back in his peaceful home during the years that followed the Revolution.

REVOLUTIONARY PILGRIMAGE

We proposed to spend the day upon our trip. So in the morning, fairly early, with two congenial friends we started out from Washington, taking our luncheon with us in the motor. On the way we made a stop in Alexandria to visit Christ Church, so intimately connected with his devotions. There is his pew; there the very communion-table used in the services that he attended. Then, driving on again, we crossed the causeway over which he came to church and in the woods beyond, just before reaching Mount Vernon itself, we enjoyed our picnic lunch.

The first view of the house that you obtain from this road is that of the less-known west front—the façade that faces the park and greensward, a fair and simple design, full of dignity and quiet repose.

I have never yet seen Mount Vernon but I have instinctively felt thankful that the "Father of his Country" should have bequeathed it such a heritage. For its effect upon the beholder is most agreeable, no matter what his standards may be. It is truly a gentleman's abode, neither too big and pompous for a republic's first citizen, nor yet so meek and lowly as to be unbefitting a nation's hero, a great leader of men.

And its grounds are so beautiful—fair Virginia hillslopes set out with stately trees and ornamental shrubs, with the Potomac encircling their bases in its wide embrace. As I stepped upon the terrace that overlooks these lawns on a still gray day in May, the placid waters of the river were unruffled by any breeze and mirrored

MOUNT VERNON

the white sails of a boat or two that lay becalmed upon them. Beyond, on the opposite shore, the Maryland hills rose green and misty, spotted with a dwelling here and there, but quite as Washington used to see them as he sat under his cool high portico.

Washington's Home at Mount Vernon

There, in the shadow, I always like to sit and dream after the day's excursionists have departed by boat and train (and that is why I planned to come by motor), and, quite alone, to recall the memories of the house and its long-departed occupants.

I like to forget the hero, the Washington that we have seen crossing the Delaware, reining up his horse between the lines at Princeton, or praying in the snow at Valley

REVOLUTIONARY PILGRIMAGE

Forge, and to remember only the simple country gentleman, as he depicts himself in a letter written to Madame de Lafayette soon after the close of the war:

"Freed from the clangor of arms and the bustle of a camp, from the cares of public employment and the responsibility of office, I am now enjoying domestic ease under the shadow of my own vine and my own fig-tree; and in a small villa, with the implements of husbandry and lambkins around me, I expect to glide gently down the stream of life, till I am entombed in the mansion of my fathers.

"Come, then, let me entreat you and call my cottage your own; for your doors do not open to you with more readiness than mine would. You will see the plain manner in which we live, and meet with rustic civility; and you shall taste the simplicity of rural life. It will diversify the scene, and may give you a higher relish for the gayeties of the court when you return to Versailles."

This is the Washington of Mount Vernon, as he intended himself to be. But, of course, his dream of perfect rural felicity could not come true. The glamour of his past achievements hung too close about him, and, as the spring advanced and the roads were freed from mud and snow, visitors began to arrive and invade his privacy: old soldiers, officers, members of the Congress, and friends, among whom was his dear Lafayette, come to remain with him for a fortnight in the little room up-stairs that still bears his name.

After the summer had passed the great French sculptor, Houdon, arrived to model him for the legislature of Vir-

MOUNT VERNON

ginia, he having consented to make the long voyage from Paris as much as a tribute to the hero as to fulfil this commission, for, as he said to Jefferson, who invited him: "It would be the glory of my life to be enabled to place my name upon the plinth of a statue representing that good and great man." And so he did inscribe himself upon the pedestal of the masterpiece that he created: "fait par Houdon, citoyen français, 1788."

In his journal Washington thus notes Houdon's arrival and the sittings that followed:

"*Oct. 2nd, Sunday.*—After we were in Bed (about eleven o'clock in the evening) Mr. Houdon, sent from Paris by Doct. Franklin & Mr. Jefferson to take my Bust in behalf of the State of Virginia, with three young men assistants, introduced by Mr. Perin, a French Gentleman of Alexandria,—arrived here by water from the latter place. . . .

"*7th, Friday.*—Sat to-day, as I did yesterday, to Mr. Houdon, for my Bust.

"*10th, Monday.*—Observed the process for preparing the Plaister of Paris & mixing of it according to Mr. Houdon. . . .

"*19th, Wednesday.*—Mr. Houdon, having finished the business which brought him hither, went upon Monday (17th) with his People, work, and implements in my Barge to Alexandria to take Passage in the Stage for Philadelphia next morning."

Thus we see that but two weeks were required to make the studies necessary to create the statue that now stands under the dome of the State Capitol at Richmond—the

REVOLUTIONARY PILGRIMAGE

finest presentment of our national hero that we possess and one of the masterpieces of modern portrait sculpture. It has the look, the size, and the serene spirit of the man whom "nature," as the Comte de Moustier expressed it in his account of the inauguration, "had distinguished from all others by his appearance. He had at once the soul, the look and the figure of a hero . . . and in his manners, he had the advantage of joining dignity to great simplicity."

Houdon has succeeded in giving us this aspect of him, depicting Washington in the uniform that is still to be seen in the National Museum in Washington—the coat with wide facings that he wore when he resigned his commission. His right hand, gloved, rests upon a walking-stick; his left arm upon a tall group of objects of symbolic meaning: a plough, fasces, his sword, and his cloak thrown over the whole. These are the only trace of symbolism. The remainder is frank portraiture without idealization of any kind, remarkably convincing and lifelike in every detail.

At Mount Vernon Washington, in his dress, threw aside even this much of the retired commander-in-chief, riding forth in the morning, after his breakfast of "Indian cakes, honey and coffee," attired, as Mr. Custis describes him, "in plain drab clothes, a broad-brimmed white hat, a hickory switch in his hand and carrying an umbrella with a long staff, which is attached to his saddle bow."

He personally managed his own large estate, putting

MOUNT VERNON

into its supervision the same admirable attention to detail that he bestowed upon all his work. His home had run down greatly during his long absence at the war and he proceeded to repair it and build the additions made necessary by his broader life. He endeavored also to retrieve his private fortune, so impaired by his service in the army, for which he would accept no pay. So these first few years of retirement became profitable as well as pleasurable ones.

His daily routine of life was most methodical. In the morning hours he visited his farms, talking to and overseeing his negroes and inspecting his fine animals—his horses, cattle, sheep, and his splendid mules, sixteen hands high, bred from a union of his own coach mares with asses sent him by the King of Spain. He was very fond of his gardens and, from his diary, you may trace him to the Mill Swamp, the Dogue Creek, and other localities along the Potomac in quest of ash-trees, crab-apples, mulberries, white thorn, and other specimens to add to his arboretum. He even went farther afield and brought hemlocks from Occoquan and acorns and buckeyes from the Monongahela; while Arthur Young, the agriculturist, sent him seeds from England and Thomas Jefferson shrubs from Monticello.

The grounds at Mount Vernon contain many trees that he set out, and so I never enter the formal garden, with its old box hedges prim as a *parterre de broderie,* that I do not seem to see him walking in the pathways or talking interestedly to the gardeners.

REVOLUTIONARY PILGRIMAGE

Before three o'clock he returned to the house for the quiet dinner in the small dining-room. This apartment, as well as the other rooms of the lower floor, still vividly recalls his home life.

I can see him shut in his panelled library on rainy days, among his books and papers, using the very inkstand that is closed in one of the cases, or dictating to his secretary Mr. Tobias Lear. I can see him receiving visitors in the "west parlor" with its French furniture, corner mantel, and general air of ceremony. I can see him on occasions leading his guests to the "banquet-hall," where it was his custom, at these larger and more formal dinners, to seat his wife at the head of the table. If there were other ladies, these sat about her. His secretary was placed at the foot of the table to make himself agreeable to the lesser people near him. Washington seated himself at the middle of the board with the more distinguished guests about him at either hand or directly opposite.

"Nothing could exceed the order with which his table was served. Every servant knew what he was to do and did it in the most quiet and yet rapid manner." He himself was frugal in his appetites, usually refusing the more elaborate dishes provided for his friends. He drank a "mug of small beer or cider" and a glass or two of fine old Madeira with his favorite toast, "To all our friends."

In the evening, at candlelight, he read the news or listened in the music-room to pretty Nelly Custis as she played the harpsichord that still stands by the door, or, at times, accompanied her upon the flute that lies upon it.

MOUNT VERNON

The precious objects displayed in cases in all these rooms recall his tastes and associations as well as the homage of his distinguished friends. There are his dress swords; his walking-stick presented by his ally the King of France; a Sèvres clock and rose-jars sent him by Lafayette, and another unique object from the same donor—the great iron key, token of despotism, about a span in length, that once locked the main portal of the Bastille. Lafayette accompanied this last gift with a letter that concluded as follows:

"Permit me, my dear general, to present you with a picture of the Bastille, such as it was some days after I had ordered its demolition, with the main key of the fortress of despotism. It is a tribute which I owe as a son to an adopted father—as an aide-de-camp to my general—as a missionary of liberty to its patriarch."

After six years of retirement at Mount Vernon Washington's peaceful life was broken into and he was again summoned to serve his country and to become its first President. But, the eight years of his office ended, he returned again to his old home to resume his quiet life. He wrote at this time to his former secretary of war, James McHenry:

"I might tell you that I begin my diurnal course with the sun; that, if my hirelings are not in their places at that time, I send them messages of sorrow for their indisposition; that, having put these wheels in motion, I examine the state of things further; that the more they

REVOLUTIONARY PILGRIMAGE

are probed, the deeper I find the wounds which my buildings have sustained by an absence and neglect of eight years; that by the time I have accomplished these matters, breakfast (a little after seven o'clock) is ready; that this being over, I mount my horse and ride round my farms, which employ me until it is time to dress for dinner, at which I rarely miss seeing strange faces—come, they say, out of respect for me. Pray would not the word curiosity answer as well? . . ."

Washington soon tired of these strangers' visits, and invited his favorite nephew, Lawrence Lewis, to come to live with him at Mount Vernon "to ease me of the trouble of entertaining company, particularly of nights, as it is my inclination to retire (and, unless prevented by very particular company, I always do retire) either to bed or to my study, soon after candlelight."

So a new member was introduced into the household and his coming brought a romance. Nelly Custis, now grown to womanhood, was the youth and gayety of the house and the ray of brightness in all its gatherings. Lawrence Lewis quickly fell in love with her, and Washington was greatly pleased when he won his suit in spite of numerous rivals.

The young people were married in the early days of 1799, and remained on at Mount Vernon. The year passed happily until nearing its end.

On the 11th of December Washington noted in his diary that there "was a large circle around the moon." The next day, upon his morning ride, he was caught in the snow-storm that this circle presaged. He returned

MOUNT VERNON

as usual in time for his three-o'clock dinner, but so late that, despite protests from his secretary, he sat down to the table in his damp clothes.

The next day he complained of a sore throat. This grew worse on the day following, and, early on the morning of the 14th, he awoke with a violent chill. Mrs. Washington sent for Mr. Lear, his secretary, who tells us that when he reached the bedchamber he "found the general breathing with difficulty, and hardly able to utter a word intelligibly." Doctor Craik was hastily summoned, then Doctor Brown, and finally Doctor Dick. All realized the gravity of the illness. He sat up twice during the day, but experienced great difficulty in breathing. Toward evening he failed rapidly.

Room in Which Washington Died

Mr. Lear, the only eye-witness who has left an account of Washington's last moments, thus describes the final scene:

"About ten minutes before he expired (which was between ten and eleven o'clock) his breathing became easier. . . . I saw his countenance change. I spoke to Doctor Craik, who sat by the fire. He came to the bedside . . . and put his hands over his eyes, and he expired without a struggle or a sigh.

REVOLUTIONARY PILGRIMAGE

"While we were fixed in silent grief, Mrs. Washington, who was sitting at the foot of the bed, asked with a firm and collected voice, 'Is he gone?' I could not speak, but held up my hand, as a signal that he was no more. ''Tis well,' said she, in the same voice, 'I shall follow him; I have no more trials to pass through.'

"At the time of his decease, Doctor Craik and myself were in the situation before mentioned. Mrs. Washington was sitting near the foot of the bed. The general's servant, Christopher, who had been in the room and standing nearly all day, stood near the bedside. Caroline, Molly and Charlotte were in the room, standing near the door."

Always, as I look through the door into that south bedroom, this is the picture that I see: the general lying upon the bed that still stands between the two windows; Martha Washington sitting in the chair near its foot; the doctor, Mr. Lear, and the old negro body-servant standing by the bed; the three black housemaids huddled in a group near the door. After his death, as was the custom, this bedroom was closed, and Martha Washington went to occupy the room above that bears her name.

Washington's body was brought down-stairs and laid in the drawing-room, and later, when the time for the funeral approached, was placed under the great white portico that fronts the Potomac. The funeral was held on Wednesday, the 18th of December. I quote from an account, written in the taste of the time, in the Ulster County *Gazette*, published a few days later:

MOUNT VERNON

"In the long and lofty *Portico*, where oft the Hero walked in all his glory, *now* lay the shrouded corpse.... On the ornament at the head of the coffin, was inscribed Surge ad Judicium—about the middle of the coffin GLORIA DEO—and on the silver plate,

General
George Washington
Departed this life, on the 14th December
1799, Æt. 68.

"Between three and four o'clock, the sound of artillery from a vessel in the river, firing minute guns, awoke afresh our solemn sorrow—the corps was moved—a band of music with mournful melody melted the soul in all the tenderness of woe. The procession was formed and moved on in the following order:

> Cavalry \
> Infantry } with arms reversed \
> Guard /
> Music
> Clergy
> The general's horse with his saddle,
>   holsters and pistols.
>   Cols.   C   Cols.
>   Simms   O   Gilpin
>   Ramsay   R   Marsteller
>   Payne   P   Little
>   S
>   E
> Mourners
> Masonic Brethren
> Citizens

"When the procession had arrived at the bottom of the elevated lawn, on the banks of the Potomac, where the

REVOLUTIONARY PILGRIMAGE

family vault is placed, the cavalry halted, the infantry marched toward the Mount and formed their lines . . . the funeral service was performed . . . and three discharges by the infantry, the cavalry and 11 pieces of artillery which lined the banks of the Potomac back of the Vault, paid the last tribute to the entombed Commander-in-Chief of the Armies of the United States and to the departed Hero."

The vault here mentioned is the old one—the ancient family vault down toward the river. Washington's body lay within it for thirty years and then was moved to the newer vault, where it now reposes—the final resting-place, built according to his wish and in the spot that he had designated in a clause of his will. Now that it is shaded by trees and partially overgrown with vines, it is not as unsightly as once it was; for, both in material and design, it leaves much to be desired, but so hallowed are its memories, so august the presence that one feels within, that all else is forgotten in the contemplation of the simple sarcophagus of the Father of his Country, the man who, by his ability and courage, his uprightness and self-sacrifice, won the admiration of the world.

WASHINGTON

WASHINGTON

ONLY a few miles from Mount Vernon now spreads the great "Federal City" that Washington founded and that has become the living embodiment of his name—the monument he builded to himself without knowing it; the enduring evidence of his breadth of vision; of his power to see, in a wilderness dotted with the tepees of the Powhatan Indians, the fair city of his imagination.

It is indeed difficult for the visitor of to-day to conceive that this splendid city was a pathless forest but a little more than a century ago and that a traveller* "after riding over an extensive tract of level country somewhat resembling an English heath" and traversing a forest "came out upon a large spot cleared of wood, in the center of which" he saw a building "commenced on an extensive scale"—the Capitol.

Washington, from the very inception of the idea, insisted, despite the jealousies of the States, the intrigues of Congress, and the greed of landowners, upon carrying out his vast plan in its entirety and hewed from the forests along the Potomac, streets that "looked like broad avenues in a park bounded on each side by thick woods."†

And that is why I think of our national capital, as we see

* Thomas Twining, writing in 1796. † Francis Baily.

REVOLUTIONARY PILGRIMAGE

it to-day—the most beautiful city in our country and the pride of the nation—as his memorial.

He was aided, in the great task that Congress had laid upon him, by his secretary of state, Thomas Jefferson, an ardent devotee of the arts and a student of architecture, as the State Capitol at Richmond, the University of Virginia, and his own handsome home, Monticello, all designed by him, still testify. A man of broad vision, he caught at once Washington's great conception and even went so far as to draw a tentative plan of the proposed city that has been preserved and, in many respects, resembles the one finally adopted.

But these two executives had the foresight to choose an artist—a man of genius and imagination—Pierre Charles L'Enfant, to put their ideas into concrete form, and to this man we owe the admirable plan of our national capital. Major L'Enfant was a Parisian, son of a "painter in ordinary to the King in his Manufacture of the Gobelins." Coming to America in the fall of 1777, he enlisted as a volunteer in the American army and, early in the following year, was made a captain of engineers. He was six feet tall and possessed a finely proportioned figure, while his prominent nose betokened that obstinacy and "untoward disposition," as Washington expressed it, that was his final undoing.

Engaged on public work in New York City when he heard of the final decision of Congress regarding the new capital, he at once made application for the task of drawing up a suitable plan, for, says he:

WASHINGTON

"No nation, perhaps, has ever before had the opportunity offered them of deliberately deciding on the spot where their capital city should be fixed, or of combining every necessary consideration in the choice of situation, and although the means now within the power of the country are not such as to pursue the design to any great extent, it will be obvious that the plan should be drawn on such a scale as to leave room for the aggrandizement and embellishment which the increase of the wealth of the nation will permit it to pursue at any period, however remote. Viewing the matter in this light, I am fully sensible of the extent of the undertaking and, under the hope of a continuance of the indulgence you have hitherto honored me with, I now presume to solicit the favor of being employed in this business."

His offer of services was accepted, and after making a careful survey of the site, L'Enfant submitted his first report, selecting unerringly "the most desirable positions for to erect the Publique Edifices," and scorning the regulation squares—the block plan of Philadelphia (and would that other of our city planners had followed his example!) as too tame and monotonous to suit his fervent fancy for, says he, with unquestionable truth:

"It is not the regular assemblage of houses laid out in squares and forming streets all parallel and uniform that is so necessary. . . . Such plans indeed, however answerable they may appear on paper, or seducing as they may be on the first aspect to the eyes of some people . . . become at last tiresome and insipid, products of some cool imagination, wanting a sense of the grand and

REVOLUTIONARY PILGRIMAGE

truly beautiful, [which is] only to be attained where nature contributes with art to diversify the objects."

So, when he finally perfected his plan, he made

"the distribution regular with streets at right angles, north-south and east-west, but afterwards I opened others on various directions as avenues to and from every principal place . . . to serve as do main veins in the animal body to diffuse life through smaller vessels in quickening the active motion of the heart."

Such were the practical ideas of the man who made Washington unique among our American cities, most of which lack these "main veins" that would be such an addition to their life. He plotted the great public buildings as we see them to-day: the Capitol on "Jenkin's Hill," "the presidial palace," as he called the White House near the "three grand Departments of State"; and a great equestrian figure of Washington (which it was hoped Houdon would execute) at the end of the Mall, where the obelisk now stands.

But, like many a genius, he was erratic. His dreams went farther and he conceived a city in which the public edifices should first be erected and then the lots sold for residences to be built in conformity with these monuments, as in the Place Vendôme or the Place de l'Etoile in Paris. It may be imagined how such ideas were received by the pioneers of that day—poor and battling with a wilderness. Troubles with the commission arose

WASHINGTON

and developed into a deadly quarrel that finally ended in his being deprived of his work.

Through all his trials Washington remained his comprehending friend, understanding and approving his dreams and his big ideas that were, indeed, too vast for his day. L'Enfant's later life became embittered and

Tomb of Major L'Enfant at Arlington

toward its close he lived as a dependent, with William Dudley Digges in Maryland, at whose house he died and was buried in the family plot. But in 1909 his remains were disinterred, conveyed under military escort to the rotunda of the Capitol, where they lay in state, and then taken for reburial to the National Cemetery at Arlington.

There they now lie upon the spot perhaps where he and Washington often stood to talk over the fair city

REVOLUTIONARY PILGRIMAGE

of their dreams. For, from Major L'Enfant's grave on Arlington Heights you obtain one of the finest views of Washington City, that spreads its vast parks, its shaded avenues, its noble distances along the Potomac, the pale shaft of the monument, simple, upright as the noble man it commemorates, rising quite near at hand, and the Capitol rearing its dome beyond "with majestic aspect over the Country . . . advantageously seen from twenty miles," as L'Enfant himself foresaw it would be.

Down in the public buildings of the city are treasured some of the most precious relics of our national hero that we possess. In the National Museum is kept the uniform to which I have already alluded—the one he wore when he resigned his commission at Annapolis. Here are also his camp writing-desk; his shaving-case with the tarnished mirror that reflected his face each morning; his mess chest, but twenty-two inches long and fifteen wide, that contained all his cooking-apparatus; the pole, pegs, and part of the canvas of his campaign-tent. How simple all these objects are! How little like the camp equipage of other great commanders!

In the library of the State Department, closed in a case, lies his sword of battle, heavier and less showy than those at Mount Vernon—its broad blade, slightly curved, being made for action and not for ornament. The hilt is of ivory, of a pale-green color, wound round with silver wire, and between the guards there is an embossed trophy of arms. The blade is incased in a black leather scabbard, engraved with the name of its maker—J. Bailey,

WASHINGTON

Fish Kill, which town was one of the principal depots of the American army.

This war sword was one of the four that he bequeathed to his nephews, with the injunction that they should never "unsheath them for the purpose of shedding blood, except it be in self defence, or in the defence of their country and its rights; and in the latter case to keep them unsheathed, and to prefer falling with them in their hands to the relinquishment thereof."

This injunction was the spirit of the Revolution. And it should be our spirit to-day: never to be the aggressor, but to defend our country, our liberty, and our honor to the uttermost, and to have by us, "prepared," weapons in prime condition—an army and navy adequate to perform this duty.

INDEX

'76 STONE HOUSE, 139
181ST STREET, 169
34TH STREET, 165
55TH BRITISH REGIMENT, 198
6TH BATTALION, 325
71ST REGIMENT, 301
7TH VIRGINIA REGIMENT, 198
ABERCROMBIE, Gen 59 Lt Col 331
ADAMS, 13 19 22 254 John 252-253 258 Mr 14 16-17 Samuel 10
ADAMSES, Two 250
ALBANY, 60 87 100 106 117-118 120 150
ALBANY POST ROAD, 128
ALCOTT, Family 25
ALEXANDRIA, 348 351
ALLEN, Capt 31 Ethan 3 51 58-59 81-82
ALLENTOWN, 269
AMBOY, 204-206
AMHURST, Jeffrey 59
AMWELL MILITIA, 204
ANBUREY, 73 104-105 Thomas 61 72 102 107
ANDERSON, John 127-129
ANDRE, 128 137-139 141-143 209 267 Capt 264 John 127 129 Maj 4 130 136 234 263 265
ANNAPOLIS, 347 368
ANTHONY'S NOSE, 134
ARBUTHNOT, Adm 273 287
ARCH STREET, Philadelphia 261
ARLINGTON, 15 17 367

ARLINGTON HEIGHTS, 368
ARMSTRONG, 229 231
ARNOLD, 93 106-107 112 123 126 128 130 136-139 Benedict 59 127 267 Maj Gen 129 Margaret 267
ARNOLD TAVERN, 204
ASHEVILLE, 307
ASHLEY RIVER, 286-287
ASSANPINK CREEK, 184 186-187 191
BACHE, Mrs 263-264
BAILEY, J 368
BAILY, Francis 363
BALCARRAS, Earl 105
BALTIMORE, 177 234 343
BARRETT, Amos 27 32-33 36 James 28 Nathan 24
BASKING RIDGE, 176
BASSETT HALL, 323
BASTILLE, Key To The 355
BATTEN KILL, 102
BATTERY, 147 153 Charleston 274 284
BATTLE LAWN, 33
BATTLE OF PRINCETON (Painting), 196
BATTLE PASS, 157
BAUME, 84 Col 83 85
BAYLOR, Col 181
BEACON HILL, 12
BEAR TAVERN, 183
BEDFORD, 32 34-36
BEMIS'S HEIGHTS, 113

REVOLUTIONARY PILGRIMAGE

BEMIS'S HEIGHTS TAVERN, 113
BEMIS HOUSE, 113
BENNETT, James Gordon 169
BENNINGTON, 5 51-52 76 79 82-83 85 87 93 101 181 299 Battle Of 82
BENNINGTON MONUMENT, 80
BERGOINE (sic), Gen 104
BERKELEY, Norbonne 320
BETSY ROSS HOUSE, Philadelphia 261-262
BEVERLEY DOCK, 126
BEVERLEY ROBINSON HOUSE, 126-128
BIDDLE, Edward 251
BILDRICA, (Billerica) 32 36
BILLERICA, 32 36
BILLINGSPORT, 216 228
BIRMINGHAM, 183-184
BIRMINGHAM MEETING HOUSE, 218 220 223 225 227
BLAIR, 321
BLAND, Richard 251
BLAZING STAR TAVERN, 178
BLOOMINGDALE, 163
BLUE RIDGE, 297 307
BLUE RIDGE MOUNTAINS, 296
BOAKE, Abel 223 Sarah 223
BOQUET RIVER, 62
BORDENTOWN, 177 186-187
BOROUGH CHURCH, 342
BOSTON, 7 9 14-15 31 37 39 41 46 48 51 114 152 254 256
BOSTON NECK, 14 47
BOTETOURT, Baron De 320
BOTTA, Carlo 190
BOWLING GREEN, 147 149 154
BOWMAN, Samuel 139
BRANCHVILLE, 290
BRANDYWINE, 4 217 Battle Of The 226-228
BRANDYWINE (CREEK), 244

BRANDYWINE (RIVER), 215 218-220 222 225
BRANT, 90 97 100 Joseph 88 Mary 98
BREAKNECK, 123
BREED'S HILL, 40 42-43
BREYMAN, 107 Col 112
BREYMAN'S HILL, 112
BRIGHTMAN'S FARM, 112
BRINTON'S FORD, 220
BROAD RIVER, 289 296 301
BROAD STREET, Charleston 274 278 New York 347 Philadelphia 249
BROADWAY, 149-151 169-170
BROOKLYN, 157-158 162
BROOKLYN HEIGHTS, 154-155
BROOKLYN NAVY YARD, 155-156
BROWN, Dr 357
BRUNSWICK, 193 204 206
BRUTON CHURCH, 321
BUCKMAN TAVERN, 18
BULL HEAD TAVERN, 178
BUNKER HILL, 12 32 37 39-40 42
BURGOIN (sic), Gen 104
BURGOYNE, 32 40 44 59 62 69-75 82-83 86-87 101-102 106-107 111-112 114 119 134 215 244 294 312 343 Gen 43 61 111 117 Lt Gen 60
BURTON, Miles 274
BUTTRICK, Maj 28 31
CADWALADER, Col 172
CAMBRIDGE, 12 15 28 37 39-40 46 114 262
CAMBRIDGE COMMON, 46
CAMDEN, 294-295 297 308
CAMERON, Henry C 197
CAMP SCHOOL, At Valley Forge 242
CAMPBELL, 107 298

INDEX

CAMPBELL (cont.)
  Lord William 279 283
CAMPFIELD, Jabez 211
CAPE FEAR, 312
CAPE HENLOPEN, 215
CARLETON, Sir Guy 60-61 149
CARLSON, R 13
CAROLINAS, 39 290 299 312-313 325 The 271 273
CARPENTER'S HALL, Philadelphia 250-251 256
CARPENTERS' COMPANY, 252
CARRINGTON, Col 45 Henry B 244
CARTER, Mrs 118
CARTER'S GROVE, 322-323
CARY, Mary 322
CASTLE CHURCH, 97
CASTLETON, 64 76-77
CATAMOUNT TAVERN, 81
CATAWBA REGION, 300
CATAWBA RIVER, 289
CATSKILLS, 121
CHADD'S FORD, 215 217 219-220 222-223 225 227
CHAIN BATTERY WALK, 126
CHAMPLAIN CANAL, 70
CHAPEL OF EASE, 342
CHARLES, Prince Of England 341
CHARLES RIVER, 14-15
CHARLESTON, 155 216 273 279 285-286 289-290 294 305-306 Battery 305
CHARLESTOWN, 12-14 36 40 42-43 45 313
CHARLESTOWN BRIDGE, 42
CHARLESTOWN NECK, 14
CHARLOTTE, 295 297 300 307-308
CHARLOTTESVILLE, 317
CHASTELLUX, 120 137 249 327 Marquis De 117 118 263
CHATTERTON HILL, 167
CHESAPEAKE BAY, 216 290 313 326 341 343
CHESTER VALLEY, 241
CHESTNUT STREET, Philadelphia 250 254
CHEW, Benjamin 233 Mrs 235 Peggy 234 267
CHEW FAMILY, 235
CHEW HOUSE, 230-231 233
CHRIST CHURCH, 13-14 348
CHURCH, Dr 13
CINCINNATI, Society Of The 122
CLARK, 23 Jonas 19 Mr 22 Rev Mr 13-14 Thomas 194-196 William 194-196
CLARKE, 289
CLEVELAND, 298 Col 296 John 296
CLINTON, 39-40 155 287 327 Gen 43 George 121 152 Gov 241 Henry 149 Sir Henry 134 266 269 273 275 286 289 313 325-326 331-332
CLIVEDEN, 233-234
COBBLE HILL, 47
COCHRAN, John 211
COCK HILL FORT, 168
COEVILLE, 114
COLFAX, Gen 210
COLUMBIA, 296
CONANT, Col 12-14
CONCORD, 3 11 16-17 24 26-28 34-36 39 51 318
CONCORD GREEN, 25 32
CONGAREE (RIVER), 292
CONNECTICUT, 51-52
CONSHOHOCKEN, 228
CONSTITUTION ISLAND, 125-126 130
CONTINENTAL CONGRESS, 202 253 256 First 252 260

CONWAY, Gen 244
CONWAY CABAL, 244
COOLEY, Rev Dr 183 185
COOPER RIVER, 287
COPLEY, 256
COPP'S HILL, 11-12 41-44
CORNWALLIS, 4 12 155 158 175 177 191-195 220 227 287 290 294-297 300-301 306-308 313 317-318 325 329-330 332 335 338-341 343 Earl 312 Gen Lord 224 Lord 176 289 326
COURTENAY, Wm A 306
COWPENS, 5 234 296 301 304-307
CRAIGIE HOUSE, 46
CRAIK, Dr 357-358
CRAM, Ralph Adams 130
CROSSWICKS, 269
CROWN POINT, 58-59 62
CULPEPPER MEN, 325
CURTIS, Miss 264
CUSTIS, 321 Mr 352 Nelly 354 356
CYPRESS HILLS, 156-157
DAMAS, Comte De 118
DANA, Richard Henry 38
DANUBE, 97
DARKE, William 209
DARRACH, Lydia 261
DAVIS, Capt 31
DAWES, William 17
DE BARRAS, 326
DE FERMOY, 181
DE GRASSE, 260 341 Comte 326
DE HEISTER, 156-157
DE KALB, 294-295
DE LA PLACE, Capt 53
DE PEYSTER, Abraham 297
DEANE, Silas 250
DECLARATION CHAMBER, Independence Hall 256
DECLARATION OF INDEPENDENCE, 202 234 255 257 259 262 Reading Of 154
DEEP RIVER, 312
DELANCEY, Capt 265
DELAWARE RIVER, 161 177-179-182 187 189 206 216-217 229 249-250 266 269 349
DELAWARE BAY, 215
DELAWARE REGIMENT, 196
DIAMOND, William 23
DICK, Dr 357
DICKINSON, John 251
DIGGES, William Dudley 367
DILWORTH ROAD, 227
DO-VE-GAT (Coeville), 114
DOBBS FERRY, 127
DOGUE CREEK, 353
DORCHESTER HEIGHTS, 40 47
DRAKE, Samuel Adams 44
DUCHE, Rev Mr 253
DUNDAS, Col 332
DUNDERBERG, 134
DUNMORE, Lord 324 342
DYER, Eliphalet 250
EAST 34TH STREET FERRY, 164
EAST FALLS, 238
EAST RIVER, 154 158 162-164 182
EDISTO INLET, 286
EIGHTH STREET, Philadelphia 259
ELIZABETH RIVER, 342
ELK HILL, 317
ELKTON, 216
ELLINGTON, Rev Mr 276
EMERSON, Phoebe Bliss 27 Ralph Waldo 25-26
ENGLAND, 353
ENGLISHTOWN, 269
EQUINOX HOUSE, 79
ERCOLE, 166
ERSKINE, 208

INDEX

FALMOUTH HARBOR, 246
FATLAND FORD, 228
FAYETTEVILLE, 312
FELTHAM, Lt 54
FENIMORE COOPER, 73 88
FERGUSON, 298-299 Maj 297
FERMOY, Gen De 65
FIRS, 127 137
FISH CREEK, 87-88
FISH KILL, 369
FISHER, Elijah 104 210-211
FISHKILL, 103-104 112 121-122
FISK'S HILL, 24
FITCH TAVERN, 35
FITZGERALD, Col 198
FIVE MILE CREEK, 191
FLATBUSH, 156-157
FLATBUSH PASS, 157
FLATLANDS, 157
FLEMING, Capt 196
FLUSHING, 163
FONDA, 98
FORBES, Maj 71
FORD, Jacob 208 Mrs 210
FORREST, Capt 186 Thomas 185
FORT ANN, 69 71-72
FORT CARILLON, 58
FORT CLINTON, 133-134
FORT DAYTON, 89 92 94
FORT DEFIANCE, 63
FORT EDWARD, 5 69 71-73 75 82 101
FORT EDWARD CREEK, 73
FORT GEORGE, 153 168 170 (Fort Amsterdam) 147
FORT GREENE, 156
FORT GREENE PARK, 156
FORT HAMILTON, 156
FORT HERKIMER, 94
FORT INDEPENDENCE, 64-65 168 181
FORT KNYPHAUSEN, 166
FORT LEE, 170 175
FORT MERCER, 229
FORT MONTGOMERY, 133-134
FORT MOTTE, 290 292
FORT MOULTRIE, 281-282 285-287
FORT NEILSON, 113
FORT PUTNAM, 130 156
FORT SCHUYLER, 87-90 92 94
FORT STANWIX, 87
FORT SULLIVAN, 279
FORT SUMTER, 280 285
FORT TICONDEROGA, 54 55 64
FORT TRYON, 168 170
FORT WARREN, 77
FORT WASHINGTON, 166-170 172 175 240 242
FOURTH STREET, Philadelphia 250
FOX, 312
FRANCE, King Of 355
FRANKLIN, 260 262-263 Benjamin 258 264 Doct 351 Mr 263
FRASER, 76-77 105-106 112 Brig Gen 62 Gen 65 69 107 114
FRAUNCES' TAVERN, 152 347
FREDERICKSBURG, Virginia 234
FREEMAN'S FARM, 105 112
FREEMAN TAVERN, 204
FRENCH, Daniel 33
FRONT STREET, Philadelphia 249
FULTON FERRY, 162
GADSDEN, Christopher 251
GAGE, Gen 37 41-42 253
GANSEVOORT, 89 92-93 Peter 87
GARDEN, 294 304 318 Alex'r 291
GATES, 106 112-113 176 295 308 Gen 74 104 110-111 260 294 Horatio 102 244
GATINOIS, 336
GEE POINT, 126
GEORGE, King Of England 276

REVOLUTIONARY PILGRIMAGE

GEORGE III, 200 King Of England 147
GEORGE WYTHE HOUSE, 321-322 327
GEORGIA, 273 286
GERMAINE, Lord 289 Lord George 190
GERMAN FLATS, 89 94
GERMANS, 105
GERMANTOWN, 228-229 232-233 236 238 244
GILPIN, Col 359
GLENN'S FALLS, 72
GLOUCESTER, 12
GLOUCESTER COUNTY, 342
GLOUCESTER POINT, 329 332
GLOVER, 181 241 Col 161 189 John 183
GOODHUE, Bertram 130
GOODRICH, Chauncy 51
GOSPORT NAVY YARD, 342
GOVERNOR'S ISLAND, 154 163
GOWANUS COVE, 155-157
GOWANUS CREEK, 158
GRAAF, Mr 259
GRAHAM, Jack 79
GRANT, 158 Gen 156
GRAVESEND COVE, 156
GRAYDON, Maj 168
GREAT PARADE, 133
GREAT REDOUBT, 114
GREEN, Gen 181
GREEN DRAGON TAVERN, 10 13
GREEN MOUNTAIN BOYS, 52 78 82-83
GREEN MOUNTAIN TAVERN, 51 81
GREEN MOUNTAINS, 39 59 71 76 78
GREENE, 3 172 192 229 231 300-301 306-308 310-312 318

GREENE, (cont.)
Gen 139 175 184 217 260 313
Nathanael 157 296 309
Nathaniel 39
GREENSBORO, 307-308
GREENWICH STREET, 151
GREENWOOD CEMETERY, 156
GREY, Gen 232
GRIDLEY, Col 40
GUILFORD BATTLEFIELD, 309
GUILFORD COURT HOUSE, 5 296 307 Battle Of 309
GUSTAVUS, 127
HACKENSACK, 170 (the) 176
HADDRELL'S POINT, Charleston 286-287
HALIFAX, 48 152 155
HAMILTON, Alexander 119 141 150 185 188 208 211 335 Col 118 340 Eliza 150 Elizabeth 119 Mrs 119
HAMPTON, 338 342
HAMPTON ROADS, 325-326 341 343
HANCOCK, 19 22 Col 18 John 10 216 256 Mr 13-14 16-17
HAND'S RIFLEMEN, 192
HANNAH'S COWPENS, 301
HARLEM, 164-165
HARLEM HEIGHTS, 167
HARLEM RIVER, 166 168 172
HARRINGTON, Jonathan 19
HARRISON, Benjamin 251
HART, Albert Bushnell 4
HARTFORD, 128-129
HASBROUCK HOUSE, 121-122
HASLET, 196
HASLET'S DELAWARES, 157
HAVERSTRAW BAY, 127 136
HAWK-EYE, 72
HAWTHORNE, 25-27
HEAD OF ELK, 216 224 327

INDEX

HEATH, 126 Gen 125
HEINRICHS, Johann 245
HENRY, Patrick 251-253 324
  Prince Of England 341
HERKIMER, 90 92 John Jost 94
  Nicholas 89 Town of 94 97
HERRICK, 85 Col 82 84
HESSIAN LION, 186
HESSIAN YAGER CORPS, 245
HESSIANS, 76 83 86 89 155-158
  166 170 177-178 182 184 186-
  187 189 209
HIGH STREET, Philadelphia 249
  261 263
HIGHLANDS, (Hudson) 123 133
  176 North Gate Of 130 North
  Gate Of The 123 South Gate Of
  130
HILLSBORO, 294
HITCHCOCK'S RHODE ISLAND
  REGIMENT, 198
HOLMES, Oliver Wendell 42
HOPEWELL, 183
HORICAN, 64
HORNET'S NEST, 308
HORRY, Col 294
HOSMER, Mr 31
HOTHAM, Commodore 155
HOUDON, 350 352 366
HOWARD, 303 Col 305 John Eager
  234 302 Peggy 234
HOWE, 39 44 48 114 153 156 161
  167 170 191 216 225 228 341
  Admiral Lord Richard 155 Gen
  43 45 101 152 163 165 177 215
  220 224 261 264 269 Lord 266
  Sir William 60 155 265-266
  Viscount 59
HUBBARD, 85 Col 84
HUBBARDTON, 77
HUDSON RIVER, 10 77 101-103
  105 107-108 112 115 117-118

HUDSON RIVER, (cont.)
  120 123-124 127 134 138 153
  163 168 170 175 215 326
HUDSON FALLS, 72
HUDSON HIGHLANDS, 130 (see
  also HIGHLANDS)
HUGHES, John 139
HUNT, Abraham 178 187
HUTCHINSON, Family 41
INCLENBERG, 164
INDEPENDENCE HALL, 233 254
  260
INDIAN, Thayendanega 88
IRVING, 210
ISLE OF PALMS, Charleston 280-
  281
ISLE OF WIGHT COUNTY, 341-
  342
IZARDS, The 276
JAMAICA, (New York) 156
JAMAICA ROAD, 158
JAMES ISLAND, 280 Charleston
  286
JAMES RIVER, 317-318 322 327
  329 341
JAMESON, Lt Col 129
JAMESTOWN, 341
JASPER, Sgt 284
JAY, John 250 253
JEFFERIS, Emmor 222
JEFFERSON, 79 299 317 351
  Thomas 257-258 353 364
JEFFERY'S FORD, 222
JENKIN'S HILL, 366
JENKS, Mr 35
JERICHO HILL, 180
JERSEY, 167 170
JERSEYS, The 173 175-176 206
JOHN'S ISLAND, Charleston 286
JOHNSON, Lt Col 129 Sir John 99
  Sir William 97-98 100
JOHNSON'S GREENS, 91

JOHNSON HALL, 98 100
JOHNSTON, 107 Col 136
JOHNSTOWN, 100
JONES, Mrs Wiley 304
JUMEL, Madame 166
JUMEL MANSION, 165 262
KEMBLE MOUNTAIN, 204 207
KENNEDY HOUSE, 149
KENNETT SQUARE, 220
KING'S BRIDGE, 153-154 167-168
KING'S FERRY, 128 134 136 138
KING'S HIGHWAY, 157
KING'S MOUNTAIN, 5 296-298 300-301 306 308
KING AND QUEEN COUNTY, 342
KING STREET, 185 187-188 Charleston 274
KING WILLIAM COUNTY, 342
KINGSTON, 121
KINGSVILLE, 294
KIPP'S BAY, 164
KIRKLAND, 97
KITSON, Henry 17
KNAPP, Uzal 122
KNOX, Col 181-182 Gen 122 189 230 240 260 Senator 240
KNYPHAUSEN, 170 226-227 Gen 220 225 266
KOSCIUSKO, 102 260
L'ENFANT, 365 367 Maj 368 Pierre Charles 364
LAFAYETTE, 3 119 227 260 317-318 325-327 338 341 350 355 Gen 222 Madame De 350
LAKE CHAMPLAIN, 49 51 54 58-59 61 64 70 101
LAKE GEORGE, 64 71
LAKE ONTARIO, 87
LANCASTER ROAD, 228
LANGDON, President (of Harvard) 40

LARKIN, Deacon 14
LATROBE, 322
LAURENS, 332 Col 141
LAWRENCEVILLE, 191
LEAR, Mr 357-358 Tobias 354
LEARNED, 241
LEE, 290 Charles 149 176 Gen 281 Light Horse Harry 310 Lt Col 291 Richard Henry 251
LEITCH, 281
LERNOULT, Capt 93
LESLIE, Gen 186
LEWIS, Gen 324 Lawrence 356 Nelly 356
LEXINGTON, 3 5 11 13-17 22-23 25 28 37-39 51-52 279 318
LEXINGTON AVENUE, 165
LEXINGTON GREEN, 17
LIBERTY BELL, 255 259
LIBERTY TREE, 9
LINCOLN, 287-288 Gen 260 286 339
LITTLE, Col 359
LITTLE FALLS, 97
LIVINGSTON, Philip 250
LONG, Col 64 69 71
LONG CLOVE, 136
LONG ISLAND, 155-156 161 163 168 182-183 Charleston 280
LONGFELLOW, 24
LONGFELLOW HOUSE, 46
LOSSING, 149
LOW, Isaac 250
LOXLEY'S HOUSE, Philadelphia 261
LUZERN, Chevalier De 210
M'CREA, Jane 73
MACDOWELL, 298
MADISON, 320
MAGAW, Col 170 172
MAGAW'S PENNSYLVANIANS, 161

INDEX

MAIDENHEAD, 191
MALCOLM, Dan'l 42 Daniel 41
MAMARONECK, 167
MANCHESTER, 83
MANCHESTER-IN-THE-MOUNTAINS, 79
MANHATTAN ISLAND, 153 163 168
MARBLEHEAD, 181 Regiment 161-162 183 189
MARION, 3 260 289-290 292
MARION'S MEN, 290 292-294
MARKET HOUSE, 231-232
MARKET STREET, Philadelphia 249 259 261 267
MARSHALL, Family 107
MARSTELLER, Col 359
MARYLAND, 349
MARYLANDERS, 161
MASSACHUSETTS BAY, 254
MATHER, 42 Cotton 41 Increase 41 Samuel 41
MAUDUIT, Chevalier De 119
MCCLINTOCK, Emory 207
MCHENRY, James 355
MCINTOSH, Gen 240
MCKONKEY'S FERRY, 179 182
MCWHORTER, Alexander 181
MECHANICSVILLE, 75 112
MECKLENBURG (COUNTY), 308
MEDFORD, 14
MEDFORD COMMON, 15
MEETING STREET, Charleston 278-279
MENDHAM, 207
MENOTOMY, 14-15
MERCER, 181 186 196 198 200-201 Gen 194-195 Hugh 197
MERRIAM'S CORNER, 36
MERRICK, Samuel 181
MERRIMAC, (ship) 343
METZ, 318

MIAMI, 307
MIDDLE SHOAL, Charleston 281 285
MIDDLESEX COUNTY, 34
MIDDLETON, 275 Henry 251
MIFFLIN, Gen 162 Thomas 251
MILL SWAMP, 353
MILLSTONE, 204
MINUTEMAN STATUE, 17 19 33
MIRALLES, Don Juan De 211
MISCHIANZA, 234 266 269
MOHAWK RIVER, 75 87
MOHAWK VALLEY, 61 87-88 93 101
MONITOR, (ship) 343
MONMOUTH, 269
MONONGAHELA (RIVER), 353
MONROE, James 185
MONTCALM, 59
MONTGOMERY, Richard 151
MONTICELLO, 258 353 364
MONTOE, Fortress 343
MONTRESSOR, Capt 163 268
MOORE HOUSE, 332 335
MORGAN, 113 301-304 310 Col 104 Daniel 112 260 300 305-306
MORGAN'S RIFLEMEN, 102 104 106 306
MORRIS, Col Roger 165 Robert 260 262
MORRIS MANSION, 169
MORRISTOWN, 140 150 203-204 206 208-209
MORTON'S HILL, 43
MORVEN, 195
MOTTE, Mrs 291 Rebecca 274 290
MOULDER'S BATTERY, 198
MOULTRIE, 281-284 287 William 279
MOUNT AIRY, 229-230
MOUNT ANTHONY, 80
MOUNT DEFIANCE, 56 58 64

REVOLUTIONARY PILGRIMAGE

MOUNT EQUINOX, 79
MOUNT HANDY, 77
MOUNT HERRICK, 77
MOUNT HOLLY, 269
MOUNT INDEPENDENCE, 58-59 62-65
MOUNT JOY, 238 240 242
MOUNT PLEASANT, 281
   Charleston 286
MOUNT VERNON, 208 327 343 345 347 349-350 352-353 355-356 368
MOUNTAIN MEN, 297
MOUSTIER, Comte De 352
MUD ISLAND, 216
MUHLENBERG'S DIVISION, 241
MUIRHEAD, George 183
MUNROE TAVERN, 17 37
MURRAY, Mrs 165 Robert 165
MURRAY HILL, 164
MUSGRAVE, Col 230
MYSTIC, 15
MYSTIC RIVER, 15
NASSAU HALL, 198-199 201
NEAL, Capt 196
NEELEY'S MILL, 180
NELSON, Gov 337 Scotch Tom 336 Thomas 337
NEW BRUNSWICK (NJ), 176 199
NEW GARDEN, 220
NEW HAMPSHIRE GRANTS, 39 51 81
NEW JERSEY, 163 175 180 191 206 215 269 347
NEW JERSEY COLLEGE, 201
NEW ROCHELLE, 167
NEW YORK, 161 163 202 215 269 273 286 289 313 325-326
NEW YORK CITY, 120 121 128 138 145 147 152 154 157 167 177 204 364
NEWARK, 176 181 208

NEWBURGH, 121-123
NEWBURGH BAY, 121
NEWPORT, 326
NEWTOWN, 180 191
NEWTOWN INLET, 163-164
NICHOLS, 85 Col 84
NICHOLS FARM, 79
NOAILLES, Vicomte De 118 332
NOOK'S HILL, 47
NORFOLK, 342
NORRISTOWN, 238
NORTH BRIDGE, 36
NORTH CAROLINA, 294 297 307 313
NORTH CASTLE HEIGHTS, 167
NORTH HOOSICK, 85
NORTH RIVER, 167 170
NORTH BRIDGE, 32
NORTON, Massachusetts 104
O'HARA, Maj Gen 339
OCCOQUAN (RIVER), 353
OLD EXCHANGE OR CUSTOM HOUSE, Charleston 281
OLD GULCH ROAD, 241
OLD MANSE, 26
OLD NASSAU, 200 202
OLD NORTH BRIDGE, 26
OLD NORTH CHURCH, 11-12 41
OLD POINT COMFORT, 341 343
OLD POST ROAD, 195 202
OLD QUAKER ROAD, 193
OLD RIVER ROAD, 183
OLD SOUTH MEETING HOUSE, 9
ONEIDA LAKE, 87
ONEIDA RIVER, 87
ORANGE COUNTY, 130
ORCHARD HOUSE, 25
ORISKANY, 5 90 94 97 101
OSBORN, Samuel 224
OSMORE (HOSMER), Mr 31
OSWEGO, 93

INDEX

OSWEGO RIVER, 87
OTTER RIVER, 77 78
PACOLET (RIVER), 296 301
PAGE, Family 34 Nathaniel 34
PAINE, Robert Treat 250
PALATINATE, Lower 94
PALISADES, 170 175
PALM BEACH, 307
PARIS, 264 351
PARKER, Capt 18 22 Sir Peter 155 279 283 285
PARKER'S FORD, 228
PATTERSON'S DIVISION, 241
PAULDING, 128
PAULUS HOOK, 153-154
PAUSCH, Capt 105
PAYNE, Col 359
PEALE, 201 Charles Wilson 200
PEARL STREET (New York), 347
PEE DEE (RIVER), 290
PEEKSKILL, 134 229
PEEKSKILL BAY, 134
PEMBERTON, Mary 264
PENDLETON, Edmund 251
PENN, William 249 261
PENNIBECKER'S MILL, 229
PENNINGTON ROAD, 184 188
PENNSYLVANIA, 206 232 263 317 Assembly Of 236
PENNSYLVANIA MILITIA, 198
PERCY, Earl 166 Lord 37 157-158 172
PERIN, Mr 351
PERRY, Sgt Maj 304
PERRY STREET, 187
PETERSBURY, 317
PHILADELPHIA, 114 154 177 202 204 206 213 215-218 228-229 233-234 237-238 245 247 249 260 263-264 269 327 341 351 365
PHILLIPS, Gen 61 111

PICKENS, 289
PINCKNEYS, The 260
PITCAIRN, Maj 19 23 26
PITT, William 278
PLACE DE L'ETOILE, 366
PLACE VENDOME, 366
PLOUGHED HILL, 47
PLUCKAMIN, 203
POMPEY, 135
POOR, Gen 241
POPLOPEN CREEK, 133
PORT HENRY, 58
PORT KENNEDY, 228
PORTER, 78
PORTSMOUTH, 318 325
POST CHAPEL, 124 130
POTOMAC, 347-348 353 358-359 363 368
POTTS, 244 Isaac 236 238 243 Stacy 187
POTTS HOUSE, 239
POUGHKEEPSIE, 121
POWDER HORN, 324
PRESCOTT, 42
PREVOST, Gen 286
PRINCE GEORGE COUNTY, 342
PRINCESS ANNE COUNTY, 341
PRINCETON, 4 176-177 181 186 191 193 197 199-200 203-204 269 349 Painting Of Battle Of 196
PRINGLE HOUSE, Charleston 274
PROSPECT HILL, 39 46-47
PROSPECT PARK, 156-157
PROVINCIAL CONGRESS, 281
PULASKI, 260 Count 210
PULLING, John 14
PUTNAM, 165 Gen 134 164 Israel 24 39 157
PYLE, Howard 218
PYLE'S FORD, 220
PYNE ESTATE, 195

REVOLUTIONARY PILGRIMAGE

PYRENEES, 76
QUAKER MEETING HOUSE, 178 189
QUAKER SPRINGS, 112
QUARANTINE STATION, 153
QUEBEC, 59 151
QUEEN STREET, 185-186 188
QUINCY, Dorothy 21 Josiah 329
RAHL, Col 177
RALL, 186-187 189 Col 177 185
RAMSAY, Col 359
RANDOLPH, 321 John 322 Peyton 251-252 323
RANGERS, 83 85
RARITAN RIVER, 176 269
RAWDON, Lord 313
READING, 228
RED BANK, 216
RED HOOK, 161
REEDY FORK, 311
REVERE, Paul 3 10-13 15 17 19 22 24 42
RICHMOND, 317 323 329 351 364
RIEDESEL, 76-77 83 Baron 63 Gen 61-62 65 105 Madame 108 117
RINGS, Benjamin 222
RIVER ROAD, 184-185
ROANOKE, 322
ROBIN, Abbe 339
ROBINSON HOUSE, 126-129 130
ROCHAMBEAU, 119 260 327 Comte De 339
ROCKY HILL, 202-203
ROGERS, 59
ROME, (New York) 87 94
ROSS, Betsy 262 George 262 Maj 332
ROXBURY, 39 47
ROYAL GREEN TORIES, 89
ROYALE AUVERGNE, 336
RUDHALL, Abel 12
RUTLAND, 76-78

RUTLEDGES, The 251
SAINT CLAIR, 59 76-77 181 Arthur 62
SAINT JAMES, 276
SAINT JAMES GOOSECREEK, 275
SAINT JOHN'S, 59
SAINT JOHN'S CHURCH, 342
SAINT LAWRENCE RIVER, 87
SAINT LEGER, 87-90 92 101 Barry 93 Lt Col 60
SAINT MARY'S CATHEDRAL, 187
SAINT MERY, Moreau De 199 201
SAINT MICHAEL'S, Trenton 178 Charleston 277 281 285
SAINT PAUL'S CHAPEL, 150-151
SAINT PAUL'S CHURCH, 342
SAINT PHILLIP'S, Charleston 281
SALISBURY, 307-310
SALUDA (RIVER), 289
SANDTOWN, 193
SANDY HILL, 73 75
SANDY HOOK, 152 215 269
SANTEE (RIVER), 290 292
SARATOGA, 60 67 69 101-102 107-108 111 114 117 210 312 343 Battles Of 104 First Battle Of 105 Second Battle Of 106
SARATOGA SPRINGS, 102
SARGENT, Col 181
SAVANNAH (RIVER), 289
SCHEFFER, Lt Col 186
SCHOOL OF PHILOSOPHY, 25
SCHOOLHOUSE LANE, 231
SCHUYLER, 72 260 Eliza 150 Elizabeth 119 211 Gen 63 71 75 77 92 101-102 111 117-119 211 Mr 120 Peggy 119 Philip 150
SCHUYLER HOUSE, 103 111
SCHUYLERVILLE, 102 108 111 117

INDEX

SCHUYLKILL (RIVER), 228 236 238 241-242
SCONNELTOWN, 220-223
SCOTT'S BRIGADE, 240
SECOND STREET, 187
SERVANT, Caroline 358 Charlotte 358 Christopher 358 Molly 358
SEVENTH STREET, Philadelphia 259
SEVIER, 298
SHAFTESBURY, 79
SHEBAKUNK CREEK, 192
SHEE'S PENNSYLVANIANS, 161
SHELBY, 298
SHERMAN, Roger 250
SHIPPEN, Margaret 267
SHUTE'S FOLLY, Charleston 281
SIMMS, Col 359
SINGLETON, 309
SIX NATIONS, 89
SIXTH AVENUE, 165
SIXTH STREET, Philadelphia 261
SKENE, Maj 69-70 82
SKENESBOROUGH, 64 69-70 72
SKIPPACK CREEK, 229
SLATE ROOF HOUSE, Philadelphia 261
SLOPER, Lt 267
SMALLWOOD'S MARYLANDERS, 157
SMITH, 128 138 Col 36 John 341 Joshua Hett 127 137
SNETZLER, John 277
SOMERVILLE, 15
SONS OF THE REVOLUTION, 347
SOUTH CAROLINA, 283 286 289 296-297 300 313
SOUTH RIVER, 64 66
SOUTH SECOND STREET, Philadelphia 261

SOUTHERN CLUB, Charleston 275
SPAIN, King Of 353
SPARKILL, 143
SPARTANBURG, 296 301 306-307
SPUYTEN DUYVIL, 168 170
STANLEY, Lord 44
STAR REDOUBT, At Valley Forge 242
STARK, 3 59 84-86 Col 181 Gen 93 John 39 83 Molly 84
STATE HOUSE, 187 Philadelphia 259
STATE STREET, 149 187 189
STATEN ISLAND, 153 155 205
STEPHEN, 181
STEUBEN, 119 260
STICKNEY, 85 Col 84
STILLWATER, 75 92 101-102 113
STIRLING, 158 181 245 Gen 186 Lord 157 161
STOCKTON, Richard 195
STONEY POINT, 136
STONY BROOK, 193
STONY POINT, 130 134
STORM KING, 123
STRYKER, Gen 194 William S 180
STUART, Gilbert 322
SUGAR HOUSE PRISON, 150
SUGAR LOAF HILL, 63
SULLIVAN, 158 185 227 229-230 232 Gen 157 181 183-184
SULLIVAN'S ISLAND, 279-281
SUMMERVILLE, 290
SUMTER, 289 292
SURRY COUNTY, 342
SUSSEX COUNTY, 342
SWAMPS, Carolina 292
SWEDE'S FORD, 228
SWEDELAND, 228

REVOLUTIONARY PILGRIMAGE

SYLVAN BEACH, 87
TACONIC RIDGE, 78
TAPPAN, 130 142 264
TAPPAN ZEE, 138
TARLETON, 298-299 302-304 310-312 317 322 Col 273 301
TARRYTOWN, 128 138 170
TAYLOR, John 114
TAYLORSVILLE, 180
TELLER'S (CROTON) POINT, 127
TELLER'S POINT, 136
THACHER, Dr 140-142
THICKETTY, 301
THICKETTY MOUNTAIN, 301
THIRD STREET, Philadelphia 250
THOMSON, Charles 252 256
THUNDER MOUNTAIN, 134
TICONDEROGA, 3-4 49 51-52 54 58-59 62-63 69 75-76 81 87 181
TOWER OF VICTORY, 122
TOWNSEND, Joseph 221
TRADD STREET, Charleston 274
TREASON HILL, 137
TRENTON, 3 175-180 182-184 187 189-191 193-194 196 203 215 269 299 327
TRINITY CHURCH, 150
TROPHY CIRCLE, 343
TRUMBULL, 188 196
TRYON, 152
TRYON COUNTY, 89
TUCKAHOE, 167
TUCKER, Col 322
TURGOT, 114
TURKEY POINT, 216
TUTTLE, Rev Mr 210
TWINING, Thomas 363
TYLER, 321 323
UNCAS, 72
UTICA, 89-90
VALLEY CREEK, 238 240

VALLEY FORGE, 5 82 228 236-238 241 243 245-246 349-350
VAN DYK, John 140 209
VAN WART, 128
VEALTOWN (BERNARDSVILLE), 176
VERDRIETIG RANGE, 136
VERMONT, 58 75-76 79 82
VERNON PARK, 233
VERPLANCK'S POINT, 134
VERPLANCK HOUSE, 122
VERPLANK'S POINT, 130
VERSAILLES, 350
VICTORY MILLS, 103
VICTORY MONUMENT, 124
VINE STREET, Philadelphia 266
VIOMENIL, Baron De 335
VIRGINIA, 290 313 315 317-318 321-327 337 347-348 350-351 University 364
VIRGINIA CONVENTION, 324
VIRGINIA UNIVERSITY OF, 79
VON DONOP, 186-187 Count 177
VON KNYPHAUSEN, Regiment 178
VON LOSSBERG REGIMENT, 178 185-186
VON STEUBEN, Baron 240 244
WALLABOUT BAY, 155
WALLER, 321 Adjutant 45-46
WALLINGFORD, 79
WALLOOMSAC INN, 80
WALLOOMSAC RIVER, 83 85
WALLOOMSAC VALLEY, 86
WAR COLLEGE, 133
WARD, J Q A 306
WARNER, Col 85 93 Seth 51-52 59 77 81-83
WARREN, Dr 9 13-14
WARREN STREET, 187-188
WARREN TAVERN, 228
WARWICK COUNTY, 342

INDEX

WASHINGTON, 3 39 48 82 102 104 121-122 129-130 134 136 139-141 143 151 153-154 157-158 161-169 175-178 180-182 184-186 188 190-192 194-195 198 202-205 207-208 210-212 215-220 222-223 225 227-229 232 236 238 241 243-245 257 261 269 317 320 322 326-327 330 332 336 338 347 349-352 354-356 360-361 363-364 366-367 (William) 303-304 Col 305 Death Of 357 Gen 118 128 149 183 273 George 46 251 254 262 359 Martha 209 358 Mrs 210 239 357 358 Portrait Of 200 William 185 260 302 310
WASHINGTON'S CROSSING, 179
WASHINGTON'S HEADQUARTERS, 238 241-242
WASHINGTON (CITY), 343 348 352 366 368
WASHINGTON HEIGHTS, 165
WASHINGTON LIGHT INFANTRY, 305
WASHINGTON MONUMENT, 234
WATEREE (RIVER), 292
WATSON, 265
WAXHAWS, 299
WAYNE, 229 Anthony 136 240 260 Gen (Mad Anthony) 135
WEEDON'S DIVISION, 241
WELLS, Family 100
WEST CHESTER, 221
WEST HAVERSTRAW, 137
WEST MEDFORD, 15
WEST POINT, 123-130 133
WESTFIELD, 204
WESTMINSTER ABBEY, 142
WESTOVER, 317
WHARTON MANSION, 267
WHITE, Bishop 254 Maj 230 234
WHITE PLAINS, 167 170
WHITE POINT GARDENS, 284
WHITEHALL, 64 69
WHITEMARSH, 261
WILBUR'S BASIN, 107 113
WILKINSON, Maj 186
WILLARD'S MOUNTAIN, 112
WILLET, 93
WILLIAM AND MARY COLLEGE, 319
WILLIAMS, 128
WILLIAMSBURG, 317-318 320 322 324-328
WILMINGTON, 215-218 245 304 312-313
WILSON, Ens 339-340 Jonathan 35
WINNSBORO, 300 308
WINSTON, 298
WINTER HILL, 47
WIRT, William 323
WISSAHICKON (RIVER), 238
WISTER, John 233
WISTER MANSION, 233
WITHERSPOON, John 202
WODFORD'S BRIGADE, 240
WREN, Sir Christopher 150
WRIGHT TAVERN, 26
YADKIN (RIVER), 308
YORK RIVER, 329 331-333
YORKTOWN, 3-4 325-326 328-330 332 336 338 340-341 343
YOUNG, Arthur 353

www.ingramcontent.com/pod-product-compliance
Lightning Source LLC
Chambersburg PA
CBHW060937230426
43665CB00015B/1981